Fei Xiaotong Studies
Volume II

《费孝通研究》 第二集

Globalization of Chinese Social Sciences book series ②

中国社会科学全球化系列丛书 ②

Fei Xiaotong Studies

Volume II

《费孝通研究》 第二集

Edited by

**Stephan Feuchtwang, Xiangqun Chang
and Daming Zhou**

With Assistant Editors Nick Prendergast and Costanza Pernigotti

GCP **Global Century Press
全球世纪出版社**

新世界出版社

Globalization of Chinese Social Sciences book series, Vol. 2

Fei Xiaotong Studies, Vol. II
Edited by Stephan Feuchtwang, Xiangqun Chang & Daming Zhou

This book first published jointly in 2016 by
Global Century Press
23 Austin Friars, London EC2N 2QP, UK
and
New World Press
24 Baiwanzhuang Road, Beijing 100037, China

British Library Cataloguing in Publication Data
A catalogue record for this book is available from the British Library

ISBN 978-1-910334-10-2 (paperback, English); DOI https://doi.org/10.24103/GCSS2.en.pb.2016
ISBN 978-1-910334-11-9 (hardback, English); DOI https://doi.org/10.24103/GCSS2.en.hb.2016
ISBN 978-1-910334-08-9 (paperback, Chinese); DOI https://doi.org/10.24103/GCSS2.cn.pb.2016
ISBN 978-1-910334-09-6 (hardback, Chinese); DOI https://doi.org/10.24103/GCSS2.cn.hb.2016

中国社会科学全球化系列丛书 第二卷

《费孝通研究》第二集
[英] 王斯福、[英] 常向群、周大鸣 主编

此书由以下两个出版社于2016年合作出版
全球世纪出版社
23 Austin Friars, London EC2N 2QP, UK
新世界出版社
中国北京市西城区百万庄大街24号

该书编入大英图书馆的公开数据中的图书馆编目

ISBN 978-1-910334-10-2 (平装·英文版); DOI https://doi.org/10.24103/GCSS2.en.pb.2016
ISBN 978-1-910334-11-9 (精装·英文版); DOI https://doi.org/10.24103/GCSS2.en.hb.2016
ISBN 978-1-910334-08-9 (平装·中文版); DOI https://doi.org/10.24103/GCSS2.cn.pb.2016
ISBN 978-1-910334-09-6 (精装·中文版); DOI https://doi.org/10.24103/GCSS2.cn.hb.2016

CONTENTS

DOI https://doi.org/10.24103/GCSS.en.0

General Preface to the Globalization of Chinese Social Sciences book series

Xiangqun Chang

The phrase 'globalization of Chinese social sciences' came out of a discussion with Professor Stephan Feuchtwang at the London School of Economics in 2010 about the title of a book commemorating the 100th anniversary of Professor Fei Xiaotong's birth. The first volume (in both English and Chinese) was published in 2014 by Global China Press alone and in 2015 jointly with New World Press. The dissemination of 'Chinese social sciences' covers a very wide range, in which the promotion of Fei Xiaotong's work is only the first step. We therefore decided to use 'globalization of Chinese social sciences' as the name of a book series in order to promote representative Chinese social scientific works. Here I shall briefly outline the key developments in 'Chinese social sciences' after 1949[1].

Institutions and resources

In China, the National Philosophy and Social Science Planning Group of the CPC Central Committee is the highest body in the Chinese social sciences. The group operates through the National Planning Office of Philosophy and Social Science. Its National Social Science Foundation is commissioned by the Department of Social Sciences of the Ministry of Education, the Research Bureau of the Chinese Academy of Social Sciences (CASS) and the Research Division of the Central Party School, to be in charge of universities, the institutions of CASS and the central State organs, respectively, with responsibility for the application of research projects, management of funds and evaluation of results. The National Philosophy and Social Science Planning Group also owns the National Social Sciences Database, which was established by CASS and developed by its Library in 2013. It is a national-level, open-information platform for Chinese social sciences. In 2015, the Chinese Social Sciences Year Book series (15 volumes to date) was published, representing the high standard of work in the field.

CASS consists of hundreds of research institutes, centres and related professional organizations, such as the Social Sciences in China Press (SSCP), Social Sciences Academic Press (SSAP), Chinese Social Sciences Net and its blogs and the journal Social Sciences in China and its site and blogs, the English version of which is now published by the Taylor and Francis Group. In 2015, the journal Social Sciences in China Review was founded. It aims 'to evaluate

---

[1] Before 1949 see: *Social Engineering and the Social Sciences in China*, 1919-1949, Yung-chen Chiang, (Cambridge University Press, 2006).

academic results based on national conditions, introduce a high standard of research results and create a system of academic discourse in contemporary China, comprehensively promoting Chinese philosophical and social scientific work in the world'. In recent years, the CASS Forum has also gained a strong reputation at home and abroad. In addition, there are a huge number of Academies of Social Sciences at province and municipality level. They also have their own publications on social sciences based on their work at the local level.

There are about 2,500 universities of different types in China. Some belong to the Bureau of Higher Education of the Ministry of Education, some to State ministries and commissions and others to provincial and municipal governments, and more one quarter are private universities[2]. In 2001, the Department of Social Sciences, Ministry of Education, built the humanities and social sciences services professional portal, the China Academic Humanities Information Network. It became the centre of information, online publications and the dissemination, management and public enquiry services for humanities and the social sciences. All the universities have different faculties and departments and research centres for different topics. Almost all have their own publishers, which publish academic journals and books. Social scientific work will be published in philosophy and social sciences edition. It is worth mentioning a few examples of universities' contributions to providing services or promoting Chinese social sciences at the national level.

In 1998, Nanjing University and the Hong Kong Polytechnic University developed a Chinese Social Sciences Citation Index and the academic series of the Chinese Humanities and Social Sciences Citation index. It led to the foundation of the Chinese Social Science Research Assessment Centre in 2000.

Tsinghua University and Tsinghua Tongfang Holding Group established China's National Knowledge Infrastructure (CNKI) in 1999. It was supported by the Education Ministry, Science and Technology Ministry, Propaganda Ministry and General Administration of Press and Publications, with self-developed cutting-edge Chinese digital library technologies and grid resources as a sharing platform. It built the most comprehensive system of Chinese academic knowledge resources – the China Integrated Knowledge Resources Database – covering journals, dissertations, newspapers, proceedings, year books, reference works, encyclopedias, patents, standards, S&T achievements and laws and regulations and some well-known foreign-language resources from Springer, Taylor & Francis and Wiley, forming a complete knowledge service network. The system is the core of the China knowledge resource base, encompassing a total of 101.9 million articles that include a large amount of social scientific work, some of which have been translated into English.

---

[2]   见：《2015年全国教育事业发展统计公报》，中国教育部(see: The 2015 National Education Statistics Bulletin, Ministry of education of China), 2016-07-06. http://www.moe.gov.cn/srcsite/A03/s180/moe_633/201607/t20160706_270976.html

Fudan University is a top-class locus for the internationalization of Chinese social sciences. It founded China's first national institute for advanced studies of social sciences (Fudan-IAS for Social Sciences). The founding Dean, Professor Deng Zhenglai, also founded the Chinese Social Science Quarterly in Hong Kong as early as 1992, which was re-established in 2008. In the same year, he founded China's first English-language journal on social sciences, the Fudan Journal of the Humanities and Social Sciences (FJHSS). Unfortunately, Deng passed away in 2013. His successor in Fudan-IAS, Sujian Guo, Professor of the Department of Political Science at San Francisco State University, USA, also became Editor of the FJHSS, which is now published by Springer.

Methodology

Some recent views need to be mentioned here. In 2011, Professor QIAO Xiaochun of the Institute of Population Research at Peking University gave a lecture entitled 'Chinese social science: how far away from science?' at a number of universities, including his own and Shanghai University of International Studies, China Youth University for Political Science, Huazhong University of Science and Technology and Zhongnan University of Economics and Law. He believed that Chinese social science occupies no position or status in world academia, and therefore enjoys no right of discourse. This is because methodologically Chinese social sciences have a strong speculative character, in contrast to the empirical studies on which general social sciences are based. However, in his 'Understanding the future' lecture in 2016, Professor Yu Xie of Princeton University and Peking University issued more balanced statements. On the one hand, he observed, scientific studies have three characteristics, namely objectivity, experience and repeatability. On the other hand, he put forward three principles, variability, social grouping and social context, which provide a methodological basis for social scientific research. Xie suggested that in today's China it is very important ever to carry out social scientific research on China scientifically since Chinese society has been changed all round significantly and still changing[3].

In 2014, XIONG Yihan, Associate Professor at Fudan University School of International Relations and Public Affairs, published an article entitled 'The internationalization of social science and native language scholarly writing in China'[4]. He criticized the phenomenon of 'academic nationalism' that wants to boycott internationalization, but also took issue with the 'colonial academic' who

---

[3]   谢宇：今天在中国做社会科学太重要了，也太幸运了，环球科学("未来科学"论坛演讲) [XIE YU, Today it is so important and so lucky to conduct social scientific research in China (a speech at the Future Forum, Beijing), *Scientific American*, 2016-07-26, http://oicwx.com/detail/1102356

[4]   熊易寒，中国社会科学的国际化与母语写作，《复旦学报(社会科学版)》，2014年第4期。[XIONG Yihan. The Internationalization of Social Science and Native Language Scholarly Writing in China, *Fudan Journal* (Social Sciences), No. 4, 2014.]

lacks local consciousness. He thought it very important that 'Chinese scholars should apply scientific research methods, actively participate in international academic dialogue and competition, invent dominant theoretical paradigms and set up research agendas with international colleagues. Even first-class Chinese writing with a global perspective is an integral part of the internationalization of social science in China.'

XIANG Biao, Professor of Social Anthropology at Oxford University, who graduated from the Department of Sociology, Peking University, in the mid-1990s, recently published an article on 'The ending of the "intellectual youth" era of Chinese social sciences'.[5]Scholars born before the 1960s, who received an incomplete education but had experience in rural China, have nearly all left their leadership or teaching posts. In contrast, post-1970s scholars, who received continuous formal education but without experience outside educational institutions, became the mainstream of academia. Xiang believes that the evolution of modern Chinese social science resembles the changes that have taken place between different generations of academic practice, knowledge acquisition and accumulation. Nevertheless, as Yefu Zheng, Emeritus Professor of Sociology at Peking University, pointed out, professors in the Department of Sociology at Peking University who were born before 1960 had still not retired; scholars' influence does not depend on their posts. Professor TIAN Song of Beijing Normal University also questioned whether the 'intellectual youth' era had ended. He maintained that the phenomenon of the post-1970s becoming mainstream is more of an academic management change[6].

The methodological character of Chinese social sciences is a very large topic. Recently we found a problem with translating the phrase '哲学社会科学' into English. It was in a speech at the Symposium of Philosophical Social Sciences by XI Jinping, President of China, on 17 May 2016.[7] Xi obtained a PhD from the Department of Sociology, School of Humanities and Social Science at Tsinghua University, in 2002. Our professional translator translated 哲学社会科学 into English as 'philosophical social sciences' based on the contents of the speech. Our copy editor accepted it, as did our academic adviser, Professor Martin Albrow, a founding editor of International Sociology and former President of the British Sociological Association. Moreover, inspired by it, when writing speech notes in preparation for attending a high-end international conference on China studies in

5   项飙，中国社会科学"知青时代"的终结，《文化纵横》，2015年第12期。[XIANG Biao. The ending of 'Intellectual youth' era of Chinese social sciences, *Beijing Cultural Review*, No.12, 2015]

4   田松，是代际替换，还是制度变更？《社会科学报》2016年3月10日第8版 [Tian Song. Is generational change or institutional change? *Social Science Weekly*, Shanghai Academy of Social Sciences, 10th March 2016, p10]

7   习近平，《在哲学社会科学工作座谈会上的讲话》，2016年5月18日，新华网 [XI Jinping, Speech at the Symposium of Philosophical Social Sciences, 18th May 2016. Xinhua Net. http://news.xinhuanet.com/politics/2016-05/18/c_1118891128.htm]

October, he titled his speech 'Philosophical social science as a bridge from "Belt and Road" to global governance'. But, as the editor of this book series, when I was finalizing the English translation of Xi's speech, I had to change 'philosophical social sciences' to 'philosophy and social sciences'. This seemed to coincide with the letter of Xi's speech, but from the methodological point of view, some important characteristics of Chinese social sciences were lost.

Globalization of Chinese social sciences

The 'globalization of Chinese social sciences' is a live issue. The direction and outcomes of globalization of Chinese social scientific studies are neither Western nor Chinese, but add concepts, theories and methods derived from studying countries like China, which have a long history, huge population and complicated society, to the sum of human knowledge. This idea first appeared in 'A Chinese phase in social anthropology'[8], the Malinowski Memorial Lecture by Maurice Freedman given at the London School of Economics and Political Science in 1962. Two years later, Freedman made another speech on an occasion when area studies were being discussed, with the title 'What social science can do for Chinese studies[9], in which he distinguished sinology from Chinese studies and emphasized the need to study China social-scientifically. Both Martin Albrow and Stephan Feuchtwang were research students, respectively in the Departments of Sociology and Anthropology at LSE, under the supervision of Maurice Freedman, and this affected their academic careers throughout their lives.

Martin Albrow helped many Chinese scholars to publish their articles in International Sociology in the 1980s when he was editor of the journal[10]. After 1990, he devoted himself to promoting the idea of globalization and became one of its international representatives. Nowadays, he helps promote Chinese social scientific work as part of the globalization of Chinese social sciences; at the same time, he attempts to insert the concept of transculturality into mainstream academia, as well as exploring the contributions of Chinese social sciences in the process of transculturalization. Details of this can be seen in my introductory paper launching the Journal of China in Comparative Perspective, entitled 'Transculturality and the globalization of Chinese social sciences: vocabulary, invention and exploration'[11].

---

[8]   Maurice Freedman, A Chinese Phase in Social Anthropology, *The British Journal of Sociology*, Vol. 14, No. 1, 1963.

[9]   Maurice Freedman. What social science can do for Chinese studies, *The Journal of Asian Studies*, Vol. 23, No. 4, 1964.

[10] Martin Albrow. A Chinese Episode in the Globalization of Sociology, *Journal of China in Comparative Perspective*, Vol.1 No.2, 2015. Its Chinese version see: 马丁·阿尔布劳, 社会学全球化过程中的中国片段, 《中国比较研究》, 2015年第1卷第2期。

[11] Xiangqun Chang. Transculturality and the Globalization of Chinese Social Sciences: Vocabulary, Invention and Exploration, *Journal of China in Comparative Perspective*, Vol.1 No. 1, 2015. [常向群, 文化与中国社会全球化: 词汇的发明与发掘《中超文化国比较研究》, 2015年第1卷第2期]。

Stephan Feuchtwang founded the China Research Unit at City University in 1973 when he worked there. It was the first organization dedicated to social scientific studies on China in the UK. Since 1998, when Feuchtwang was at the London School of Economics, he devoted himself to the creation of comparative studies of China. He appreciated Fei Xiaotong's comparative perspectives and theoretical conceptualization of the differential mode of association and organizational mode of association (Gary G. Hamilton's translation of 差序格局 and 团体格局[12]) and elaborated them with his own translation[13]. In 2013, after its gestation, birth and early years of growth of the China in Comparative Perspective Network (CCPN) at LSE, he supported changing its name from CCPN to CCPN Global, as CCPN completed the process of becoming independent from the LSE.

In addition to the above, some scholars are also dedicated to Chinese social sciences in the USA. For example, Professor Daniel Little, Chancellor at the University of Michigan-Dearborn, presented a paper 'New developments in the Chinese social sciences' at a conference Mapping Difference: Structures and Categories of Knowledge Production, 19–20 May 2006, at Duke University. As early as 1989, he published Understanding Peasant China: Case Studies in the Philosophy of Social Science, which was translated into Chinese and published in 2009[14]. In 2010, Gary Hamilton, Professor of Sociology and International Studies at the University of Washington, presented a paper entitled 'What Western social scientists can learn from the writings of Fei Xiaotong'[15] at the international conference at LSE, Commemorating the 100th Anniversary of Professor Fei Xiaotong's Birth. Hamilton speaks highly of Chinese social sciences' methodological contribution to general social science methodology. A recent example was seen at the Young Scholars conference Social Sciences and China Studies, 20–21 May 2016, organized by the Fudan-UC Center on Contemporary China at the University of California, San Diego. These are joint efforts to promote Chinese social sciences from both Chinese and American scholars. All in all, a huge amount of work is being done all over the world in different disciplines studying China social-scientifically – too much to be mentioned here.

---

[12] Xiaotong Fei. *From the Soil: The Foundations of Chinese Society*, A translation of Fei Xiaotong's Xiangtu Zhongguo, by Gary Hamilton and WANG Zheng. University of California Press, 1992.

[13] Stephan Feuchtwang. Social egoism and individualism: surprises and questions from a Western anthropologist of China – Reading Fei Xiaotong's contrast between China and the West, *Journal of China in Comparative Perspective*, Vol.1 No. 1, 2015. Its Chinese version see: 王斯福, 社会自我主义与个体主义 —— 一位西方的汉学人类学家阅读费孝通"中西对比"观念的惊讶与问题, 《中国比较研究》, 2015年第1卷第1期。

[14] Daniel Little. *Understanding Peasant China: Case Studies in the Philosophy of Social Science*. (Yale University Press, 1989). Chinese version: 李丹《理解农民中国——社会科学哲学的案例研究》, 江苏人民出版社2009年.

[15] Gary Hamilton. What Western social scientists can learn from the writings of Fei Xiaotong, *Journal of China in Comparative Perspective*, Vol.1 No. 1, 2015. Chinese version: 韩格理 (Gary G. Hamilton), 费孝通著作对西方社会科学家的启示, 《中国比较研究》, 2015年第1卷第1期。

In the Preface of this book, Feuchtwang stated that Fei Xiaotong is probably the highest-ranking policy-influencing anthropologist ever, who profoundly influenced social policies in China's development[16]. In his Preface to *Peasant Life in China*, Malinowski noted that Dr Fei promised that after he returned to China he would work with Chinese colleagues to undertake the comprehensive reform of China's economic, social, cultural, political and belief systems[17]. Taking the opportunity of commemorating the 100th anniversary of Fei Xiaotong's birth to launch the initiatives of globalization of Chinese social sciences, is for promoting the results of comprehensive studies in China and Chinese society by Chinese and non-Chinese scholars into the human knowledge palace. In his speechon Chinese philosophy and social sciences, XI Jinping mentioned LSE graduate Fei Xiaotong's name, which is no accident. As the highest-ranking policy-maker, Xi has promoted the all-round development of Chinese social sciences (see Appendix E). We believe that this may not only affect the process of globalization of Chinese social science but could also have far-reaching historic impact on China's participation in global governance and society building and the sustainable development of a global society.

August 2016 revised

---

[16] Stephan Feuchtwang. Preface, *Journal of China in Comparative Perspective*, Vol.1 No. 1, 2015
[17] Bronislaw Malinowski. Preface, in Hsiao-Tung Fei (Fei Xiaotong), *Peasant life in China*, London: Routledge, 1939.

DOI https://doi.org/10.24103/GCSS2.en.2016.1

Preface[1]

Stephan Feuchtwang

I remember Professor Fei with fondness; I think everybody who met him probably does. He smiled a lot, with a most benign look. But he was not at all complacent. Indeed, he was critical, curious and enquiring, as you can tell from his publications up to the very last. I would go further: he had such a strong sense of his own direction that it was difficult for me to know what he was making of what I said to him on the few occasions when we met.

Outside China and China studies he is not well known, and this is not surprising since he focused so resolutely on how his sociology and anthropology could help the Chinese people. He deserves to be well known for the fact that he is probably the most committed and eventually the highest-ranked policy-influencing anthropologist ever. But he certainly also thought of himself as a contributor to the social sciences, particularly sociology and anthropology, more generally. And he did not just study China. One of the points of this volume is to explore and expound his anthropology and sociology for a wider readership.

Each chapter, and the Appendix, contains what we consider to be contributions made by Fei's writings on China to a more general social science, either as a deliberately comparative concept or as a mode of analysis that can be applied elsewhere.

Fei Xiaotong's first contribution is his best-known and deliberately comparative conceptualization of the basis of Chinese social relations. It is a formulation invented by Fei, which is best left in Chinese: *chaxugeju*, two translations of which are expounded here – the differential mode of organization, and social egoism – compared and contrasted by Fei with secularized and Protestant Christian individualism. I would add, here, that *chaxugeju* is also comparable as a civilizational hierarchy in contrast to Hindu caste and sub-caste hierarchy, and the hierarchy of Euro-North-American industrial capitalist class and status, each with their own units of social mobility up and down the respective hierarchies, each encompassing from the top down in different ways. I hope to elaborate this comparison in a forthcoming book. In this book, apart from the various expositions of *chaxugeju*, there is also its extension and elaboration by Chang Xiangqun into a larger concept of interpersonal relations, *lishang-wanglai*, which takes into account a great many studies in China of 'face', the

---

[1] *Editor's note:* This Preface was written in August 2011. The author listed some of Fei Xiaotong's contributions based on the articles published here. After the event in memory of Fei Xiaotong's 100th anniversary at LSE 2010, the editors have received and collected many articles. Their views have not been included in this Preface.

art of connections, and the ethics of human relatedness, besides and beyond Fei's own. This elaboration is based on Dr Chang's own restudy of Fei's Jiangcun, namely the village of Kaixian'gong in Wujiang county, Jiangsu province, in the delta of the Great River, the Yangtze. But it is set, as Fei's original concept was, in readiness for comparison with other conceptions of interpersonal relations and their cultivation in other kinds of society. The discussions with Dr Chang in the Appendix bring out the possibilities of such comparison.

The second contribution is a continuation of the theme of comparison, but through a methodological imperative of self-reflection and self-exposition by anyone, native or not, embedded within a particular society but already partially disembedded by the task of studying it. Self-exposition refers especially to the untranslatability, or partial translatability, of the language of social reflection used by social actors in the society concerned. But exposition must persist in finding roundabout ways in another language of conveying what is not directly translatable. All the best ethnographies do this, without conceding to the obscurity of either a cultural relativism or a cultural chauvinism that reduces Chinese or any other culture to just itself. In some of his late publications, Fei turned this into a special kind of self-reflexivity. It is not the reflexivity of English-language anthropology celebrated in the widely read and followed chapters (except that by Talal Asad) edited by James Clifford and George E. Marcus in *Writing Culture* (Berkeley: University of California Press, 1986). In these chapters anthropologists seek to make explicit and to overcome the formerly implicit power relations between the anthropologists and their subjects of study. They seek to overcome these power relations by raising the statements and expositions of the subjects to a status equal to those of the anthropologists who bring them to the attention of a readership, while Asad points out the inherent and unavoidable power relation of writing in English. Fei's is a quite different reflexivity and has so far been confined to the Chinese language. It is a cultural reflection in which he uses the concepts derived from a culture to reflect upon itself, and crucially in addition to reflect on and with its 'heart' – the feelings as well as the reason and concepts that key words or phrases convey. One section of the Appendix expounds Fei's notion of 'heart'. Might there be a comparison and contrast here with a key text in English-language Cultural Studies, Raymond Williams' *Key Words* (Oxford University Press, 1984)? In any case, although confined to the study of China, Fei's example can be followed and varied by anthropologists seeking the culturally reflective terms of the societies and cultures they study and inhabit. And they would have to do this without insisting that only these terms are appropriate, because they want to be read in other languages and with other words and concepts, including those of the social sciences to which they contribute and into which they are finding roundabout ways to translate these culturally specific reflective words. Their very conceptualization depends on this effort of translation. Only by making this effort do they become applicable and open to comparison, though translation is merely a first step.

The second contribution is all about Fei's studies of villages in China. It would appear to be only about the study of China, no more and no less. But it does raise several more general methodological problems. Of what is a village study a so-called 'case'? And, if it is a 'case' of something claimed to be 'China', is it the appropriate unit of study?

One answer to the first question is to suggest that a village is an example of a 'community' and that Fei was following in the footsteps of the American Chicago School of urban sociology in pursuing 'community' studies, which are studies of localities within which most, but not all, relations in which the inhabitants engage are confined. Of course, urban studies since then have found just as often if not more often that the radiation of relationships from any one household goes far beyond their neighborhood and its radii do not coincide with those of neighboring households. They are especially differentiated by class and occupation. Similarly the relationships radiating, on the principles of *chaxugeju* and *lishang-wanglai*, from the households of a village are certainly not confined to the village but at the very least to a marriage area linking several villages, and those villages are linked in their economic activities with small towns. Fei was acutely aware of this and indeed he made small towns his basic unit of study after his classic village studies. This problem of the appropriate unit of study for qualitative fieldwork – within what range are most relations stemming from households confined in their coincidence, so that this unit is the best for intensive local studies – is common in a market economy and a state that defines the limits of local political relations. A good ethnography, precise in its descriptions, expounding well the local terms used for discussing social relations, is already a contribution to potentially comparable ethnographies and the economies and states in which they are set.

Then there is the question of how to generalize to the whole of that economy and state from selected case studies. Fei hoped to do this, first by village studies but then by small-town and regional studies, by comparing them and inducing from this comparison a typology of their differences, which were called, by him and by policy-makers, 'models' of different paths of development within the same political economy. Could this method be copied elsewhere, outside China? Perhaps. Could it ever become exhaustive, covering the full range of differences to be found in a country at one time? I doubt it.

Finally, there is the question of what is a study a 'case'? Were Fei's studies cases of economic development or more? They can as well be read as case studies of gender relations, or of kinship relations, to be compared not only within China, as in Chapter 4, but with other such case studies from other contexts altogether, of development, of gender relations and of kinship relations.

The fouth contribution continues with a discussion of these questions: how and for what were Fei's studies carried out, and how can they be extended to other studies in China up to the present day? But in this chapter we come to Fei from the opposite direction, in fact from two directions. One is from outside China to his concepts. The very question of whether Fei's work, in his own estimation, should be a contribution to the 'luxury' of anthropological theorizing is raised in relation to the work of English anthropologists. Concepts from general sociology, chiefly that of urban Euro-North-America, are applied to his concepts of *chaxugeju* and economic enterprise. Readers will have to settle for themselves whether these outside concepts have to be changed in their application to Fei's Chinese concepts and studies. What further steps must we take in accepting Fei's works into anthropology, or into the sociology of social capital, or into management studies?

The other direction is from his work on other peoples in China than the Han majority to the question of 'China'. What is 'China' as bounded by its present borders, including the large border regions that Fei helped to define? How different are these border regions from the other regions of China? More currently, less historically, how are their separate paths of development, or modernizations in the plural, to be nurtured and acknowledged even as their differences grow while their sharing a state and an economy brings them together? Several potential comparisons suggest themselves, for instance with the Russian Federation of States or with India's adivarsi (tribal peoples), though none have been carried out yet.

The fifth contribution based on an article we come at last to some country-to-country comparisons, though they must be suggestive of the far greater potential for comparison. Comparison of kinship systems, based on Fei's Kaixian'gong, and of border regions based on his Chinese border region studies, are the most anthropological. Comparison of the construction of garden cities as communities with Fei's small-town studies and policies is more sociological and has more to do with planning. And two further reviews of the relationship of Fei's anthropology to general and comparative studies extend the discussion relating to the second and the fourth contributions.

Finally, the six contribution is about Fei's life and work, indeed to his life as a work of Chinese political history. In his later years and since he died China has become a world power of which the rest of the world has necessarily taken notice, not least the social scientists of the English writing world. Coming from several disciplines and not specializing in the study of China, some of them seek and find in Fei's works at least two things. One is a set of clues to the workings of Chinese society. The other is his example and the way in which the study of China can be an example of world anthropology or global sociology. Again the potential is clear, but its realization is yet to be accomplished. And that is the message of every part of this book. The potential for comparison, contrast, and contribution to general social sciences has, we hope, been made clear. Its realization is to be accomplished by further work.

DOI https://doi.org/10.24103/GCSS2.en.2016.2

Introduction[1]

Xiangqun Chang

The year 2016 will be another significant year for honouring Professor Fei Xiaotong (1910–2005), because it is the 80th anniversary of his fieldwork in Kaixiaogong Village (of which the academic name is Jiangcun). His most famous book, *Peasant Life in China* (1939), was based on this fieldwork. Peking University and Nanjing University are jointly organizing an international conference entitled 'Jiangcun Fieldwork and the Sinicization of Social Sciences' on 22–23 October 2016 at Maogang Community, where the village is located.

This issue is publishing two articles from the conference marking the 60th anniversary of Fei Xiaotong's fieldwork in Kaixiaogong Village. They are 'A practical-minded person—Professor Fei's anthropological calling and Edmund Leach's game', by Stephan Feuchtwang, and 'A swan's trace in snow: unexpected visits, fieldwork and the anthropology of Fei Xiaotong', by Charles Stafford, and both are published here for the first time in the West. They are not only new to readers outside China but also important in helping readers understand the development of Chinese social sciences.

I should highlight that both the above articles deal with China or the Chinese in comparative perspective, either between anthropologists or their work on China and other countries or regions. On the merit of comparative studies on China, we specifically invited Chie Nakane to contribute an article 'China and India: an anthropological view in relation to cultural peripheries'. Chie obtained her PhD in Japanese and Indian Studies at the London School of Economics in 1957. This article applies a comparative perspective between Japan and China with India and Tibet, where she conducted her fieldwork with help from Fei Xiaotong. She presented this paper at the 'First Fei Memorial Lecture', on the first anniversary of Fei's death, 16 December 2006, at Peking University. Its Chinese version was published in the *Journal of Peking University* (Philosophy and Social Sciences), 2007, no. 2. *JCCP* is proud to be publishing the first English version of this work.

---

[1] This Introduction was originally written as the Editorial for *Journal of China in Comparative Perspective*, Vol.1 No.2. 2015. I use it as an Introduction for this book since the main articles are selected from *JCCP*. But I would like to add that Appendix A was taken from *Chinese for Social Sciences* (Vol. 1, 2016), edited by Dongning Feng. Chinese for social sciences' or 'Chinese language for Social Sciences' is a branch of 'Chinese for Specific Purposes' (CSP), like 'Chinese for science and technology' or 'business Chinese'. This innovative idea was first developed by CCPN Global. The source articles in this volume have been published in *JCCP*, the only peer-reviewed academic journal for social scientific, humanities and comparative studies of China in the world. The General Preface and Appendix D serve as general info for all the books in this book series.

This issue also includes two papers from scholars of the younger generation. They are 'A comparative study of family in China and Japan', by Hong Park, and 'The road to the cities: interpreting some theoretical perspectives on migration and urbanization by Fei Xiaotong and Ebenezer Howard', by Zhiming Wu and Ye Liu. They were selected from the papers that we invited for the international conference 'Understanding China and Engaging with Chinese People – Commemorating the 100th Anniversary of Professor Fei Xiaotong's Birth', 5–8 December 2010, at LSE. One is an empirical study-based article by Hong Park, who is a Korean Chinese and has been studying and working in Japan for more than two decades, but who also did her fieldwork and paid many field visits in Kaixiangong Village. The other is a documentary-based article originally written in Chinese and published in China by Zhiming Wu of Renmin University of China. In his absence, Ye Liu, the then CCPN research assistant, revised the Chinese version significantly, translated it into English and presented it at the conference.

A section on 'Reflection and Prediction' is included in this issue. My own reflection here will trace back nearly 80 years, to the time when Fei Xiaotong finished his PhD thesis at LSE and then published it as *Peasant Life in China* (1939). Malinowski regarded the book as 'a landmark in the development of anthropological fieldwork and theory'. In 1962, the Malinowski Lecture was given by Maurice Freedman. In this lecture, entitled 'A Chinese phase in social anthropology', Freedman encouraged social anthropologists to study societies with long and complex civilizational histories, such as that of China, and expressed his belief that the future course of social anthropology lay in this type of study.

The reflective paper is entitled 'A Chinese episode in the globalization of sociology', by Martin Albrow. Like Stephan Feuchtwang, Albrow also received supervision from Maurice Freedman and listened to the lecture mentioned above when he was a research student in the Department of Sociology at LSE. In the 1980s, Albrow was President of the British Sociological Association (BSA) and the founding editor of *International Sociology*. In this article, Albrow observes that 'Chinese papers contributed to a developing debate about the globalization of sociology, its signification and the universalistic credentials of sociology. This episode illustrates the ongoing reflexivity of sociology when in encounters between cultures it seeks to overcome conceptual differences by attending to common features of the human condition and challenges that confront all humankind.'

The predictive article is 'Post-nationalist anthropology? Anthropologies today in their nationalist traditions, cosmopolitan ethos and collaborative possibilities', by George E. Marcus. It is based on the author's lecture at the event 'To Commemorate the Centenary of Professor Fei Xiaotong's Lectures – World Anthropologies and China Anthropology' on 20 June 2010, held at Peking University and jointly organized by the Department of Sociology and Institute of Sociology and Anthropology, Peking University, the Department of Anthropology, Sun Yat-Sen University, School of Ethnology and Sociology, the

Central University for Nationalities, School of Nationalities, Yunnan University, and the Department of Sociology, Shanghai University. In this article, Marcus offers 'a vision for world anthropology as an organized project' and predicts that 'World anthropology at its most pragmatic and accessible is embedded in such contemporary initiatives of collaborative, creolized training that continue to operate at a situated scale of enquiry, cultivated by and emblematic of our discipline.'

In the 'Dialogue and Comments' section, a full account is published of 'A dialogue between a Western scholar (Gary G. Hamilton) and a Chinese scholar (Xiangqun Chang) on Fei Xiaotong's contributions to sociology and anthropology' (the abridged version was published under the title 'China and world anthropology: a conversation on the legacy of Fei Xiaotong (1910–2005)' in *Anthropology Today*, Vol. 27, no. 6, 2011). It can be seen as one of efforts of the 'world anthropology organized project' that Marcus proposed. After reading the above dialogue, Bettina Gransow offered her 'Comments on the dialogue on Fei Xiaotong's contributions'. Readers will enjoy this for themselves, but I should like to draw attention to earlier work by sociologists inside and outside China in the 1990s. According to Albrow, 'the sinification and globalization of sociology that could almost be taken as a textbook case of the issues involved in indigenization'. He introduced Gransow's work (1993), in which she 'surveyed the different tendencies in intensive debates among Chinese sociologists in Taiwan, Hong Kong, the United States and the People's Republic.' He cited Gransow's conclusion that 'the endeavour towards the sinicization of sociology led to a learning process about sociology's cultural and civilizational ties, a learning process which sharpened the senses for the relative limits set within the context of cultural semantic patterns, even if a universal approach was taken.'

Finally, I should mention two pieces in the 'Feedback and Comments' session. They are 'From cross culture, interculture to transculture – reading "Universal dream, national dreams and symbiotic dream: reflections on transcultural generativity in China–Europe Encounters"', by SHEN Qi, and 'Making space for "transculturality" – a response to SHEN Qi', by Shuo Yu. Readers will find both papers very interesting and thought-provoking, especially if they have read the original article in *JCCP* 1.1.

DOI https://doi.org/10.24103/GCSS2.en.2016.3

A Practically Minded Person
Fei Xiaotong's Anthropological Calling and Edmund Leach's Game[1]

Stephan Feuchtwang

Abstract: This is a continuation in print of the conversation between two famous anthropologists, Professors Fei Xiaotong and Edmund Leach. It compares their two callings, or senses of vocation, as anthropologists and puts each into their historical context. To this it adds consideration of Maurice Freedman, a British anthropologist of Chinese society. It praises Fei for his patriotic and critical anthropology; it praises Leach for his critical and committed anthropology, which frees the discipline from its functionalist limitations; it praises Freedman for his critical extension of the concept of the corporate lineage beyond functionalism and into history. With Fei, it criticizes the narrowness of much anthropological writing for purely academic readerships, but comes to the conclusion that at its best anthropology is an independent and open critical vocation.

Keywords: Fei Xiaotong, Edmund Leach, Maurice Freedman, patriotic anthropology, anthropology as a calling

On his eightieth birthday, reflecting on his personal experience as a Chinese anthropologist and contrasting his kind of anthropology with that of his classmate in London, Edmund Leach, who also became a famous anthropologist, Professor Fei wrote this:

> I admire Edmund Leach for his profound knowledge of philosophy and his excellent... academic training. I hardly doubt that the answers a practical minded person like myself can give to his questions sound convincing. But when I think about it, I admit that what would have seemed to him overly credulous and plodding in me is neither the result of chance, a personal trait of mine or prejudice born of private experience. I could not help but fall under the influence of some traditional credos, two in particular: first, that every single person shares the responsibility for the rise or fall of his nation; and second, that we study in order to apply what we learn. These two time-honoured Chinese maxims sum up my basic attitude towards learning. (Fei Xiaotong 1992)

---

[1] This paper was first presented at a conference in 1996 with Professor Fei Xiaotong in Wujiang County, celebrating sixty years since he first studied Kaixiangong. It was published in Ma, Zhou, Pan and Wang (eds.) *Tianye Gongzuo yu Wenhua Zijue* (*Fieldwork and Cultural Consciousness*), Beijing: Qunyan Chubanshe 1998:1141–1166. It has been slightly revised by the author before it was published in this journal.

In this paragraph Professor Fei describes his calling as an anthropologist. It is a scientific calling, but it also stems from a Chinese intellectual tradition of duty and engagement.

When I read this passage I feel myself being addressed in several ways and pushed in more than one direction. As someone who during my own academic training was very excited by the ideas of Edmund Leach, and in particular by the publication of the first Malinowski Lecture, which he gave in 1959, entitled 'Rethinking Anthropology', I feel I must say something about his kind of anthropology. But I am also someone who has spent most of his life studying Chinese society, and therefore one for whom Professor Fei's works are classics. Not only did they form part of my ethnographic training, but I have in recent years been involved through a Chinese colleague and research student, Chang Xiangqun, with the longitudinal study of Kainxian'gong itself, which Fei started and has so generously shared.

As a student of rural society in China I am drawn to Professor Fei's practical concerns and his Chinese identity. But my identification with China is through professional interest and personal friendships. I am not a resident or a citizen of China. I come from outside China as a successor to the tradition of Leach's anthropology.

In his reflections, Professor Fei distances himself from Leach not only as a different kind of anthropologist but as a Chinese one. I feel bound to exercise whatever I have learned through my knowledge of China and from working with Chinese colleagues in the social sciences to deepen the dialogue that Professor Fei has opened between himself and Edmund Leach. In his own paper for this conference (published in advance as 'Chongdu "Jiangcun Jingji × xuyan"' (Re-reading the preface to *Peasant Life in China*), Beijing Daxue Xuebao, 1996: 4, pp. 4–18) Professor Fei again addresses Leach and in addition refers to a lecture given by my teacher Professor Maurice Freedman's Malinowski Memorial Lecture in 1962, only three years after Leach gave the first. Freedman's view of the lessons that the anthropological study of China can teach will be an addition to my dialogue with Professor Fei.

In furthering this dialogue between English and Chinese anthropology, I feel I am crossing zones between different senses of time and between different histories. Professor Fei has lived, in his own person and in his identification with the Chinese people, through the ups and downs of an historical turmoil far longer-lasting and more disturbing (and also far more full of hope as well as despair) than Britain's, even when you include the Second World War. He has wanted to use anthropology to shape and affect and to prevent the destructiveness of social change, even while fully recognizing that it is always to a great extent unpredictable.

A patriotic profession

Leach and Freedman were deeply involved in the Second World War, but professionally as anthropologists they were far more identified with anthropology itself than with the politics and development of their country and people.

Leach was interested in generalization by mathematical and imaginative induction from single studies. He was against the comparative method of typologizing. Professor Fei is in favour of typologizing in order to make practical policy for China. Models, the more dynamic and developmental version of types, are Professor Fei's way of expanding small-scale studies to the complex whole of contemporary Chinese society. Professor Fei's public and self-professed history is the history of modern China and the service that sociology or social anthropology can render it. Professor Leach's public and self-professed history, in contrast, is that of anthropology and the service he can render it. Not only do we have different histories, each with its own pace – a faster pace in China, a slower one in Britain, each disturbed by different catastrophes of war – but we also have quite different subjects of history: anthropology in and for China; anthropology as such in Britain.

For Leach, the mission of anthropology is to expose and question ethnocentricity. In both 'Rethinking Anthropology' and the chapter of *Social Anthropology* (1982) entitled 'My Kind of Anthropology', Leach promoted intensive and local studies in order to obtain from them insights that might be true for enquiry into any human society. His aim was to increase the capacity to question and to locate the assumptions both of the people studied and of the anthropology being used to study them.

For Professor Fei as a patriotic and a practical anthropologist, the problem is quite different. He considers Leach's quest for generalization to be a luxury enjoyed by the secure academic in a wealthy nation engaged in a playful as distinct from a practical study: 'an intellectual game for showing off one's talents' (Fei 1992: 13). Professor Fei's is a patriotic anthropology. By patriotic I do not mean nationalist; I mean only the motivation and the professed dedication to work for the good of one's people. But this does not exclude a broader, humanistic and comparative vision. 'I believe that we who study man are duty-bound to nurture the spirit of tolerance' (Fei 1992: 20). Nor does it exclude a scientific ethic: the spirit of enquiry, empirical testing, and of debate.

Interestingly, for Professor Fei the experience of being attacked and being prevented from writing during two decades (1957–1980) of persecution made him 'stateless in a sociological sense' (*Current Anthropology*, 29(4), 1988: 654). He was reduced and at the same time elevated to a detached humanity. But, for him, even this was an historical humanity: humanity in movement, humanity as the self-consciousness of nature in evolution. Unlike at the beginning of this century, there are few if any Western anthropologists now whose humanity would be so cosmic and historical. Such optimism is lost in the planetary concepts of interdependence and in the doubts about direction and development with which we in academies of the developed world view the world.

In the same interview with an American fellow anthropologist, Burton Pasternak, Professor Fei frequently used 'we' to identify himself with the Chinese people and to unite his personal history with that of China. We are far more likely to use it to represent ourselves as part of the academic profession in that country than to represent ourselves as one of its people.

One has a mission of popular advancement. The other has a mission of scepticism and critical appraisal. Both are based on empirical enquiry and the development of concepts useful for analysis and open to question. But the primary purposes seem to differ.

Placed in the context of a patriotic anthropology, fieldwork is a way of building up generalizations about a whole people, out of the local histories, local cultures, local economies and other conditions of its social life. It is part of the efforts of local historians and folklorists whose works enter huge compilations of publication and documentation which are then stored in the archival knowledge of a nation and used by its politicians to forge its identity, both singular and plural. Some of Professor Fei's work on ethnic minorities served such a purpose. But Professor Fei's slow project of building a typology of models of development (1996: 9) is a different project altogether. So dynamic a project is nothing like the static typologies of whole societies undertaken by the structural functionalists who were criticized by Leach for trying to be natural historians of society and culture. It also differs from the sorting out of peoples by governments for the purpose of rule. Its anthropological hallmark is still local, small-scale study. But isn't it also in another Chinese, a revolutionary and now governmental tradition of on-the-spot observation of processes of change, which can become models for emulation elsewhere? In any case, the anthropologist doing this kind of work is a channel through which the different local conditions, local traditions and local creativity can inform and influence national policy and show how it is being implemented and what is going wrong as well as what new directions it could take.

I want to underline another aspect of this work, which I think is of equal importance. Anthropologists' publications are a means by which localities can learn about each other. This is the anthropologists' equivalent of the opinion poll. It creates the sense of a people, its variations, its tensions, and its changing composition. The boundaries of a nation and the assumption of unity within them are of course built into such a project. It would be politically dangerous to assume otherwise. But what distinguishes the anthropologist's carrying out of this kind of enquiry from the government official's enquiry and also from a social survey is that the anthropologist's report places the local facts in a local context and enables an understanding of the local people in their own terms. What it brings to a wider view are not simply the facts of a condition or a new way of dealing with a problem. It brings to the larger view the social creativity of the people studied.

Furthermore, since it is an academic report, it raises professional and critical questions of the validity and reliability of the facts presented. As a professional act, a field report should be open to reinterpretation or modification by other fact-finders and analysts. The fieldwork report is an act of representation and it should be open to challenge as a misrepresentation. When this occurs in the language of and in publications that can be read by the subjects of the study themselves, it is a representation of a people to itself. Native anthropology has this dynamic dimension, which removal to an international forum does not have. If my analyses of Chinese villages and towns were translated into Chinese, they too would have this dynamic dimension, but I myself would be removed, as I live in another country. Mine is therefore more of an academic than a patriotic profession, while Professor Fei's is more patriotic as well as being an academic profession.

An academic profession

In 'Rethinking Anthropology' Leach pointed out that unexamined assumptions are imported into and imposed by typological frameworks. They come from two sources, neither of which are questioned or acknowledged: one is the society studied and the other the psychological and philosophical preoccupations of the anthropologist's own society. In his last book, *Social Anthropology* (1982), to which Professor Fei refers, Leach gave the very same reasons for saying how difficult it is to be an anthropologist of one's own society. It is difficult to avoid bringing unquestioned assumptions into reported facts and it is hard to avoid drawing generalized conclusions from a single study, which the native anthropologist takes to be typical of his own society. At the same time Leach praised Professor Fei for his success in overcoming this propensity. He praised Fei for maintaining the stance of a professional anthropologist in the particularly difficult circumstances of self-involvement because of his patriotic mission, which was (in my words) to promote action to change the subject of his study and to treat at least some of its subjects as agents of their own change.

According to two of his students, Leach inherited and passed on to them two ideas about anthropology from Malinowski. One was that action is not rigidly constrained by cultural rules; statistical norms are likely to diverge from ideal norms; there is room for individuals to make self-serving choices. The other was that anthropology reveals both the familiarity of the exotic and the exoticism of the familiar (Fuller and Parry 1989: 12).

The first idea made Leach more willing to discuss social change and action than other British structural anthropologists, such as his colleague at Cambridge University, Meyer Fortes. 'Where Fortes focused on jural order... [and] the priority of descent over relations based on local contiguity, Leach insisted on the over-riding significance of local organization and property relations...[in which] kinship relations are merely an idiom for talking about property relations .... [E]ven for the African societies for which it was originally developed, the "descent paradigm" was a distorting lens which severely undervalued locally-based relations of economic co-operation and conflict' (Fuller and Parry 1989: 12).

Similarly, in *Political Systems of Highland Burma*, Leach established that idioms of tribal belonging were used for talking about political relations. The same people in one generation might say they were of one tribe and in the next of another. Kachin political institutions and ritual meanings changed as their tensions developed and burst into another set of relations in cycles of change from egalitarian anarchic community to hierarchical organization and back again, precipitated by power-seeking individuals. Leach taught his students to recognize the ambiguities and contradictions with which people live, and to avoid over-coherent accounts of cultures.

His idea of structure was at one time modelled on mathematics, but it was not a statistical means of generalization. It was a mathematics of relatedness, not an algebra of functional equations, and was even further from a functionalism of needs. Here he departed radically from Malinowski and from the other British structuralists of social systems. Leach drew an analogy for his kind of structural generalization from topology, which is a kind of geometry. It starts from the content and contrast between concurrent relations, and examines what happens when these contents and contrasts are varied across cultures ('Rethinking Anthropology': 7–8). At the same time, as I have already pointed out, he stressed the actor using the rules of relatedness. For Leach, case studies, however small or large, can be compared according to the variation of complementary and different kinds of relationship and of the different and contrasting contents of those relationships. Such comparison could include a great many cases, as in his example in the Malinowski Lecture, which took in his own work on the Kachin, along with Malinowski's Trobriands and Meyer Fortes' Tallensi, and a number of others. But it always included by implication his own society and its cultural rules. This was putting the second idea taken from Malinowski into practice, to treat the familiar as strange and the strange as familiar.

This second idea combined with the first one on the creativity of individual actors to produce the anthropology he consistently practised and taught. He nurtured in his students a capacity to generalize and to avoid agonizing over cultural relativity, and he took this way of thinking beyond the academic world. Over-arching his writing and his teaching was his constant willingness to challenge orthodoxies and engage with a wider audience (Fuller and Parry 1989: 14). Like Professor Fei, he was passionately committed to the belief that anthropology can tell us something significant about ourselves and so should address a wider public than academic anthropologists. For instance, Leach hoped the essays contained along with his Malinowski Lecture in the book entitled *Rethinking Anthropology* would 'provoke some readers to doubt their sense of certainty' (Leach 1961: v). For a wider audience, in the last of his famously provocative Reith Lectures, which were broadcast on British radio in 1967, Leach urged his listeners 'to keep on remembering the total interconnectedness of things as distinct from their separate isolated existence'. He reminded them that they are in a dynamic not a static relation to each other (Leach 1968: 77). From this he derived the principle that we have to take responsibility for our interconnectedness, and for the changes we can bring about, to weigh the effects of what we do and to avoid the destructiveness of separation and fragmentation which breeds fear and violence among peoples: 'It is nationalism, not technology which is our contemporary disaster,' he claimed, since for him nationalism was 'the lamentable delusion that only the separate can be free' (Leach 1968: 90).

Leach deliberately avoided preaching. He was against moralizing. He warned of the dangers of doctrines of universal truth and moral judgment. But he did enjoin the practical ethic of an anthropologist, which is consistent with the condemnation of doctrinal creeds of universal judgment. Fieldwork and the reading of ethnographies are the disciplines through which connection as a practical ethic is formed, and by which the professional calling of an anthropologist is transmitted. The human beings and social states that are the subjects of anthropological study do not have to be distant or even present. 'Fieldwork' can take the form of secondary analysis or historical research. Whatever its materials, fieldwork is always the contemplation of others as selves and of self as other. Fieldwork training and ethnographical education discipline students into acknowledging their otherness by an enquiry which requires us to learn what the other knows. We are trained to accept the differences between us without fear or prejudice and then to try to convey their distinctiveness by cross-cultural means of description and explanation. Leach's cross-cultural generalizations included the Judeo-Christian-Muslim Bible as well as the myths of other cultures.

The anthropology of a large society: Maurice Freedman and Professor Fei

There is a similarity between Leach's concentration on the human actor and Professor Fei's focus on the self in a much-changed and changing China during the 1930s. Recent writing by Chinese anthropologists of China has taken up Professor Fei's idea of Chinese social structure starting from a moral person, a self at the centre of social networks, governed by circles of closeness and distance, in different categories of kinship and friendship obligations derived from Confucian, Daoist and Legalist ideals, like the circles cast by a pebble thrown into water (Feuchtwang 2014: 75–95). This idea and the idea of the importance of neo-Confucianism as a governing ideology have been used to attack the same descent paradigm that Leach attacked and which was applied by Maurice Freedman to the study of Chinese kinship relations.

The attacks by Chinese anthropologists are part of an intense search for a more faithful anthropology of China by native Chinese anthropologists. In the place of Freedman's concentration on the structures of corporate groups, we have Professor Fei's self and its family connections or the neo-Confucian ideology and its use by the imperial Chinese state to maintain governmental order. Lineage becomes an idiom rather than a social being. Lineages or sub-lineages, where they occur as local groups, are placed in an historical moment and in regional conditions.

The overwhelming importance of seeing things in an historical perspective, and having to locate social institutions in a continuous history of slow or sudden change may be a Chinese contribution to anthropology. There may be a peculiarly Chinese way of conceiving history. But in itself the importance of history is not peculiar to studies of China or to Chinese scholars. It has become a commonplace of anthropology since the attacks on structuralism for ignoring agency and change.

It is true that, in the West, Freedman's analyses and models of local lineages and their segmentation became a paradigm for anthropological studies of Chinese society, which concentrated on the south-eastern provinces. More recently they have been the basis of debate on the social history of Chinese kinship as a whole. This is because Freedman was so successful at making the detailed records of other people's first-hand observations of local, rural organization in south-eastern China intelligible as lineage organization. His object was Chinese society as a whole, and his promotion in 1962 of a Chinese phase in anthropology served, as Professor Fei has pointed out (1966), to urge upon anthropologists the study of large-scale societies and civilizations. Far from presenting ahistorical structures, as the structural functionalists had done, Freedman took pains to point out that this meant conducting historical studies. By this he meant studies of social change as well as the use of the rich documentation of change that the Chinese and other written cultures provide.

Freedman's conception of local lineages as corporate groups that have competitive advantages in the political and agrarian conditions of south-eastern China became something to argue for, to qualify, or to contest. Unfortunately, some of the contestation ignores the historical and political dimensions of Freedman's analyses. Freedman had taken what was a paradigm for classifying small-scale societies in Africa, Asia and the Pacific into categories according to different principles of descent and marital location. While Leach attacked this typological framework for what he called butterfly collecting, a false notion of scientific generalization, Freedman attacked it in another way.

In applying the descent paradigm to a large society with a state and a long written history, Freedman consciously changed the African conception of a lineage. In his hands it became applicable to a social organization that could not be fitted into the categorization of whole societies. He knew this and made it a part of his writing. Freedman showed that property relations, wealth and status aspirations in China affected the formation, the management and the genealogies themselves of local lineages and their segmentation (Freedman 1974). A system of descent was, according to him, only one sub-system among others with different rules or principles of organization. But unlike Leach he never tried to make cross-cultural generalizations. From his studies of Chinese society it is possible to derive a general concept of society as a number of principles of organization which cut across each other in the formation of social institutions. But he worked on this conception only for China.

Despite his efforts, the Chinese case and the anthropology of China have remained cut off from the kinds of generalization that Leach so successfully advocated and himself contributed to anthropology. Perhaps the increased number of studies by Chinese and foreign anthropologists will achieve for China a place in generalizations about social relations, or about the formation of nations, or about family and kinship as idioms of relatedness. I hope we can achieve this together.

A practical ethic and its institutionalization

Certainly there is a difference in our habitual conceptions of self. The individual, for Leach, is a self in its social relations, a self for whom the discourses and conventions of a culture orient action, but are also used politically or for self-interest. Rules are not as rigid as to predict in action what they prescribe as ideals. As I have already remarked, this conception has some similarity with Professor Fei's idea of ego-centred networks. But the self in each case is quite different. Professor Fei's is a Chinese, neo-Confucian self. Leach follows Malinowski in assuming the self to be, as his students have pointed out in a critical remark, 'the maximizing individual of Western utilitarian theory, and it is hard to accept the assumption that either the Kachin tribesman or the Sri Lankan villager is quite such a simple soul' (Fuller and Parry 1989). Here Leach himself is caught out making an unquestioned assumption, derived from his own historical culture. But this criticism by his students is a good example of the spirit of anthropology for which Malinowski and Leach stood.

Criticism, and the development of concepts by which it can be carried out, serves a purpose, although it is not the same as the purpose that takes priority for Professor Fei. Academic anthropology's purpose is to search out alternative possibilities, other realities than those to which our thought and the discourses of our times have been confined. Of course, criticism can become play, as Professor Fei warns us. It easily and often turns into a criticism from the sidelines, without commitment to any reality or any change of direction except a romantic wish to preserve critical purity.

It is a pretence of not being involved in the ideologies, governments, and common senses that make up the realities it criticizes. It sounds radical but it takes no risks, because it commits itself to no direction or governmental possibility. It cannot make choices because it favours instead an idealized political community and assumes a separate and totalized ethical position. It is so disengaged that the realities it criticizes from outside can easily accommodate it. Such critiques are a kind of political romanticism (Minson 1993: 6–11).

But the profession of anthropology does, I think, imply an ethico-political position which need not be that of romanticism. I speak only for a possibility that I see. Others probably act on different premises. But it seems to me that implicit in a scientific profession to generalize to humanity from local and intensive empirical studies there is a practical humanism. It is a disciplined capacity to listen and to see, withholding judgment. It is a training to respect what is said and done by others before judgment. It is to allow the theories and even the frameworks of the theories with which the study was conceived to be open to question. It is to welcome the unexpected and to be prepared to think about why it was not expected, and so to overhaul theory and framework.

Professor Fei described precisely this when he wrote that in fieldwork the anthropologist uses his own experience as a guide, not as an imposition. He agrees with Leach that study of others is to be valued as a reflection on one's own theories and expectations: when something is observed which from one's own experience is unexpected, that is a high moment of learning, because one then begins to ask more and to differentiate the culture and society of the people studied from one's own (Fei Xiaotong 1996: 11). To differentiate is not to assume that the other is the same as oneself: to assume this would be to find in the unexpected something backward or inferior, which is to assume that the other is an earlier version of oneself in the same evolutionary history, whether it is a relatively recent evolution called development or modernization, or a longer evolutionary history of universal stages of the human species. It is instead to ask what the differences are between our conditions and their conditions, our and their histories as human beings. The answers will be generalizations about the co-relation of variations in productive technology, ecology, climate, economy, cultural transmission and social structure which pertain to any place or moment of human social histories.

The willingness to do this has been professed by anthropologists since Malinowski as the central point of doing fieldwork. Equally often, the risks involved in doing it, in being challenged by our work of explication and cultural translation, are minimized. We reduce these risks by assuming the authority of the language of anthropology into which the language of the place and people studied is translated. The act of cultural translation often does not allow the discourse and the statements of the subjects of study to question the validity of the language into which they are translated. Yet in principle the subjects of study are our equals as thinking and questioning human beings, though they are not the same as us.

It is true that few people want to be or are driven to engage in cultural translation as a profession. It is therefore wrong to expect them to have developed the concepts and generalizations that result from this activity. It is foolish to expect everyone to be an anthropologist. But it is possible for anyone to be an anthropologist and it should be possible for any language to be disturbed into anthropological usage. So we should, ideally, leave ourselves and our writings open to such disturbance. But too often we protect ourselves from it.

The main self-critical thrust in English-language anthropological writing has been to point out this failing. Such self-criticism continues earlier critical examination of the relationship between anthropology and colonialism. What the more recent, post-colonial self-criticism has pointed out is not just that the language of international anthropology is usually English, but that its authors and readers protect themselves in an institutional life with academic conventions and rhetorical ways of establishing evidence and authority (Asad 1986: 159)

Academic protection is a protection from challenge. It is a protection not as easily available to sociologists of their own countries. The native anthropologist is a sociologist in the sense that his or her work will be in the language of and in publications available to people who can read and check the evidence more easily because it is in their own country. Even so, academic life and its conventions erect defences for the sociologist too. We write for each other. The game of research in the established academies is one of satisfying referees. Referees are fellow academics who have acquired or been appointed to positions of authority in which they judge the worth of a project or where they can decide whether its written results can be published. We pursue financial support, judge whether fellow academics should receive such support, and then write for referees and conference audiences. Research topics are defined in increasing part by academic and business advisers to the funds that finance the research. Academic promotion depends upon records of funding and publication. This, then, is the academic game: a game of referees which prevails throughout the wealthy countries of the world as well as in China now. It describes a closed circle. Within it are smaller rings of area and discipline specialists. They are the small readerships upon whom academic reputations rest and among whom rivalries rage.

The Chinese academy is also protected. But it is less wealthy and, in the social sciences at least, less well established than its Western counterparts. Anthropology has had to begin again at least three times in China. It is also organized along very different lines, with large research academies outside universities funded mainly under annual and five-year governmental plans and by research contracts on agreed projects with foreign institutions. University research is itself funded to some extent by government plans. There is more reference to governmental than to fellow academic authority than in Western countries. Furthermore, the budgetary constraints are greater and the range of research topics are confined far more to urgent questions of policy – what the funding council in the UK calls 'applied' and 'strategic' topics, rather than the purely scientific.

The point I wish to draw from this is that Professor Fei and Professors Leach and Freedman have acted in different institutional environments as well as different histories and that these environments have influenced and significantly differentiated their professional callings. From Malinowski onwards, from the establishing of social anthropology as an academic profession in the 1920s, anthropologists in England have been more removed from government than is anthropology in China. But I think these differences are only relative ones, differences of priority. We share a calling to a critical, empirical discipline which is based on the study of others, respectful and curious about our differences.

The combination of academic and patriotic professions

In China today there is a new generation of anthropological researchers and teachers, and with it will emerge a new Chinese academic tradition of fieldwork and its practical ethic. The new generations will combine the academic and the patriotic professions of anthropology in ways that they will create. Recently Chinese anthropologists have begun to apply their concepts to the study of non-Chinese societies. I hope one will do so in the UK. I wonder what those concepts will be.

References

Asad, Talal. 1986. 'The concept of cultural translation in British social anthropology' in James Clifford and George E. Marcus. *Writing Culture*. Berkeley: University of California Press.

Fei Xiaotong. 1992. 'The study of man in China – personal experience' in Chie Nakane and Chien Chiao. eds. *Home Bound: Studies in East Asian Society*. Tokyo: The Centre for East Asian Cultural Studies.

费孝通：《人的研究在中国 — 个人的经历》，载《读书》，1990年第5期。

—1996年，《重读<江村经济>·序言》，《北京大学学报(哲学社会科学版)》，第4期 [(Fei Xiaotong. 1996. "*Chongdu 'Jiangcun Jingji xuyan*'" (*Re-reading the preface to Peasant Life in China*). Beijing Daxue Xuebao (*Journal of Peking University: Philosophy and Social Sciences*, No 4)].

Feuchtwang, Stephan 王斯福. 1998. A Practically Minded Person: Fei Xiaotong's Anthropological Calling and Edmund Leach's Game, 马戎、周星、潘乃谷和王铭铭 主编.1998年，《田野工作与文化自觉》，北京：群言出版社，第1141-1166页[Ma Rong, Zhou Xing, Pan Naigu and Wang Mingming. eds. 1998. *Tianye Gongzuo yu Wenhua Zijue* (*Fieldwork and Cultural Consciousness*). Beijing: Qunyan Chubanshe: 1141–1166].

— 2014. 'Social Egoism and Individualism: Surprises and Questions for a Western Anthropologist of China Reading Professor Fei Xiaotong's Contrast between China and the West', *Journal of China in Comparative Perspective*, Vol. 1 (2):75-95.

王斯福：《社会自我主义与个体主义 — 一位西方的汉学人类学家阅读费孝通 "中西对比"观念的惊讶与问题》，《中国比较研究》，2014年第1卷第2期第185-201页.

Freedman, Maurice. 1963. 'A Chinese Phase in Social Anthropology', *British Journal of Sociology* 14(1): 1–19.

— 1974. 'The politics of an old state; a view from the Chinese lineage', in John Davis .ed. *Choice and Change; Essays in Honour of Lucy Mair*. Monographs on Social Anthropology No. 50, London: Athlone Press: 68–88.

Fuller, Chris and Jonathan Parry. 1989. '"Petulant inconsistency"? The intellectual achievement of Edmund Leach', *Anthropology Today* 5(3) (June): 12–15.

Leach, Edmund. 1961. *Rethinking Anthropology*. LSE Monographs on Social Anthropology No 22. London: Athlone Press.

— 1968. *A Runaway World?* Reith Lectures 1967. London: British Broadcasting Corporation

— 1970. *Political Systems of Highland Burma: A Study of Kachin Social Structure*. LSE Monographs on Social Anthropology. London: Athlone Press.

— 1982. *Social Anthropology*. Glasgow: Fontana.

Minson, Jeffrey. 1993. *Questions of Conduct*. London: Macmillan.

Pasternak, Burton and Fei Xiaotong. 1988. 'Interview'. *Current Anthropology* 29(4): 637–662.

DOI https://doi.org/10.24103/GCSS2.en.2016.4

A Swan's Trace in Snow
Unexpected Visits, Fieldwork, and the Anthropology of Fei Xiaotong[1]

Charles Stafford

Abstract: This speech takes 'a swan's trace in snow' from Fei Xiaotong's poem as a cue, briefly outlines certain influences on Fei's anthropology and on anthropology more generally. It emphasizes fieldwork takes place in particular historical contexts, which helps to shape anthropological knowledge. It also briefly discussed the author's own research in Taiwan in relation to other researchers working in other very different places. It attempts to underline the significance for social anthropology of fieldwork, and to echo Professor Fei's calls for a revitalised, and fieldwork-based, Chinese anthropology. Finally it suggests that anthropology must be comparative to truly engage with modern, and international, anthropological debates.

Keywords: fieldwork, comparison, ethnography, concepts, the Anthropology of Fei Xiaotong

Modern anthropology produces complicated, and at times strangely overlapping, itineraries, and these complicated itineraries help to produce anthropological knowledge. For example, in 1936 Fei Xiaotong – himself from Wujiang County and already a veteran of research on Yao Mountain – returned here to conduct fieldwork in Kaixiangong, after which he travelled overseas to England. There he studied at the London School of Economics under Malinowski (a Pole in exile), and became the student, colleague and friend of Malinowski's first PhD student – Raymond Firth (a New Zealander). Together – and primarily through fieldwork in the Trobriands, in Tikopia, in Kaixiangong and other places – these men contributed to what is almost wistfully called 'British' social anthropology. Although Professor Firth is in good health and spirits, and wished to attend this workshop in honour of his friend, he knew that the long journey here would be a tiring one. For this reason (and also because I now teach at the LSE as an Oklahoman in exile), I've travelled from London to Wujiang county as his representative. So it goes in this

---

[1] This is a speech given on the occasion of the celebration of 60 years anniversary of Fei Xiaotong's fieldwork in Kaixiagong Village, in Wujiang, September 1996. It was published in Ma, Zhou, Pan and Wang, eds. *Fieldwork and culture consciousness (Tianye gongzuo yu wenhua zijue)*. Beijing: Qunyan Publishing House. 1998: 374-399.

particular century. In any case, I should properly begin by noting that as of 1996 Raymond Firth and Fei Xiaotong are friends of some sixty years standing.

I recently spoke with Raymond and Rosemary Firth about the period (1936-38) when Professor Fei was a research student at the LSE. They mentioned that in the summer of 1938, shortly before his return to China, Fei visited their cottage in southern England, and wrote two short verses commemorating the occasion. In these, he expresses his surprise at finding away from the noise of London a place which reminds him in certain ways of home-thoughts amplified in his brief introduction to the poetry:

> The muddy wall and grass roof (of Firth's cottage) take me back to my native land on the left of the Yangzi River. From a distance I see the plain – the scattering of cattle and sheep. Is it possible that in southern England there remains this old country? Viewing the scenery, I sing the following two rhymes (i.e. his two verses). They are not good enough to be considered poetry—but they are like the 'swan's talon' (*hongzhao*), a mark of my unexpected visit[2].

The final reference is to the Chinese idiom *xueni hongzhao* (雪泥鸿爪)– literally, 'a swan's talon-mark in snow', which means the trace of a past event. It is obviously true that a complex trail of events had resulted in Fei's departure from 'the left of the Yangzi River', his arrival in London and his short visit to a cottage in the English countryside. And one can imagine – in the context of Fei's complicated and sometimes terribly difficult life – why that particular idiom (which describes a vanishing trace) should have come to mind.

In what follows, I would like to take 'a swan's trace in snow' as my cue, and briefly outline certain influences on Fei Xiaotong's anthropology and on anthropology more generally. The obvious place to start is with encounters between scholars and – this, for me, is the important part – those which occur during fieldwork. However 'unexpected', both kinds of encounters take place in particular historical contexts, and they help to shape anthropological knowledge. In order to illustrate this, I will also briefly discuss my own research in Taiwan in relation to that of colleagues working in other, very different places. In this way, I will attempt to underline the significance for social anthropology of fieldwork, and to echo Professor Fei's recent calls for a revitalised, and fieldwork-based, Chinese anthropology. I will also suggest that this anthropology must be comparative if it is to truly engage with modern, and international, anthropological debates.

The impulse to see it firsthand

If Fei Xiaotong was preoccupied with China while visiting the English countryside at the end of the 1930s, this seems consistent with the aim he set for himself at the beginning of that decade as an undergraduate at Yanjing University,

---

[2] Editor's note: it was Professor Fei's translation, slightly revised by the author. However, it was only partially translated. See the completed notes and poem in the Chinese version.

where he was the student of Wu Wenzao[3]. 'Ever since that time,' he told Burton Pasternak, 'I have been driven to understand China in order to understand Chinese problems' (Pasternak 1988: 639). The question for Fei was how best to develop these understandings, and the strategy he eventually adopted reflects several key influences.

Aside from the impact of his Chinese teacher (and later colleague) Wu Wenzao (Fei 1996b), Fei has also acknowledged the influence of the Chicago sociologist Robert Park. Park taught field observation at Yanjing, as Fei recounts, by leading his students around the streets of Beijing – 'he wanted us to see it firsthand' (Pasternak 1988: 639, also see Fei 1996b). In this way the 'abstractions' of Chinese society became more concrete and sociology could be based, at least in part, on the everyday experiences of ordinary people. Later, under the guidance of the Russian physical anthropologist Shirokogoroff at Tsinghua University, the emphasis for Fei was once again on concrete observation. Fei suggests this was precisely why he turned towards anthropology: 'I was interested in the methodology of fieldwork, and I knew that anthropology was the fieldwork discipline' (Pasternak 1988:639). It was Shirokogoroff who encouraged Fei to delay going overseas for postgraduate study in order to first conduct field research in China. The resulting project among the Yao apparently represented for Fei Xiaotong something of a conversion. As he told Pasternak, 'When I went to Yao Mountain it was as a physical anthropologist, but I came away a social anthropologist' (Pasternak 1988: 641). Tragically, as most of you will know, this project ended in serious injury to Professor Fei and in great personal loss (Arkush 1981: 68).

While recovering from these events, Fei went to stay with his elder sister Fei Dasheng who was living in the Wujiang County village of Kaixiangong. Here she was helping to promote new techniques of farming and silk-cultivation. As Arkush notes, her interest in these issues almost certainly helped inspire her younger brother's own focus on rural industry (Arkush 1981: 68-9). In any case, it was during this time of recovery that he gathered the material on life in Kaixiangong which he took with him to London in 1936 and which he wrote up under the supervision of Malinowski.

I briefly outline these events in order to make an important, if perhaps obvious point: that before Fei Xiaotong's arrival in London, his thinking was already the product of a complex personal history. In addition to his own upbringing and early education, this included contact with Chinese, Russian and American scholars, as well as encounters with the people of Yao Mountain and Kaixiangong. During these years his presence in particular circumstances, at particular times, obviously depended in part on unforeseeable histories – an accident, the presence of his elder sister in the countryside, and so on. And in the background of these seemingly

---

[3] For discussions of Fei's career, see Arkush (1981), Pasternak (1988), Guldin (1994) as well as Fei (1995a,1995b,1996b).

contingent personal circumstances stood the history of modern China, and the Chinese crisis which so preoccupied Fei Xiaotong and other scholars of the day.

Malinowski and the LSE

When Fei arrived at the London School of Economics in 1936, carrying with him the traces of these past events and influences, he was entering what was, by many accounts, a genuinely exciting intellectual environment. Malinowski, Firth and others were helping shape the relatively new discipline of social anthropology, and Malinowski's famous seminar at the LSE was the focal point. As Fei has observed: 'Those of us who participated in that seminar were aware that we were encountering the frontiers of the development of science' (Pasternak 1988: 642). Here Fei could make sense of his material from Kaixiangong, not least through listening to what other anthropologists were saying about their own ethnography.

Part of the excitement of the LSE and of the seminar obviously derived from the charisma of Malinowski himself, and Fei has acknowledged the Polish scholar's influence on his own intellectual style:

> He caught everything. He said very little, but always the right thing. He made all the right points. And by listening, you learned how to approach a problem, how to represent it, how to analyze it (Pasternak 1988:642).

Much has of course been written – both good and bad – about Malinowski, and Professor Fei has himself recently prepared a discussion of his work (Fei 1995a, 1995b). Here I simply wish to draw attention to several points Fei makes concerning the historical circumstances of Malinowski's career, and of his own time in London. As he notes, this period between the two world wars was a time of great change. The British Empire was declining, the colonies were moving towards independence, and anthropology itself was entering a new era. Fei suggests that Malinowski, as a Pole and an outsider, was highly sympathetic (*tong Qingxin* 同情心) towards the colonised, and notes that the London School of Economics was itself a centre of progressive and radical thought (1995b: 3). It is also significant, as Adam Kuper has stressed, that Malinowski's students at the 'academically unconventional' LSE included an unusually high proportion of foreigners (i.e. non-British) and of women (Kuper 1983:70-1). All of these factors influenced the newly evolving discipline of social anthropology.

The point for Fei (as for Kuper) is that the impact of Malinowski and the development of anthropology at the LSE and beyond, should be seen in historical context. More generally, Fei comments that 'If someone becomes a great writer in a particular era, this is itself a product of that era'.[4] He underlines this point by recalling a verse written in honour of the great Tang Dynasty poet Li Po (Li Bai):

---

[4] My translation, 'Yigeren neng chengwei yige shidai de dashoubi, keyi shuo shi shidai zaocheng de' (Fei 1995b:3).

The meaning of the verse (by the Qing Dynasty poet Huang Zhong-ze) is that Li Po's poetry was not written byLi Po himself. Instead, when he was drunk, his hand was taken by the *hongmeng* – the 'primordial energy' of the unformulated universe – which then wrote verses for him. This so-called 'primordial energy' we can understand to mean the historical era. And can we not also say of Malinowski's writings, which so influenced people, that detached from his own era he could never have written them? (Fei 1995b:3)

In making these observations, Professor Fei has in mind not only the pattern of history in relation to his Polish teacher of the 1930s, but also in relation to his Chinese students of the 1990s – 'perhaps now', he says, 'the *hongmeng* will seek another hand', and perhaps this will be in China (1995b:3). In an interview and article published this year, Professor Fei has again reiterated his hope that Chinese anthropology will make a significant contribution not only to scholarship, but also more generally to the Chinese people (1996a, 1996b).

What anthropology takes seriously

But why should anthropology, which is after all only one among many human sciences, be in a position to do such a thing? Perhaps the answer lies in the method which attracted Fei Xiaotong to the discipline in the first place: fieldwork. This may seem an obvious, and perhaps even banal, observation, but it deserves restating and rethinking. Of course, many methodological issues confront anthropologists, and Professor Fei has recently discussed some of these. For example, how appropriate and useful is contemporary village-based fieldwork in China, given China's long recorded history, and given the regional (and interlocking rural-urban) structure of much Chinese social life (Fei 1996c)? These and other methodological questions merit careful consideration. But I personally hope that long-term participant-observation fieldwork – including research about the small, often seemingly insignificant, details of everyday life – will remain an important part of' Chinese anthropology, not least because it facilitates anthropological comparison. Such comparison adds to a tradition which has already produced important insights about collective human life, insights which arguably have philosophical, scientific and political implications.

I suspect that much of the interest of Malinowski's LSE seminar was generated by its extraordinary and unprecedented subject-matter: material collected through intensive and long-term participant-observation in almost willfully obscure places. More to the point, this style of research was an attempt, however flawed, to document and take seriously the lives and experiences of people who were largely ignored by other academic disciplines. Thus it was that these forgotten people (e.g. the Trobrianders studied by Malinowski and the Tikopians studied by Firth) were themselves direct participants in a flow of ideas which was, at least in the context of Western scholarship, fundamentally radical. Of course, anthropology develops in part through the scholarly exchange of ideas, and through the influence of teachers such as Malinowski and Professor Fei. But anthropology also helps circumvent received wisdom – including the wisdom of its very own teachers – through fieldwork, i.e. through its active engagement with the lives of people who are, in most intellectual contexts, invisible.

At first glance this 'invisibility' could hardly apply to much-studied China. But as Professor Fei noted many years ago, histories and accounts of China have often ignored the way in which ordinary Chinese – of whom, after all, there are some hundreds of millions – go about their lives: '...the majority of the population, engaged in the hard work of production, leaves little impression on observers and little trace in historical documents' (1946:1). This absence is one of the reasons Fei's research in Wujiang County was of such interest to Raymond Firth, Malinowski, and other anthropologists. Fei's ethnography documented a rural Chinese way of life about which little was known, and which was itself under threat. But it also documented a much more general phenomenon, involving shifts in the global economy, which anthropologists of the time had not yet begun to grapple with.

One central conclusion of *Peasant Life in China* is of course the significance, for the people of Kaixiangong, of stable rural industry (Fei 1939).[5] Although we now take it for granted that anthropologists might study industry and industrialisation, this focus was an unusual one among anthropologists of the day. The straightforward thesis of Fei's book is that some form of rural industry was absolutely vital to the people of Wujiang County, because farming alone could not support them in an adequate standard of living. And if rural industries were undermined (whether through international competition or government policy) the people would suffer. These conclusions and their ramifications for much of the rest of China, have been confirmed in the most dramatic way by subsequent events.

Now we might ask why Fei Xiaotong was able to see a reality about rural industry which others, including many intellectuals and policy-makers, seemed ignorant of, and which most anthropologists were not addressing. Part of the answer is surely that he joined his sister in a place where the realities were there to be seen, living amongst people who could help explain these realities to him. In other words, Fei was influenced in this direction not only by teachers such as Wu Wenzao and Robert Park, he was also influenced by his encounter with the people of Kaixiangong. This encounter, in turn, was reconceptualised, in relation to other ethnographic encounters, at Malinowski's LSE seminar. His conclusions should be seen as a distillation of these various influences, including the 'long conversation' of participant observation fieldwork – both his own and that of other anthropologists.

---

[5] For a more recent view of Kaixiangong, see Fei (1983).

Fieldwork and Chinese relatedness

Now I'd like to briefly consider what is, on the surface, a very different topic – my own fieldwork in relation to Chinese kinship – in order to illustrate some of the points I've been making about anthropology, and about ethnographic comparison. What follows is simply an informal reflection on these themes, and I suspect that what I say will seem obvious to many of you here today.

As an outsider to Chinese society – i.e. as someone who knew of China only through representations of that place – I went into the field with many preconceptions. Through reading ethnography and history, I came to understand, among other things, that kinship – here meaning patrilineal and patriarchal kinship – was terribly important. Chinese rural society, as I understood it, was focused on agnatic groups which were concerned with the strict maintenance of boundaries. Chinese kinship was about descent, and it was exclusive both in principal, and in practice. Senior men were in firm control of the significant rituals of kinship (as they were of all public affairs), and of women – who, after all, were 'outsiders'.

I developed this image in part from my undoubtedly superficial reading of works about elaborate lineages in south China, and about the Chinese past. My subsequent experiences in contemporary Taiwan and north China, and more extensive readings of Taiwanese and Chinese ethnography, have in some ways, confirmed the original impression. People in these places certainly say and do things which imply the significance of 'exclusive' kinship, of patrilineal descent, of ancestors, of ties of blood, and so on, not to mention the insignificance of women, etc.

They also, however, say and do things which imply something else – and, in the context of fieldwork, this 'something else' generates certain confusions. For example, I was at first surprised, given my preconceptions, by the Chinese emphasis on friendship, on children and on the future, rather than on ancestors, the elderly, and the past. I was also surprised by the power and autonomy of Chinese women. These realities, encountered during contemporary fieldwork, partly reflect a shifting balance of power in China (between old and young, between men and women) which is a matter of recent history. But I can honestly say that my reactions to these realities – surprise – also reflects my misunderstanding of kinship in general, and of Chinese kinship in particular.

It might have helped had I noticed Professor Fei's warning about over-estimating, or misinterpreting, the significance of kinship in China:

It is true that in China kinship is the key to social organization, but it would be wrong to think that kinship is itself so dear to the people. Kinship is only a means by which social groups are organized for different purposes. I do not think that kinship possesses any force of extension by itself and is valued as such (Fei 1948:6).

On the surface, this extraordinary statement seems to contradict many of our assumptions about China. But perhaps more importantly, it helps place 'organized groups' in the context of the much more diffuse kinds of relatedness which one encounters when conducting fieldwork in Chinese communities.[6]

But let me explain what I mean by 'diffuse kinds of relatedness'. This is simply to say that one obviously encounters many kinds of relationships in Taiwan and China, and that these are constructed in many different ways. Friendship is crucially important, but so are forms of kinship which seem (at least on the surface) idiosyncratic. These relationships often seem to be constructed or 'built up' through almost imperceptibly small and diffuse interactions – rather than being 'given'. But then the same could be said of the supposedly 'given' relationships of standard patrilineal kinship – if only one could see beyond the rhetoric.

If I understand anything about Chinese kinship, and Chinese relatedness, it is partly because of encounters during fieldwork which have helped to set me straight. For example, when I first moved in 1987 to the Taiwanese fishing community of Angang I lived for some months in a teacher's dormitory at the local middle school. The young teachers living there – my first Taiwanese friends – were 'outsiders' to the local community. They maintained close contact with their own families, but while in Angang (i.e. almost all of the time) their lives revolved primarily around their very demanding work. They also built for themselves, with some care and determination, a social life which centred on the teachers' dormitory – they cooked and ate together, they entertained themselves, they occasionally fought, and a couple of them even fell in love and thought about getting married. None of these young people expected to remain in Angang. And yet their temporary presence there unquestionably had an impact both on them and on that place, not least because of their responsibilities to local children, for whom they were expected to be 'models' (Stafford 1995:56-68).

The first kinds of relationships I observed in Taiwan were thus not (for the most part) based on kinship they were instead those between colleagues, and between teachers and schoolchildren. But what is it that makes these people 'related', if only in a transient way? This kind of relatedness seems not to be given, rather it seems partly constructed through actions: through sharing food, through providing lessons, and so on. In this way people appear to create, within a cultural framework, their own connections. Now it is tempting to contrast this with ties of kinship, which – powerful illusion – do not seem transient, and which appear as given rather than created. But surely – as anthropological studies of kinship have repeatedly shown – seemingly 'natural' ties between persons are also historically situated *products* of human thought and action.

This is perhaps easier to see in apparently idiosyncratic situations. Again, allow me to illustrate with material from Angang. In order to escape, during the first weeks of fieldwork, from the rather boring routine of the school, I often

---

[6] Donald R. DeGlopper has also argued against the view that China is necessarily 'familistic', and his own research in Taiwan has focused on the (non-kinship) relationships of small businessmen (DeGlopper 1995).

jumped the school fence. As it happened, the closest thing to the school fence was a small shop which sold, among other things, cigarettes, betel nuts, beer, rice wine, snack foods and spirit money. The people who ran this shop were very kind to me and they were, I suppose, my first 'Chinese family'. But they were so unusual that I seriously thought it might be better to ignore them! The shop was entirely managed and run by a middle-aged woman, who was very highly thought of by the locals. Hers was an energetic and friendly operation, and anyone loitering about the place, including me, would be asked to help. Her husband, for various complicated reasons, was hardly ever resident and normally lived elsewhere in Taiwan. But they had four daughters who – when not studying or working outside of Angang – helped their mother in running the shop. Both husband and wife were 'outsiders', and they had neither sons of their own, nor a local kinship network. In classical Chinese terms it all sounds rather unfortunate. They were my first example of Chinese kinship in practice, but they were a bad example of patrilineality because the men and the ancestors were somehow missing. What was striking was the extent to which this absence didn't seem to matter.

What *did* seem to matter was that the women in this family had between themselves significant ties, including emotional and economic ties, and that they, as a unit, had significant emotional and economic ties to the local community. Some of this could perhaps be explained with reference to descent. The daughters were born (so it seems) with a 'natural' connection to their mother and father, and in theory they would later be 'married out' to another patriline. But the relationships I observed were in fact being produced according to other idioms. To put it briefly, they were effectively making themselves related through processes also found in seemingly more conventional families, and even found outside of kinship altogether. What were these?

In my ethnography of Angang (Stafford 1995) I discuss how relationships between parents and children are constructed, in part, around a 'cycle of *yang*' (养). On the surface, parents obviously *yang* children – meaning that they 'raise' them, feed them, provide education, and so on. The detail of this provision is very complex. For instance, 'feeding' might include providing the religious charms which are eaten by children (thus symbolically placing the writing of gods within their bodies). But however it happens, the fact of receiving *yang* from one's parents is crucial for children, not least because it compels a return. They are morally obliged to *yang* or *fengyang* their parents, meaning to respectfully support them, once they have grown old.

The idea of a 'cycle of yang' fits very comfortably with standard notions of Chinese patrilineal descent. Sons are expected to have sons, to support their parents in retirement, and to maintain ancestral rituals. Why do they have these obligations? In part because of descent – because they are the blood and breath of a patriline – but also because of *yang*, i.e. because they have been raised by their parents, and owe them life-long support. For daughters, the situation is clearly different, and the obligations are (at least in theory) displaced. They receive *yang* from their natal homes, 'marry out', and then provide *yang* to their husbands' parents. Their own fathers and mothers, meanwhile, receive *yang* from their brothers' 'incoming' wives – so that reciprocity of *yang* is theoretically always sustained within the patrilineal framework. From this perspective, it almost seems that descent and *yang* merge.

But the 'cycle of *yang*' may also at times be seen as standing in opposition to patrilineal descent. I think this is partly what Margery Wolf had in mind with her notion of the 'uterine family', based around a mother and her children (Wolf 1972). To the extent that a woman commands the loyalty of her sons – a loyalty produced in part through her provision of *yang* – she is at least potentially undermining their commitment to patrilineal ideals, and their obedience to patriarchal authority.

But – to return to the example of my shop-keeping family – here there was scarcely a patriline to undermine, and the significant loyalty was mostly between women. These women were producing a life-long connection between themselves, they were 'making kinship'. Although this kinship was perhaps not of the textbook kind, it was very real for them, and it reveals much about Chinese relatedness. And once one begins to conceptualise Chinese relatedness in this way, even the most conventionally 'patrilineal' family may also be seen as the end-product of active processes, including the cycle of *yang*.

The perhaps obvious point I am trying to make – certainly obvious to anyone who is Chinese – is that there are, in China, ways of producing relatedness between persons which are not necessarily about descent, and also sometimes not about kinship at all. This may involve the sharing of food, the sharing of housing, the sharing of humour, the sharing of work, and so on, processes which are observable (if one can be bothered to look) in everyday life. The very first 'family' I encountered in China – a woman shopkeeper, her daughters and their network of friends – showed me this in the most striking way, as did the teachers in the Angang Middle School. But I confess that it has taken me some time to register these realities about Chinese relatedness.

Insights from comparative ethnography

Seeing them clearly is something which has come partly from fieldwork, but also partly from my contact with two anthropologists – both close friends and colleagues from the LSE – who have worked in very different places. (As I said at the beginning, modern anthropology produces strangely overlapping itineraries). Both of them have analysed forms of relationships which on the surface, seem very un-Chinese.

The first is Janet Carsten, now of the University of Edinburgh (since I have already alluded to the international nature of 'British social anthropology', I might note that she is the daughter of central Europeans who immigrated to Britain in the 1930s). Carsten conducted long-term fieldwork in Langkawi, a Malaysian fishing village, and her research thus falls within the more general anthropology of southeast Asia. She stresses the 'processual and transformative nature' of Malay kinship, and focuses especially on the significance of shared food and shared residence:

> Ways of living and thinking about relatedness in Langkawi lead me to stress a processual view of personhood and kinship. It is through living and consuming together in houses that people become complete persons – that is kin. The core substance of kinship in local perceptions is blood, and the major contribution to blood is food. Blood is always mutable and fluid – as is kinship itself (Carsten 1995:224).

On the surface, the notion which Carsten puts forward of 'fluid' or 'mutable' Malay kinship seems dramatically different from the standard view of Chinese kinship – which, as I have noted, is often assumed to be rigid and exclusive. And yet, many of the details she provides about the production of relatedness in Langkawi – e.g. through the sharing of food and the sharing of grandchildren – find echoes in my own Chinese ethnography (see also Carsten 1989, 1991, 1992, 1997). Of course, I wouldn't try to suggest that Chinese and Malay kinship are the same, or even that they are similar, but thinking about Malay kinship has helped me to question my assumptions about the 'given', non-processual, nature of Chinese kinship.

I would also like to mention the influence of a second colleague, Rita Astuti – an Italian now teaching at the LSE – who conducted fieldwork among the Vezo people who fish along the Western coast of Madagascar. Astuti has stressed the remarkable fluidity – at least in certain contexts – of Vezo identity. The Vezo have a highly performative and present-oriented notion of identity. This is not 'given' by birth, and so it is not an 'ethnic identity' in the usual sense of this term. One can effectively 'become Vezo' by living among them and doing what they do, and one can stop being Vezo by moving away from the coast and stopping fishing. It is hard to imagine a similar thing being said about 'becoming Chinese', and yet reading Astuti's work has made me rethink Chinese processes of identification. The Vezo, after all, also have a rather more rigid notion of identity, especially in relation to death and burial, and Astuti's work focuses on the tension between these two principles (Astuti 1995a, 1995b).

Fluid Vezo notions of identity, kinship and personhood obviously bear comparison in certain key respects, with those from Langkawi – and this in spite of profound differences – partly because they both fall within the Southeast Asian cultural area. But anthropologists of China might also learn a great deal by reading about places of this kind. By studying places with malleable (and in some cases seemingly 'creative') kinship and identity we might reformulate the notion of China as a place where rigid patrilineal kinship, as such, is all-important, or where social identity is given and unchangeable. For me, this reformulation has occurred partly because of fieldwork – e.g. because of my experiences with the schoolteachers and shopkeepers of Angang, among others – but also because of my contact with fieldworking anthropologists who have never set foot in China. I believe that this process, which is largely about listening and watching, and then comparing, is an important, and sometimes even radical, intellectual exercise.

References

Arkush, R. David. 1981. *Fei Xiaotong and Sociology in Revolutionary China*. Cambridge Mass: Council on East Asian Studies. Harvard University Press.

Astuti, Rita. 1995a. *People of the Sea: Identity and Descent among the Vezo of Madagascar*. Cambridge: Cambridge University Press.

— 1995b. 'The Vezo are not a kind of people: identity, difference and "ethnicity" among a fishing people of western Madagascar', *American Ethnologist* 22(3): 464-482.

Carsten, Janet. 1989. 'Cooking money: Gender and the symbolic transformation of means of exchange', in Jonathan Parry and Maurice Bloch, eds. *Money and the Morality of exchange*. Cambridge: Cambridge University Press.

— 1991. 'Children in between: Fostering and the process of kinship in Pulau Langkawi, Malaysia', *Man* 26: 425 -443.

— 1992. 'The process of childbirth and becoming related among Malays on Pulau Langkawi', in Goran Aijmer (ed.) *Coming into Existence: Birth and metaphors of birth*. Gothenburg: IASSA.

— 1995. 'The substance of kinship and the heat of the hearth', *American Ethnologist* 22(2): 223-241.

— 1997. *The heat of the hearth: the process of kinship in a Malay island community*. Oxford: Oxford University Press.

DeGlopper, Donald R. 1995. *Lukang, Commerce and community in a Chinese city*. Albany: University of New York Press.

Fei Xiaotong 费孝通.1939. *Peasant life in China*. London, Routledge & Kegan Paul.

— 1948. 'Peasantry and Gentry: an interpretation of Chinese social structure and its changes', *American Journal of Sociology* 52: 1-17.

— 1983. *Chinese Village Close-up*. Beijing: New World Press.

— 1995a. 《从马林诺斯基老师学习文化论的体会》，北京大学社会学与人类学研究所资料 [Cong Malinnuosiji Laoshi xuexi wenhua lun de tihui ('My experience of studying cultural theory with Teacher Malinowski'). mimeo, Beijing: Institute of Sociology and Anthropology, Peking University].

— 1995b. 《讲课插话》，北京大学社会学与人类学研究所资料 ['Jiangke chahua' ('Additional comments on the lecture'). mimeo, Beijing: Institute of Sociology and Anthropology, Peking University].

— 1996a. 《关于"人类学研究与文化交流"访谈 》《北京大学学报》，第1期第4-6页 [Interview on 'Anthropological Studies and Cultural Communication', Beijing Daxue Xuebao, 1:4-6].

— 1996b. 《开风气，育人才》《北京大学学报》，第1期第14-19页['Kai feng qi, yu rencai' ('Start a new trend, cultivate talented people'). Beijing Daxue Xuebao, 1: 14 -19].

—1996c. 《重读<江村经济>》《北京大学学报》，第4期第4-18页 ['Chongdu 'Jiangcun jingji, "xuyan"' (Rereading the preface to Peasant Life in China), Beijing DaxueXuebao.4:4-18].

Guldin, Gregory Eliyu. 1994. *The Saga of anthropology in China*. Armonk, NY: M. E. Sharpe.

Kuper, Adam. 1983. *Anthropology and Anthropologists: the Modern British School* (revised edition). London: Routledge and Kegan Paul.

Pasternak, Burton. 1988. 'A conversation with FeiXiaotong', *Current Anthropology* 29(4): 637-62.

Stafford, Charles. 石瑞.1995. *The roads of Chinese childhood*. Cambridge: Cambridge University Press.

— 1998. A Swan's Trace in Snow: Unexpected Visits, Fieldwork, and the Anthropology of Fei Xiaotong, 马戎、周星、潘乃谷和王铭铭 主编，1998年，《田野工作与文化自觉》，北京：群言出版社，第374-399页[Ma Rong, Zhou Xing, Pan Naigu and Wang Mingming. eds.

1998. *Tianye Gongzuo yu Wenhua Zijue (Fieldwork and Cultural Consciousness)*. Beijing: Qunyan Chubanshe: 374–399].

Wolf, Margery. 1972. *Women and the family in rural Taiwan*. Stanford, Stanford University Press.

DOI https://doi.org/10.24103/GCSS2.en.2016.5

China and India
An Anthropological View in Relation to Cultural Peripheries[1]

Chie Nakane

Abstract: China and India are two ancient civilizations. The two nations are very different in general impression. According to personal living and research experiences in the two nations, the author found out significant commonness based on a huge continental society with a long history. Tibet is located between China and India. The author observed different attitudes of Han people and Hindus towards Tibetans, which is related to characteristics of two civilizations and the nature of two societies. Regarding the acceptance of Buddhism, finally the author discusses the different attitudes of Tibetans, Han people and Japanese.

Keywords: cultural peripheries, Hannization, Sanscritization, Buddhism

It is a great honour for me to be invited by Peking University to speak as the first lecturer in the lecture series in memory of Professor Fei Xiaotong. In this talk I do not intend to make a comparison between China and India per se. What I discuss here is largely related to my anthropological experiences in both countries. My special research field has been in Tibet, which I approached from the Chinese Mainland as well as from the Indian Himalaya. I have lived for several years in both countries. When I came to India (Calcutta) for the first time in 1953, everything appeared so exotic to me, but, strangely enough, I soon sensed a kind of similarity in the atmosphere to what I had experienced before in China (Peking). This relaxed me and made it easier to start life in India. Later I came to realize that such a feeling must have come from the atmosphere that only a huge continental society with a long history could produce. In fact, China and India exemplify noticeable commonalities, although we generally get an impression that these two societies are totally different.

Now let me proceed by pointing up some distinguishable aspects that are to be seen in both societies, in respect of socio-geographical settings; effects of

---

[1] This article is based on the 'First Fei Memorial Lecture', by Chie Nakane, on the December 16, 2006 at Peking University. It was originally written in English, translated in to Chinese by Rong Ma, and published in the *Journal of Peking University (Philosophy and Social Sciences)*, 2007, No2. Thanks to the author who has kindly provided us with the English version. It is published for the first time in JCCP 1.3.

Hannization and Sanscritization; and contrasting configurations of society. Finally, I present different manners of acceptance of Buddhism in China, Tibet and Japan.

Common features of socio-geographical settings

Firstly, both societies, China and India, comprise great regional differences with linguistic and local cultural distinctions, which correspond largely to the contemporary administrative units: 23 provinces (省) in China, and 25 states in India, leaving aside certain special areas. They are largely dichotomized in terms of north and south (as their usage of 北方人、南方人and North Indian, South Indian). These categories are also in accordance with their food habits, as the staple food in the north is wheat, while that of the south is rice.

Secondly, both societies include many minority groups, with a fairly large population of Moslems. The number of types of minority group in China comes to 56, and in India roughly 400 (without established statistics). In India they are called 'tribals' or 'tribes', and most of them are small groups, with the majority averaging more or less around 300,000 people. Most of them reside in remote hilly areas, and in some areas of less fertile plain on the outskirts of Hindu villages. They are scattered in many regions, and found in almost all states. Among these, a heavy concentration is found in the north-eastern border areas of India, including Assam State. This particular area, where hill tribes live, stretches to the hilly areas of northern Burma and continues to Thailand and up to Yunnan (云南), thus forming a wide hilly tribal belt. The natural scenery and living conditions of these peoples are basically similar, although they are diversified into many small ethnic groups. A noticeable linkage can be seen from Assam to Yunnan.

In China, besides these hill people there are several major minority groups that are not only numerous in population, but which have also been active players, as they ruled China in a certain period of Chinese history. It is understandable that research on minority groups in China has been carried out by historically oriented ethnologists. This kind of approach was best exemplified by Professor Fei Xiaotong's well-known book entitled *The Pattern of Diversity in Unity of the Chinese Nation* (中华民族多元一体格局). His discussions are largely concerned with their historical accounts, which are essential to an understanding of these minority groups. In India, research on minority groups has been carried out by physical and social anthropologists. This difference in fields thus also invites different scientific approaches.

As for the Moslem community, they form 0.7% of the total population of China[2], and 1.7% of that of India. As regards population, Moslems in India outnumber the total Pakistani population. In India these Moslems together with Hindus form the majority of the population – 93% of the total – while in China

---

[2] According to MA Rong's Chinese translation of this paper (2007), the figure of 0.7% was the figure for Hui Moslem only. The total Moslem population from 10 minorities made 1.6% of the total population of China.

Moslems are classed as one of the minority groups. Such a dominance of Moslems in India is considered to be related to the influence of the Moslem Mughal Empire, which ruled India for more than 300 years (1526–40, 1555–1858) prior to British rule, comparable to the era of Manchu rule (1636–1911). Today, the manner of distribution of Moslems is very similar in both societies, as they are scattered over many regions, and their areas of concentration are equally found in the north-western part of each respective country, Kansu[3] and Kashmir. They are particularly found in such an area as between the major population and other peoples such as Tibetans. Professor Fei designated this the 'Islamic corridor' in North-west China. Exactly the same situation is found in the north-western part of India. Whenever I entered a Tibetan area, I passed through Moslem communities in China as well as in India.

Effect of Hannization and Sanscritization

Given such great variations in the composition of a society in a vast continental area, the main contributing factor in unification and integration must be considered to be the role of Han-wen and Sanskrit. Both languages were well developed in ancient times, and their carriers have been the learned men of the upper strata of each respective society. But through the course of history the basic thought penetrated down to general population level. The characteristic culture of Han-wen is found in ethics involving political thought, while Sanskrit reveals philosophical and religious thought involving a social system. Both have contributed effectively to the development and establishing of the order and common values of society. Hannization accompanies the administrative force with the political system designed by the Center. The people under the system became part of Chinese society. Sanscritization resulted in a sociological order based on Hindu values, represented by the caste system. Those who reside closer to Hindu areas develop familiarity with the Hindu sociological order, and are likely to become members of the Hindu world. In the process, one cannot become a Hindu as an individual, only as a group. Thus Hanhua and Sanscritization have each produced a distinctive society at large, set apart from other worlds, though there are no clear borders like those of the contemporary nation states: the borders tend to be blurred.

Let me give here some examples from actual border areas. It is interesting to observe noticeable phenomena in the border areas where Hans have been in close contact with Tibetans. These contacts have resulted in not a few cases of intermarriage, in which a Han male with a Tibetan wife normally lives in the Tibetan area, although there are hardly any cases in which a Tibetan wife lives in a Han community. A Han family who have lived in a Tibetan area for several generations would become Tibetanized to such an extent that it would become almost impossible to recognize whether they are Tibetans or Hans. I have found that these local Hans are surprisingly able to overcome differences with non-Han

---

[3] In MA Rong's Chinese version he added Ningxia (2007).

peoples. On the other hand, in these areas, Tibetans, who assume the headship of local communities as well as of monasteries, speak fluent Chinese and are good at Han-wen, and they often have Chinese names besides their own Tibetan ones. It is also difficult to see at a glance whether they are Hans or Tibetans, but their Tibetan identity is surprisingly strong.

The local situation on the Indian side is quite different. Very few Hindus used to live in Tibetan areas. There have not been as many Hindu–Tibetan contacts as I found among Chinese Tibetans in the border areas. However, it has long been the practice that many Tibetans, including both nobles and peasants, visit India on pilgrimage during the winter season. They have a kind of familiarity with and admiration for India, where their Buddhism originated. Local Hindus accept these Buddhists in a friendly manner. Some of the upper-class Tibetans used to maintain a residence in the Indian Himalaya, and they have good friendships with their Indian counterparts. But cases of intermarriage have been very rare. This is understandable, as Hindus have a rule of caste endogamy, which is the traditional practice: a marriage partner should be found within the same caste, but not within the same patrilineal group.

Configuration of society

I have just mentioned 'caste endogamy'. Caste in India is a very distinguishable social system. In relation to this I would like to discuss here an important comparison of the social structures of China and India. Regarding the social structure of China, Professor Fei presented his well-known model known as *chaxugeju* (差序格局)[4]. According to this theory, with ego as the starting point, social relations expand wider and wider in concentric circles (like the forms of ripples caused by throwing a pebble into water), and ultimately reach Heaven (*Tianxia* 天下). The nature of the relations of these circles being elastic, there are no clear boundaries between groups.

When you look at Indian caste society a very different model can be exemplified. Indian society consists of numerous groups, which make a mosaic pattern. Every group, represented as being like a caste, has a clear-cut existence. A cluster of groups is formed by various factors, such as local region, similarity of occupation, and closeness of position in the caste hierarchy. Furthermore, since a caste is primarily an occupational group, every caste is characterized by one kind of occupation, so that in order to lead an ordinary life each caste needs the services of the others (normally of 30 or more different castes). Thus they have functional economic links with other castes. There are, however, no links that expand to the society at large. Nevertheless, a very important point is that, wherever you go in Indian society, you would find the same principle of the caste system, with some variations, irrespective of differences in language and customs. They share the

---

[4] Editor's note: There are more than 10 ways of translating *chaxugeju* (Fei 1985[1947]/1992) into English. We use 'social egoism' here (Feuchtwang 2014).

basic principles of the value system and behavioural patterns. So they are able to identify others without any established links: anybody could be placed on their imaginary social map. In this manner, a kind of coherence of the total society could be produced.

The pictures of the two societies so far presented reveal an interesting contrast. In spite of such different configurations of organizational structure in the two societies, a striking similarity is found in the core of social organization, that is, 'the family'. The ideal traditional type of family structure is the same in both societies. The family is structured primarily by the vertical as well as collateral relationships of family members: father–son and brothers from the same parents. This crossed structure anchors the core of the family, and the kinship relations of the members extend to outside members. Between a family and a patrilineal wider circle (宗族) there is no clear boundary. Its functional boundary may be established by certain given conditions, such as common possession of a property, or personal factors affecting the members. The recognition of patrilineal relationships in China could be extended to many ascending and descending generations – here we recall the professed Chinese ancestor worship.

The Indian version of a patrilineal group (the same structure as 宗族) is called *gotra*, which forms a segment of a caste (a caste consists of many different *gotras*). It functions as the recognition of the common membership, rather than the relationship with ascending generations. *Gotra* has a common shrine and a name. The name of *gotra* for individual members may correspond to the Chinese surname system, but it is not used in ordinary social life: under the Indian system, a wife is designated by the same surname as her husband.

In spite of the differences found between the Chinese and Indian systems, in both societies the recognition of descent (kinship) plays the primary role in underpinning social organizations. It is not so in the Japanese system: here, it is the *household unit* rather than descent in recognition of relations with outside members of a family. The succession of a family line is in fact the succession of the household (*ié*), in which only one son and his wife succeed, and the successor's brothers have to be separated, each forming another household unit. In the event that a household head (father) fails to have a son to succeed him, he chooses as an adopted son a man who might come from his own kin, or a man without any kinship relationship to him. Likewise, although the Japanese also have a notion of 'ancestor worship', the same term as is used by the Chinese, ancestors are regarded as the generations succeeding the man who first established the household, not necessarily through kinship-based genealogy. The Japanese obtained important cultural elements from China, but the social systems of the indigenous Japanese remained unchanged.

In the Japanese system, an institution such as *ié* is more important than kinship links between individuals. This point further results in the fact that networks of individuals tend to be limited, blocked by the wall of the institution to which they currently belong. At the level of institutions, networks do exist – for example, parent and child companies, which in some cases construct a gigantic congregation. Even in such cases the function of networks is limited within the institutional set-up. We Japanese are amazed by the rich functional networks possessed and utilized by Chinese and Indian individuals. In Japanese eyes, the differences and commonalities of Chinese and Indian social systems look particularly clear.

Acceptance of Buddhism: Cases of Chinese, Tibetans and Japanese

Lastly, let me discuss how indigenous cultures have accepted other cultures, taking the example of transmissions of Buddhism from India. The first Chinese translation of Buddhist texts in classic Sanskrit, including prajna-paramita hrdayam samaptan, known as the Hannya-shingyo in Japanese, was done in the year 403 by Kumarajiva (龟兹人), who was very skilled in both Sanskrit and Chinese (Han-wen). The next was done in 660–663 by the Chinese monk Hsuan Zang (玄奘), who had returned to Chang'an (长安) from India. The latter translation is the most popular.

Tibetan translations came later, as Tibetan letters were composed during the 7th century, borrowing elements from Nagari characters, which made it possible for them to translate Sanskrit texts by the 8th century. The study of Buddhism flourished in Tibet especially after the 11th century, producing very distinguished monastic scholars. Many of them studied in India, while at the same time Indian Pundits were often invited to Tibet. The Tibetan scholars in these days were called *Lotsawa* (literally meaning translators – scholars had been synonymous with translators). They tried their best to make Tibetan terms correspond to Sanskrit words and concepts. Their translations were in some cases also done jointly with Pundits. The first 'Dictionary of Sanskrit–Tibetan Buddhism Terms' was composed as early as the beginning of the 9th century. The Tibetan approach to Buddhism was scholastic from the beginning. The standard of their scholarship was very high, and it was they who formed the foundation of Tibetan Buddhism for later development. I should also mention here that Tibetan texts have a unique importance for scholars around the world working on restoring the original Indian texts, most of which have been lost in India.

In comparison, Chinese translated texts do not serve this purpose, as Han-wen translations were not literary (word-for-word) translations. They generally have the following two characteristics. One is that concepts in original Sanskrit texts are likely to be made to correspond to related Chinese concepts that already exist, without creating new words. That is, there was a tendency to sinify texts. Secondly, the original texts were normally shortened or selected parts only were translated owing to the Chinese way of articulating thoughts. Therefore, Indians' elaborate constructs of logical discourses were not translated. It seems that the Chinese did not have a taste for engaging in metaphysical discourse. The Chinese way of thinking is directed at what serves to promote righteous conduct. Chinese thinking is quite different from that of Indians. Nevertheless, the Chinese texts themselves contain their own excellent style and beautiful wording, through which profound concepts of Chinese Buddhism were expressed.

Unlike the Chinese, the Tibetans strove as hard as they could to swallow Indian logical thinking, which must be fresh for them: they have created many Tibetan conceptual terms to meet the Sanskrit. This trend was also related to the fact that many of them had direct contacts with Indian Pundits, and intimacy with Sanskrit continued throughout the development of Tibetan Buddhism. In China Buddhism began to pass its peak by the 7th century, and by the 11th century the government office of Buddhist translation, as well as the translators' employment, was terminated. It was the time when Tibetan Buddhism was entering its golden age.

Lastly, I should mention the manner of the acceptance of Buddhism, especially the use of sutras by the Japanese. Japanese people accepted Chinese versions without translating them into Japanese. The reasons for that may be as follows: by the 7th century, Chinese characters had already been transplanted into the Japanese literary strata, and beautifully composed Chinese texts also conveyed a kind of sacredness for the Japanese. They chanted these sutras with a nicely arranged Japanese pronunciation. Among all the sutras, Hannya-shingyo became the most popular for the Japanese people, irrespective of their Buddhist sect. Its short version takes less than five minutes to chant: many Japanese are able to recite it by heart. However, its meaning is not necessarily clear to ordinary Japanese, although monks and scholars have tried to explain it (in fact, hundreds of books of explanation have been published). To one degree or another, they incorporate Japanese ways of thinking. Only a few learned scholars have explored the original meaning of the Sanskrit version restored from the Tibetan texts. The best example would be by Nakamura Hajime (1960, 2003). More recently, commentaries and explanations on the same sutra by Tibetan monks have been published and translated into Japanese, including *Essence of the Heart Sutra* by Dalai Lama the 14th Tenzin Gyatso (2002), translated by Miyasaka Yuko (2004).

As seen above, the manner of acceptance of Buddhism by Chinese, Tibetans and Japanese reveals interesting differences. Such differences can be considered as due to the course of history and the innate cultural force of the respective society.

Concluding remarks

So far, I have considered distinguishable aspects of China and India as viewed from their peripheral societies, which in a way serve to allow for an effective comparison.

Today, it is a global trend that independent nations have more and more contact whether they like it or not. China and India have begun to make welcoming approaches to each other. Prime Ministers Hu Jintao and Manmohan Singh met recently, and several fields including academia are entertaining more exchanges. Such trends are much welcomed not only by the two countries involved, but also by surrounding countries and the world at large.

In the process of increasing contact, our general concerns tend to be directed towards contemporary political, economic and technological activities, but we also need an understanding of societies and how they have come to be as they are today, and of what kinds of inherent element they carry in spite of modern changes. From this we will be able to realize where we stand, and what is the best way to deal with other peoples.

References

第十四世達賴喇嘛, 2004. 《心經的本質》, 翻訳:宮坂 宥洪, 東京:春秋社, 2004 (ダライ・ラマ 十四世,ダライ・ラマ般 若心経入門, 翻訳:宮坂 宥洪, 春秋社, 2004); (Dalai Lama the 14th Tenzin Gyatso, 2004. *Essence of the Heart Sutra,* Wisdom Publications, Trans. Miyasaka. Yuko: Shunjusha).

费孝通. 1947/1985年. 《乡土中国》, 北京: 三联书店(Fei, Xiaotong. 1985 [1947]. Xiangtu Zhongguo (in Chinese), Beijing: SDX Joint Publishing Company).

— 1992. *From the Soil: The Foundations of Chinese Society.* Translation of Fei Xiaotong's Xiangtu Zhongguo with an introduction and epilogue by Gary Hamilton and Wang Zheng, Berkeley: University of California Press.

Feuchtwang, Stephan. 2014. 'Social Egoism and Individualism: Surprises and Questions for a Western Anthropologist of China Reading Professor Fei Xiaotong's Contrast between China and the West', *Journal of China in Comparative.* Vol. 1 (2):75-95. (王斯福:《社会自我主义与个体主义— 一位西方的汉学人类学家阅读费孝通"中西对比"观念的惊讶与问题》, 《中国比较研究》, 2014年第1卷第2期第185-201页).

中村元、纪野一义翻译. 1960/2003.《般若心经·金钢般若经》岩波文库 (Hajime, Nakamura and Kino, Kazuyoshi, Trans. 1960. *Heart Sutra and Diamond Sutra.* Iwanami bunko).

Chie Nakane. 2006. 'China and India: An Anthropological View in Relation to Cultural Peripheries', a lecture at the 'First Fei Memorial Lecture', Peking University, December 16 (unpublished). [中根千枝.2007. 《中国与印度:从人类学的视角来看文化的边陲》, 马戎 译, 《北京大学学报(哲学 社会科学版)》2007年第2期第143-147页。

DOI https://doi.org/10.24103/GCSS2.en.2016.6

A Comparative Study of Rural Families and Family Property in China and Japan[1]

PARK Hong

Abstract: It is interesting to compare rural families and family property in China and in Japan. The family (*ie*) in Japan is an entity mainly concerned with farm production, and it is made up of elements such as the family name, family property, family business, family status and ancestral sacrifices. The family property is exclusive (it is inherited by the eldest son alone) and perpetual. In contrast, the Chinese family (*jia*) is mainly concerned with continuing the lineal blood relationship. Family property, as the economic support base for the family, is in principle inherited equally between brothers. However, in the case of Kaixiangong Village Area 13, cited in this paper, family property seems to be treated similarly to family property in Japan. For example, in multi-son families of the 1970s, to avoid dividing the family property, only one son inherited it, while other sons married and moved in with their wives' families. Although this system appears similar to the Japanese family property system, it is essentially different in nature. This paper, taking Kaixiangong Village as an example, focuses on housing, both as a unit of living and as part of family property, and analyses the process of change in rural families and family property in Southern Jiangsu Province from an historical angle. Observation of the change in housing in Kaixiangong Village over the past hundred years reveals that the division of family property was limited, and the growth in the economic accumulation of individual families led to a steady increase in family property.

Keywords: rural families, family property, Sino-Japanese comparative studies

Introduction

Small-scale peasant economies were formed in both Japan and China in very early times. However, the social and economic organizations that supported these small peasant economies were established in very different ways in the two countries. In Japan, village communities were formed according to geographical

---

[1] During preparation of this paper, detailed instruction and assistance was offered throughout by Dr Chang Xiangqun of the London School of Economics and Political Science. Guo Aimin, Associate Professor of Economic History at Nanjing Normal University, also made valuable suggestions. I hereby express my sincere thanks to both. My thanks also extend to Mr Matthew Timothy Wills, Assistant Editor of the JCCP, Ms Costanza Pernigotti, Mr Lee Chi Ying, and Mr Sheung Kuen Poon of CCPN Global's Assistant Translators, as well as my PhD student Gao Hui Chen, for their help in different ways.

grouping, while in China they were based on clan groups formed by blood ties (Nakamura 2000). On the other hand, as indicated in the research of Fei Xiaotong, the economic network centred on markets and towns also offered strong support to small peasant economies in China (Fei 2002).

Thus the principles of small peasant family structure were different in Japan and China. Furthermore, as the Chinese clan enlarged, so the ways of inheriting family property came to differ greatly from those in Japan. This paper first compares the concepts of clan, family property and inheritance in the two countries; it then presents a case study in Japan; finally, Kaixiangong Village is used as an example to illustrate the changes in the small peasant clan in the Southern Jiangsu rural area of China in the last century, by means of an analysis of the separation of the clan and inheritance strategies.

1. Clan and family property – a comparison between Japan and China

Family inheritance in Japan

In Japan, the small peasant economy was established in the early Edo times (mid-seventeenth century). At that time, a clear distinction was made between samurais and peasants, both in status and in housing space: samurais lived in cities while peasants lived in villages. Land rent was paid on the basis of a 'village' (*mura*) by way of a peasant joint responsibility system. On the proviso that land rent was paid, the Bakuhan (the system of shogunate rule) permitted the *mura* control over their legal, administrative and judicial mechanisms, leading to the formation of 'self-ruled villages.' Peasants were ruled by the same clan group up until the Edo period (1603–1868), when they gradually became independent as *hon-byakushou* (peasants who had land use rights and were included in the Bakuhan land register, paying rent and tax to the tax through their *mura*). Hence the small peasant economy of *hon-byakushou* was established and families (*ie*) were formed. The land that they had formally contracted was now regarded as the family property of *hon-byakushou*, and the family name, family business, family status and right of sacrifice to ancestors were inherited by one son alone. Such practice became a tradition (Sekiguichi 1989; Okama 2009).

Family property was the material condition needed for the *ie* to survive. One-son heritance usually meant property passing to the eldest son, but in some cases, when conditions did not allow for this, the second son, younger sons or sons-in-law (without a blood relationship) also inherited. Therefore, the right of sacrifice to ancestors was not governed by the concept of blood relationship. This is totally different from circumstances in China (Nakane 1987). In addition, although the head of a family enjoyed absolute power, if he damaged the interests of the *ie*, he faced possible rejection by other clan members, a situation in which the *mura* could also intervene.

In brief, the *ie* tried to maintain two aspects of continuity: family status, which included the family name, family business, custody and guardianship of family members and right of sacrifice to ancestors and the maintenance of ancestral graves; and family property.

After entering the contemporary era, the promulgation of the Meiji Civil Code reinforced the rights of family heads. In addition, although the administrative organization was restructured, the *mura* was maintained. Heads of households and the *mura* served as important means by which Meiji government policy could penetrate rural areas. Meanwhile, family property as the basis of the *ie* survived. The novel *Mon and Kura* (which records family names and the process of accumulation of land as a kind of family property) was a symbol of the prosperity enjoyed by family property (Wada 1972–74). During the process of democratization after World War II, the Meiji Civil Code was modified and an inheritance system based on equal division was established. However, in actuality, the one-son inheritance system is still dominant today, except in those regions where farmland is regarded as property. In recent years, though its importance has been drastically reduced, the *mura* has been instrumental in saving Japanese agriculture, acting as a 'village-scale agricultural cooperative': therefore, it remains a relevant field of study. In view of this, rural clans and their family property remain important factors for *mura* agricultural reproduction; without them, it would have been impossible for Japan to maintain six million hectares of farmland and six million farming families (with some decrease in recent years).[2]

Stirpism in China and the inheritance of family property

Chinese families (*jia*) and family property are very different from those in Japan described above. In China, direct government rule extended only to district level up to the time of the Qing Dynasty. It was country gentlemen who formed the link between the government and the broad mass of the peasantry. Therefore, under such 'double-track politics' (Fei 1999), the *jia* could not become a unit of land ownership. It could not become an entity like *ie*, which was an essential feature of agricultural production and management at a regional level and as a permanent form of family business. Japanese clans, both materially and psychologically, took agricultural production as their main purpose, whereas the main purpose of the *jia* is the continuation of the lineal blood relationship. Family property (real estate, money and chattels) is only one (albeit very important) element of the *jia*'s financial support base.

Various arguments exist on the subject of family property. Gao Yongping explained this issue with the property inheritance principles of 'stirpism', or 'doctrine of the family line' (Gao 2006; Shiga 1950). Here the family line means

---

[2] Males other than the eldest sons became peasants or odd job workers. After entering modern times, when the domestic labour market became saturated, some of them left mainland Japan (as immigrants to Hokkaido in Japan and emigrants to foreign countries or regions, such as Korea, Manchuria, Hawaii, North America and South America).

a male adult, who does not live together with his brothers, as well as all his continuous (single-pass) ancestors and all his underage sons (or even adult son, in the case of an only child), who form a group of males related by blood (or intended male blood relation group.) (Gao 2006:173)

Family lineage is the only factor in the continuation of clan pedigree and property inheritance. When a father is the head of his family line, he naturally has the right to make decisions on family property with others outside the family. But for issues involving inheritance of family property, the case is different. In the case of an only son, he inherits directly from his father and no division of property is necessary. This was the case in Fei Xiaotong's study of Kaixiangong Village (see note 2). However, if property is inherited by more than one son, family division will take place. The ownership of the family property will be equal to the number of sons when a family is divided up. The father never has the right to distribute the property other than by dividing it equally among the sons. From this we know that the family property, no matter how much that property is worth, will be divided equally among the new family lines when the sons grow up (usually to be married and have their own children). As a result, new family lines emerge from equal-division inheritance.

In discussing the differences between the Japanese *ie* and the Chinese *jia* with respect to inheritance, a case study of a Japanese family line is presented here, followed by a study of the special characteristics of Chinese *jia* and family property inheritance as shown in Kaixiangong Village. This paper also includes a description of a Chinese family's spiritual[3] and daily life, as well as the way in which they organized production.

2. Inheritance of *ie* – the introduction of modern sericulture in Japan

In order to compare the inheritance of *jia* in China with the concept of *ie* in Japan, I draw on the research results from Hasebe (Hasebe 2009a).

Family name, family business, family status and family property in Japan

This case study concerns a rural family (family K) in Kamishiojiri Village, Nagano County, during the period from the beginning of the eighteenth century to the middle of the nineteenth century. The village is a highly developed district, known for its crop farming and sericulture. In the 140 years since family K divided from its clan (Family Z) in 1727 (see table 1), seven family heads had maintained the inheritance of their clan name (Kaheiji).[4]

---

[3] With regard to spiritual life, worship of ancestors is a major rite. For example, the No. 14 family needs to prepare two tables of feasts on the spirit festival in mid-July, by the lunar calendar. One table is for their own ancestors, and the other is for their former neighbour's ancestors, since they use the site of their neighbour's house.

[4] For more on the situation of families K and Z, see Hasebe (2009b).

The management periods of each family head are as follows. The family head of the first generation had the longest period of management, 37 years; the second family head had 27 years; the third family head had only seven years because he died at the age of 33. His brother helped manage the family as 'transitional family head' for 14 years; the fourth family head, who was the son of the third, managed his family for 32 years; after that, the fifth family head had 15 short years and the sixth 17 years. From the discussion below it can be seen that the inheritance of the family clan occurred in a difficult situation involving a high mortality rate. As regards inheritance, the first family head chose to retire at 60 to pass the management position to the next generation, and so did the second family head, who retired when he was 54 years old and died at 72. The other four family heads all took on their management position owing to the death of the previous head.

Table 1: The inheritance of family K (Hasabe 2009a, partially summarized

G	Name	YOB	Period as family head			Way of inheritance	Remark
			Start	End	Years		
①	T. F	1703	1727	1763	37	Secluded	Divided from family Z with land, started silkworm egg business
②	Y. A	1736	1764	1790	27	Secluded	
③	Y. N	1763	1790	1796	7	Died at 33	Enlarged silkworm egg business
③'	N. Y	Around 1770	1796	1809	14	Divided from family	Set up silkworm egg cooperative and became a centre (transitional family head)
④	H. K	1788	1809	1840	32	Died at 53	Maintained family business, important role in administrative aspect of the village
⑤	N. N	1813	1840	1854	15	Died at 41	Inherited family business and village cadre position
⑥	N. Ch	1820	1854	1870	17	Died at 50	Ditto
⑦		1850	1870				Set up sales company to make and sell silkworm egg paper

Notes: 1) G for genetration; YOB: Year of birth.
2) As described later, ③ 'is ③'s younger brother. After ③'s death, ③' became the transition family head. This family head title will be given back to ④, ③'s son, when he becomes an adult.

What kind of family property existed during this period? From the year 1727, when the first generation divided from its family clan, to the year 1731, when it inherited nearly half of family Z's land and became *hon-byakushou*, the land holding of the family had reached a middle to upper level in the village. Moreover, family K started a silkworm egg business in cooperation with family Z at the end of 1740. They not only made silkworm egg paper, but also sold the paper in the local and surrounding areas, building a solid relationship with sericulture famers who could make credit exchanges with the family.

The second generation maintained the existing family business, before the third generation enlarged the silkworm egg business and the 'transitional family head' set up a silkworm egg cooperative, in which he became the main figure.

With such economic power, the fourth family head played a much more important role in the administrative aspects of village life.

Thus, focusing on the silkworm egg business, family K kept on enlarging the family property, which raised their status and led to their becoming an important part of the *mura*.

The family property consisted of financial assets from their farmland and silkworm egg business. The farmland remained at the middle to upper level in the *mura* from the first to the third generation, then underwent a decrease in the fourth and fifth generations (1830–1840); afterwards, it began to pick up again. The development of the silkworm egg business played a significant role in the accumulation of financial assets. When trading with sericulture silkworm farmers, family K provided a service for families who lacked agricultural funds, in the form of sheets of silkworm eggs, and then deducted the cost from cocoons in the harvest season. Thus, the two sides formed a virtually fixed, exclusive, financial lending relationship. The period from the end of 1790 to the middle of 1910 was family K's heyday in terms of financial assets, after which came a ten-year regression leading to a low period.

The inheritance process of family K

The detailed inheritance process of the K family line is shown in figure 1. The first head of family K had four sons and two daughters. The fourth son, who was chosen as candidate 1 owing to the deaths of his older brothers, passed away after his marriage. The eldest daughter married a man from family Z, who became a live-in son-in-law and was supposed to be the second family head. However, both he and his wife died soon after their marriage, which left family K with no choice but to call back their second daughter and make her husband the family's adopted son. Eventually, the second daughter's husband, a live-in son-in-law, became the second head of the family.

It grew more complicated when the third family head took charge. The second family head had two daughters and one son; only his elder daughter survived to grow up and marry. Her husband became candidate 1 for family head. As a result of this daughter's divorce, the man she married next was chosen as candidate 2. After that, following the death of the first daughter, her husband married another woman and then left the family, which led to a marriage between his second wife and another man, who became candidate 3. Unfortunately, this couple also later left the family. Because of the death of his wife, the second family head married another woman, who had earlier been married and raised two daughters, the elder of whom was married to a live-in son-in-law, who became candidate 4 and finally inherited the position of third family head. However, he died seven years later at the age of 33.

His eldest son was too young to manage the family, so family K decided that the third head's younger brother should be a 'transitional family head' as a live-in son-in-law. This 'transitional family head' helped to manage the family for 14 years until the third family head's eldest son grew up to be the fourth head of family K. He was the only one in this family who had a smooth succession.

Thereafter, this family ran into complications again. The fourth family head had four sons and one daughter, and his eldest son became the fifth family head after his father died. This family head was involved in three marriage failures, leaving no child to take over the family and dying at the age of 41. Family K had to recall the fourth family head's third son, who by that time had got married and moved out, to be the sixth family head.

The inheritance process of the seventh generation reached modern times, but still met with some difficulties. The sixth family head had only one daughter; thus the husband of this daughter should have been the next family head. However, owing to this live-in son-in-law's misbehaviour, their marriage broke down. As a solution to this situation, family K adopted an eight-year-old boy from the same clan. After the sixth family head died, this boy inherited the family and got married at the age of 20.

In sum, the second family head was actually a live-in son-in-law, as was the third family head, whose wife was the daughter of the previous family head's second wife, with no blood relationship to family K. The fourth and the fifth family heads were both the eldest son of each generation, yet the sixth family head was actually the younger brother of the fifth family head, which meant his time as family head was much shorter. Though the seventh family head was adopted from the same clan, reinstating the blood relationship, this can only be considered as an emergency response measure.

Figure 1: Inheritance tree for family K (Hasabe 2009a)

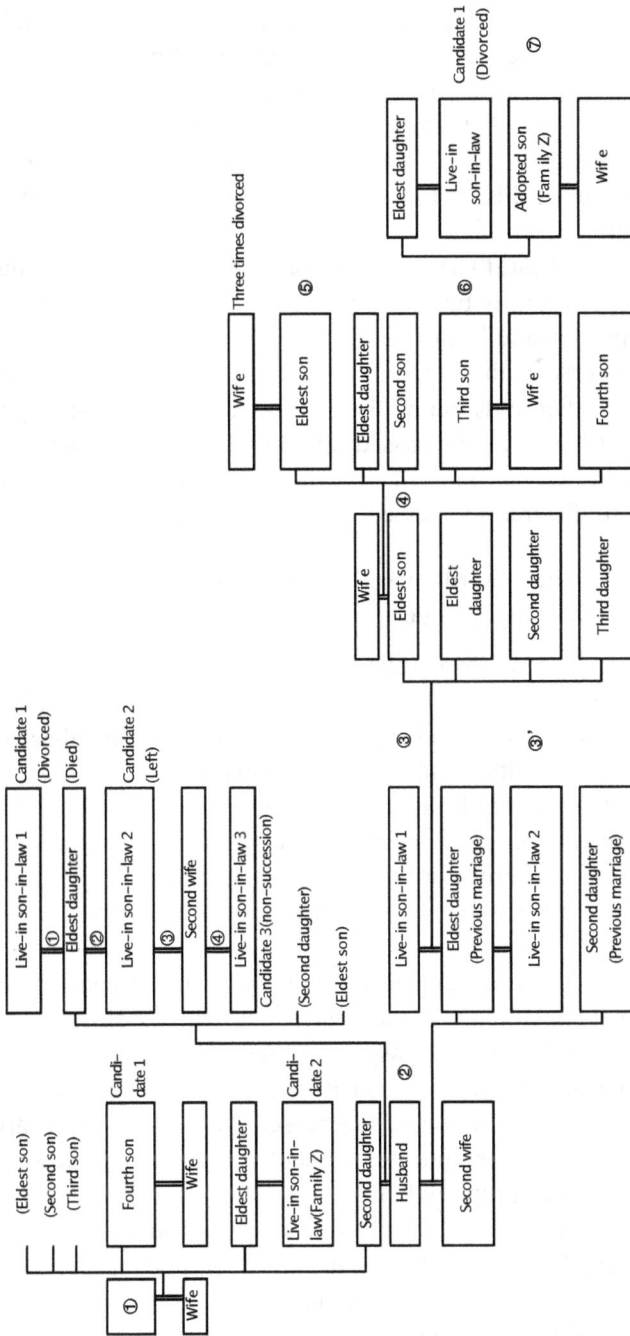

Figure 1: Inheritance tree for family K (Hasabe 2009a)

We can see that the extremely high mortality rate was a key factor in the difficulties experienced in family inheritance. As a result, there were two cases in which the live-in son-in-law inherited the family property (three if we count the 'transitional family head'), one case where the adopted son inherited and two cases in which brothers of family heads inherited (including the 'transitional family head'). Cases in which the candidate (live-in son-in-law) died made this succession more complicated. On the other hand, the inheritance of *ie* was not constrained by a need for bloodline inheritance. The case of family K includes only a few instances of this, as this relationship was cut off when it came to the third family head.

All these facts indicate that the main purpose of inheritance is that the inheritors should maintain their family business, as family property is an economic basis of a family. The family name is an important symbol of the combination of family business and property. Unlike the inheritance of *ie*, which could not be passed on, the members of family K put all their energy into making sure this economic base and their family name were passed smoothly to the next generation. Whether this thrilling, tightrope-like kind of inheritance is common or not is unknown; however, this case illustrates the essence of inheritance in Japan.

3. Inheritance of *jia* and family property in China – the case of Kaixiangong Village

The farmland in Kaixiangong Village consists of a high, four-sided ridge surrounding low-lying land, which is called *wei* (圩). Since ancient times, Kaixiangong's population to land ratio has been severely imbalanced (too high a population with too little land), and so people's occupations are relatively diversified. This diversity has been reduced since the 1920s, owing to the influence of the world economic crisis, war, chaos and the planned economy. However, industrialization in rural areas in the 1990s brought big changes to the internal industrial structure of Kaixiangong Village, precipitating a return to the diversity of former times.

Kaixiangong Village developed on both sides of the canal (known as the Xiaoqing River) at the entrance to the village. With the construction of more and more roads, the main mode of transport changed from water transport to land transport. The houses by the Xiaoqing River are now farthest from the roads. Meanwhile, the number of houses has increased rapidly and house structures are taller. The number of houses indicates the units of a clan and the size of houses represents the amount of property families own. We can use the changes in house quantity and quality to indicate the changes in clans and in family property. An analysis will be made here of changes in family property based on changes in house size. Then we will consider changes in the family tree in order to understand the independence of family members who lived with the family before and to understand the process of the division of family.

Formation of family property from the perspective of house size
Although Kaixiangong is an administrative village, the arrangement of land is still composed of four *wei*, constituting a natural village as described by Fei Xiaotong in the 1930s. The four *wei* are Xichang Wei, Nan Wei, Liangjiao Wei and Chengjiao Wei, There are also two big water masses: the Dongzhuang and Xizhuang ponds. Up to the early 1980s, transport between one *wei* and another was principally boats that sailed along the waterway. The houses extended along the bank of the Xiaoqing River with doors facing the river. The present Kaixiangong Village (natural village) consists of 15 groups. There are three *wei* in the north, with three groups in each *wei*. The Chengjiao Wei in the south consists of six groups.

Area 13 furnishes a good example. In the group, there are some historic buildings such as the Kaixiangong Silkworm Cooperative and the Shared Young Silkworm Growth Room. These sequentially became the site for the Kaixiangong Township Government after the Liberation in 1949, a production brigade office during the people's commune period and the dormitory for rusticated youth during the 'Cultural Revolution'. This location is still the centre of Kaixiangong Village (Sakashita et al. 2006). After the road was built, the area it crossed became the central area. The primary school moved to the south side of the Area 13 road in the 1990s, merging with Miaogang Central Primary School in 2008. In 2009, the Village Commission moved in.

The number of households in Area 13 is now 29, and their layout is shown in Figure 2. The houses stand in six rows. All residential houses were built in the Qing Dynasty by the Xiaoqing River (to the north of the dotted line). Up to the end of the 1960s, nothing changed the traditional historical landscape. We can see the distribution of family lines in Figure 2. Starting from the right, the sequence is Yao 1, Zhao, Yao 2, Yao 3, Zhou 1 and Zhou 2. In addition, the households in the south of the village were divided into groups by surname in 1935 (Fei 2002). The most popular surname was Zhou, in 49 households, followed by Yao in 30 households and Zhao in seven. It can be seen that many of the clans have been represented here for a long time. Before the 1960s, most houses in this area were single-storey except the house of Zhou 2, whose ancestor was a bureaucrat in the Qing Dynasty. Their house is a small, two-storey structure that is 300 years old.

Figure 2: The distribution of houses in Kaixiangong Village area 13

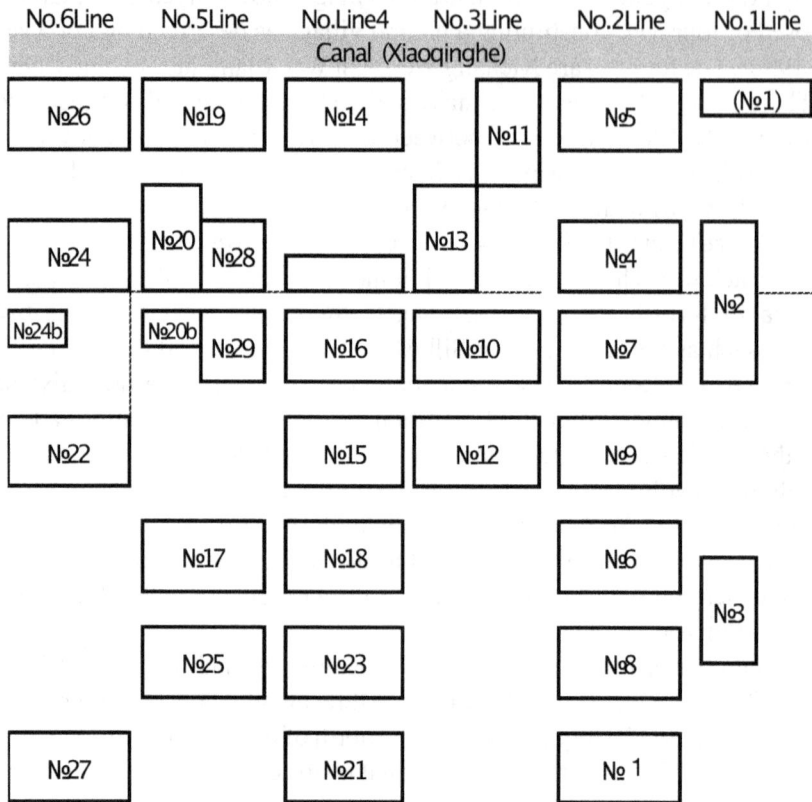

No.6Line	No.5Line	No.Line4	No.3Line	No.2Line	No.1Line

Canal (Xiaoqinghe)

№26 | №19 | №14 | №11 | №5 | (№1)

№24 | №20 №28 | | №13 | №4 | №2

№24b | №20b №29 | №16 | №10 | №7

№22 | | №15 | №12 | №9

№17 | №18 | №6

№3

№25 | №23 | №8

№27 | №21 | № 1

Houses in Kaixiangong Village were situated along both sides of the Xiaoqing River up to the 1960s. However, in the 1970s, after Deng Xiaoping came to power, a new rural plan was promulgated. The villagers replaced some paddy fields around the village with mulberry fields. At the same time, they took the opportunity to convert the paddy fields, mulberry fields and wild bamboo shoot fields in the south into housing. In Area 13, one third of families needed a larger housing space when their children reached marriageable age, so they built new single-storey houses for them. This was similar to the case of Xiajia Village studied by Yan Yunxiang (2006). In the 1980s, to improve their living conditions, their children also built new houses after they got married. These were also single-storey houses, as the village is in Heilongjiang Province, where land, natural resources and space for building are all plentiful. In Kaixiangong Village, the low-ceilinged, single-storey houses were remodelled in the mid-1980s. In the late 1980s, when the policy of openness and reform had been in place for some years, the peasant families greatly increased their income and two-storey houses became popular. This was because Kaixiangong was situated in a region with a high population, where it was necessary to maximize the use of building land. Rich families before 1949 had similarly been able to improve their living conditions by building multi-storey structures.[5] For the peasant families, silkworm breeding and wool weaving became part of their daily lives. In the late 1980s, as two-storey houses became popular, they began to have separate spaces for silkworm raising and for domestic life.

New houses had been built by 235 families in Kaixiangong Village (Nos. 1–19 groups before the merger) in 1989, accounting for 38.4% of the total number of families (612). The construction cost of a building was about 20,000 yuan and the total cost about 4 million yuan (Wang 2004: 12). The total income of the peasants in this village was 1.2 million yuan in 1985 (Shen 1993:135), showing that the construction cost represented almost their total income for four years. Afterwards, new houses were built by 51 families (with construction costs of 2.59 million yuan) in 1990, 71 families (with construction costs of 3.42 million yuan) in 1991, and 32 families (with construction costs of 1.13 million yuan) in 1992.

Table 2 shows the year of construction of the houses in Area 13. The data came from our interview. In some cases, an additional storey was added to an existing one-storey house. In these cases, the year represents the year of construction of the second storey. In the late 1980s, 17 of the 29 families built their two-storey houses. All peasant families (excluding two families with city/town household registers) had moved into two-storey houses by 1996. Luxury and villa-type houses began to appear after 2000. The difference between the rich and poor began to be reflected in the exterior of their houses.

---

[5] For a comparison of housing structures in Kaixiangong Village and Xiajia Village, see Chang (2009), sections 1 and 2 and chapter 6. For a detailed description of household types in Xiajia Village, see Yan (2009).

Table 2: Construction of two-storey houses in Area 13

Units of measure: buildings, Renminbi

Year	Two storeies	Extension	Building	Total	Net income per person
1985	2			2	659
1986	4			6	
1987	5			11	
1988	1			12	1,115
1989	5			17	1,181
1990	2			19	1,120
1991				19	1,346
1992	4			23	1,873
1993	6		2	29	2,222
1994	2	1		31	2,931
1995				31	4,078
1996	1	1		32	4,879
1997				32	4,945
1998				32	5,106
1999				32	5,117
2000				32	5,246
2001				32	5,466
2002				32	5,632
2003	2			35	6,073

Source: Interview with village committee.
Note: The information about net incomes was taken from Sakashita et al. 2006,
while the figure for 1985 was calculated based on Shen 1993.

Division of families into smaller units

The increase of houses both in number and in area in Kaixiangong Village indicates two sides of the housing issue. First, improvement was made to the crowded living conditions that existed by the Xiaoqing River before the 1960s and the increase in house numbers was a reflection of the splitting up of large families. Second, it was a reflection of children's marriages, division of families and the process of separation from the original living unit. In the next section, we will study the six rows of houses as shown in Figure 2 for an analysis of two typical clans.

Row 2: The Zhao clan (Figure 3)

Figure 3: Lineage and house divisions of the Zhao clan

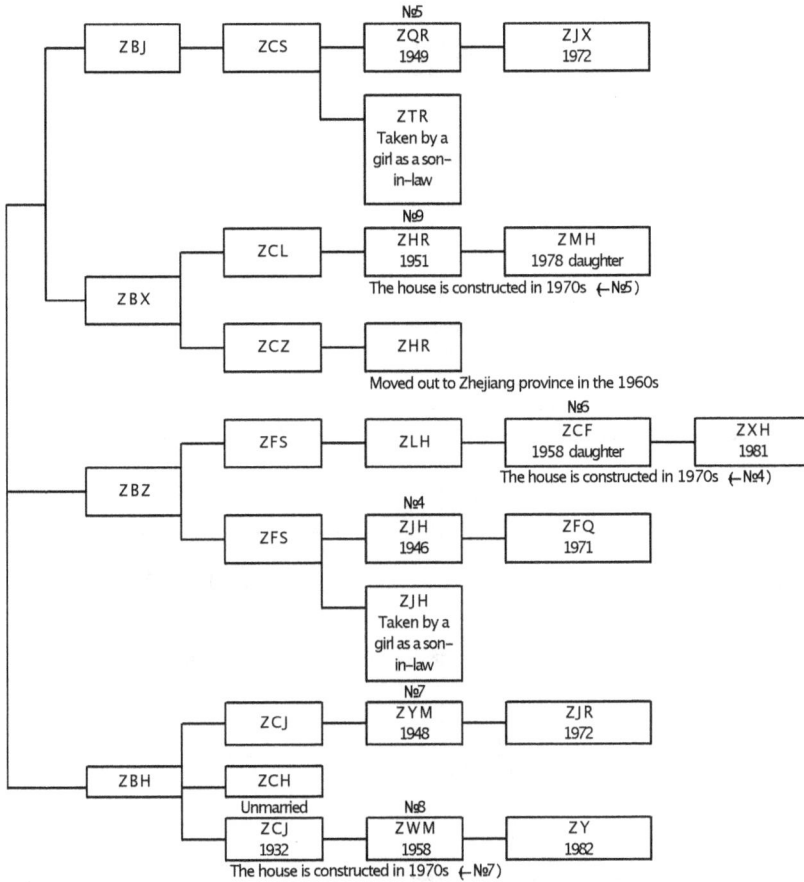

No. 5 is the closest to the Xiaoqing River. Four families (ZBJ, ZBX, ZBZ and ZBH) lived here in the past. They called themselves 'members of the same family'. They had seven rooms plus kitchens and storerooms.

No. 9's younger brother's family moved to Zhejiang Province in 1962. Then No. 9 and No. 4 separated and became independent families in the 1970s. They built new houses in row 2. Only three families (No. 5, No. 9 and No. 4) lived here after this. No. 4's son-in-law joined the family and set up an independent family as No. 6. Both No. 5 and No. 4 had younger brothers, who got married and moved to their wives' families. No division of family happened. We know that, in this clan, one family moved away and in two families one son got married and moved in with his wife's family. No new houses were built. No. 5's house had remained single-storey until the 1980s, but a second floor was added in 1985. The house on No. 7's site was built in the Qing Dynasty. There were three brothers in No. 7's father's generation. The second brother did not marry and the third one had an independent family in the 1970s. This case of division of household did not represent a division of family property.

Thus, no division of family happened in this row after the Liberation in 1949. The six families from No. 4 to No. 9 make one row.

Row 4: The Yao clan (Figure 4)

Figure 4: the lineage and divisions of the Yao clan

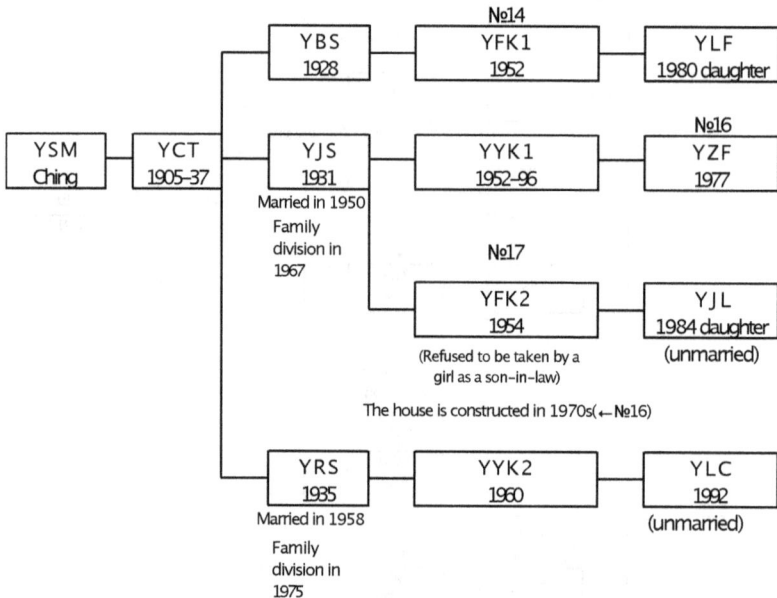

Figure 4: The lineage and divisions of the Yao clan

No. 14's father had three brothers. They once lived in an old house, built in the Qing Dynasty, by the Xiaoqing River. The layout of the house is shown in Figure 5. The three brothers got married in the 1940s–50s. There were about ten people, including the three couples and their children, living in six bedrooms. The second brother (YJS) built a new single-storey house on the site of the original livestock shed and its surrounding open space in 1967. His family moved out of the old house and set up an independent family, No. 16. (The second floor was added in 1984. A new two-storey house was built in 1994.) Then the first and the third brothers (YBS and YRS) lived in three rooms each until the third brother moved to No. 15 on the inner side of No. 16 in 1978. When they moved, they used some timber, bricks and tiles from the No. 13 house (Figure 2).

As mentioned before, the homestead (foundation of the house) of No. 15 had been used as the Silkworm Raising Co-operative and Shared Young Silkworm

Growth Room in the Republic of China, and became Kaixiangong Township Government headquarters after the Liberation. It became the production brigade office (place A), then the dormitory of the educated youth, and finally the warehouse (place B) of the production brigade in 1969. No. 14's father owned the land here in the Republic period and repurchased it after the Cultural Revolution. No. 15 bought and moved to the location (place B) in front of this house (the second floor was added in 1991). They purchased the front part (place B) and used it as a woollen sweater factory.[6] With the independence of No. 15, the units of residence became three families, that is, the number of households gradually grew to three. The old house was used by No. 15. The house was rebuilt by adding a second floor in 1984 and 1986, and then further remodelled in 1994 as a two-storey house, which is the one they still live in now. No. 16 had a younger brother, who refused to be taken by a girl of another family as a son-in-law.[7] In the 1970s, he built a new house in row 5 and set up an independent family (No. 17).

---

[6] For the job structure of the farm households of the Kaixiangong Village Area 13, see Park et al. 2008.

[7] According to Chang (2009), 'Traditionally in Kaixiangong Village a marriage that involved taking a son-in-law (*zhaonuxu*) into a family was seen as a misfortune. It meant that the family had no son, and the son-in-law's social status was low since he was poor. Nowadays more and more families accept this kind of marriage. [...] The change of the villagers to favour daughters rather than sons or to feel easy without sons might have been affected by the one-child family policy, which applied from the early 1980s.' The younger brother (No. 17) of No. 16 in this paper refused to be taken as the son-in-law in the 1970s; we infer that the reason was that he was afraid of being discriminated against.

Figure 5: housing use and building process of No. 14

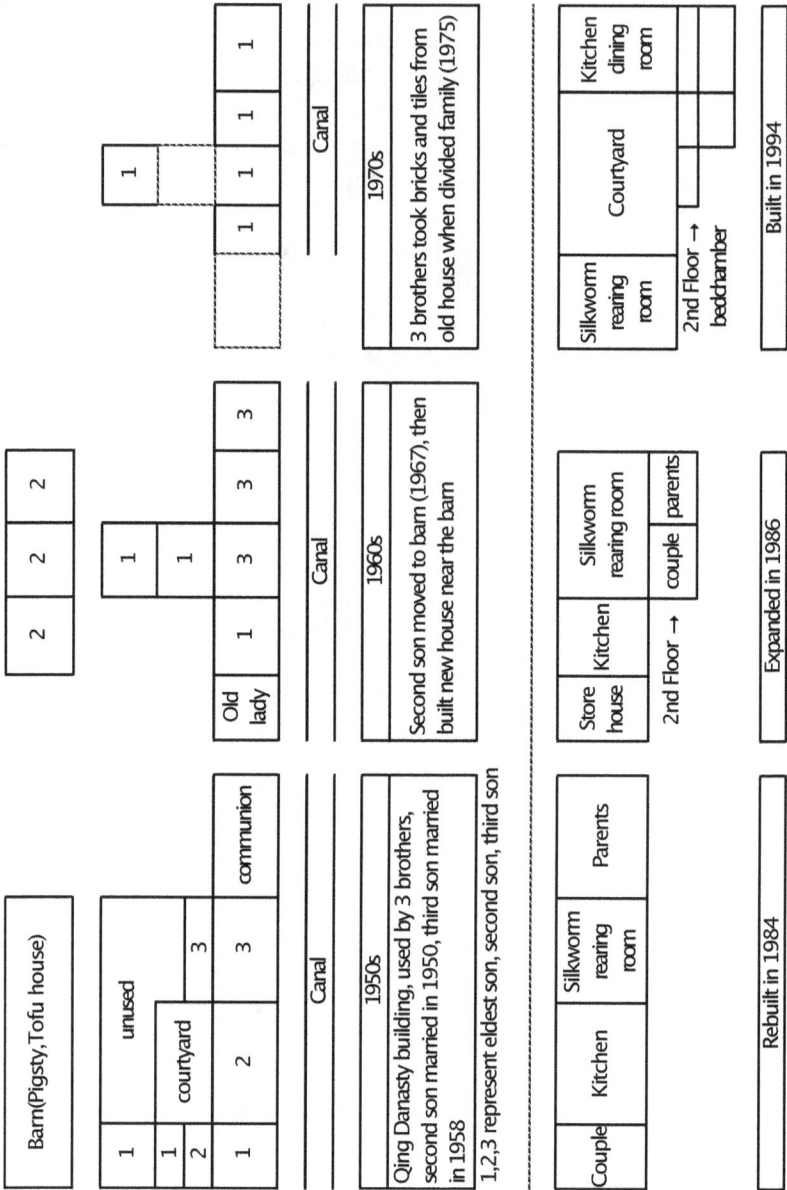

Figure 5: Housing use and building process of №14

Table 3: The number of households and their inwards/outwards mobility in area 13

	The first generation	The second generation	The third generation	Total
Number of people	21	24	24	69
Median year of birth	1922	1948	1974	
Took a husband into the family	0	2	5	7
Family division	0	3	0	3
Taken by a girl as a son–in–law	0	4	3	7

Source: Interview.
Notes: 1) 24 households (not including 5 households registered in the city). Does
           not include the people who went to live with their wife's family;
        2) When not clear, the dates of birth of the first generation were calculated
           by subtracting 25 years from the ones of the second generation.

Changes in three generations of the clans

We have investigated the changes undergone by the three generations of different clans and the changes in their living units. Division of family is rare in Area 13, as Table 3 confirms. There are 27 residential families in the group now. Information about the ages

of three of them is not known, since they hold city household registers. For the remaining 24 families, the data on the number of family heads and their status regarding moving in and moving out are sorted and entered into Table 3. It shows that there were 21 people in the first generation in Administrative Area 13. They lived by the Xiaoqing River. Among them, six people were born in the 1920s, five people in the early 1930s, and four people in the early 1940s. Their median birth year was 1922. They were young adults when the country was liberated. There were 24 people in the second generation, nine born in the late 1940s and five in the early 1950s. Their median birth year was 1948, and they got married in the 1970s. This was the same period when the first generation became independent and built new houses. The area had larger living space and more families. Among the second generation who were born after the Liberation, three persons set up independent families through division of family. (There were two families, which were not mentioned in this paper, besides No. 17.) Four men married and moved into these families. Two females became female family heads when their husbands moved into their families. The number of families grew from 21 to 24. There were 24 people in the third generation, of whom eight were born in the early 1970s and six in the early 1980s. Their median birth year was 1974. They were the generation that grew up during the reform and opening period, and none of them set up independent families through division of family. Three males married and moved into their wives' families. Five females became family heads when their husbands moved into their families. As a result, the number of families remained unchanged. In summary, only three families experienced family division. Seven males moved into families here on marriage. Seven females married and their husbands moved into their families.

Conclusion

In this paper we have considered the inheritance of family and family property with regard to two cases, Kamishiojiri Village in Japan and Kaixiangong Village in China. The significance of these two cases is as follows.

First, in Japan the *ie* is a family group bent on continuing the family business, family property and family name. This is one of the characteristics of the traditional clan in Japan. *Ie* is a constituent element of the village community. To put it more vividly, the village can be seen as a country, which has legislative, administrative and judicial powers. *Ie* is the legal structure in this country, by which every legal group has its family name, family property, family business and family status. In the case of Kamishiojiri Village, family K was one branch of the six big families (Z family clan) in their village. The primary consideration of their family inheritance was not blood relationship, but the continuance of family property. To maintain the existence of their family is to safeguard the existence of the village community. To ensure that the family property (mainly land) is sustainable, they need the family business (e.g. agriculture) to continue to thrive. The family name is the symbol of family property and possessions, i.e. a distinguishing marker.

Second, in Kaixiangong Village in China, the case of group 13 was demonstrated by changes in the housing units, and the process by which housing units of two typical families expanded was analysed. Southern Jiangsu Province is a narrow land area in a region of lakes and streams, where agricultural operations have been carried out since ancient times. Rural residents' assets are symbolized by their houses. With the development of industrialization in rural areas and the increase in peasants' income from sideline occupations, villages with dense three-storey housing are no longer rare. Before the liberation of the village, most workers were tenant peasants, few of whom had their own farmland. The houses they had lived in for generations were their own family property and were of great importance as a family asset. Among poor people, a few different lineages might live under the same roof. The houses in Area 13 extended inland from the banks of the Xiaoqing River in the 1970s, owing to the gradual improvement in living conditions and to progress in the external environment. This helped to create the conditions for division of family property and inheritance. However, only three families, including No. 17, among the more-than-one-son families in Area 13, experienced division of family. Other families kept one son to inherit the family property and any other sons married and moved to their wives' families to avoid division of family. This is unlike the traditionally equal inheritance of family property in Chinese multi-son families.

So why did this happen in Kaixiangong Village? Li Peilin explains this phenomenon:

> Always the basic way of avoiding and reducing declining risk in big families is not family division, because family division means the reorganization of property right and social relationship (Li 2002:177).

This description also applies to the ordinary villagers in our study. This is because the Chinese family (*jia*), whether large or small, mainly aims at continuation of the lineal blood relationship. The family property is its economic support. In order to be able to continue making the lineal consanguinity, in other words, to 'avoid and reduce declining risk', as Li puts it (2002), the fundamental strategy is not to have family division. In Group 13, the villagers use the method of 'live-in son-in-law', which is a folk-invented custom or a product of common practice, to avoid the division of family property when it is unable to support more than one family line.

In this way, the non-division of family in Kaixiangong in order to continue blood relationships is essentially different from the Japanese *ie* system, which aims for the perpetual continuation of family property.

However, it is worth noting that, thanks to the impact of birth control, most families in the present Kaixiangong Village have only one child, and the population is tending to decrease at the same time as it is ageing. In this situation, a form of 'two-sided independent marriage' has become popular in recent years. 'Two-sided independent marriage' means that the new couple will not live in the same house as either partner's parents but will live independently from both. In addition, a newborn's name will include the surname of both father and mother, indicating that the new family line belongs to both of the old lines at the same time. On the other hand, more and more houses have been built as family properties, which can provide a secure economic foundation for the continuation of blood relationship. However, *jia*, which meant supported blood relationship, is now in great peril. This will be the topic for further research.

References

常向群:《关系抑或礼尚往来? 江村互惠、社会支持网和社会创造的研究》，中文简体版，毛明华译，沈阳:辽宁人民出版社2009年。

Chang Xiangqun. 2010. *Guanxi or Li Shang Wanglai? – Reciprocity, Social Support Networks, & Social Creativity in a Chinese Village*. Taipei: Airiti Press).

中村哲:《近代东亚史像的重新构成》，东京：樱井书店，2000年 [Nakamura, T. 2000. *Recomposition of Eastern Asian Images in the Contemporary Era*. Tokyo: Sakurai Shoten].

费孝通:《江村经济》,北京:商务印书馆，2002年 [Fei Xiaotong. 2002. *Jiangcun Jingji* (in Chinese). Beijing: The Commercial Press].

— 1999年《乡土重建》，见《费孝通文集》第4卷，300–440页. 北京：群言出版社 [1999. *Xiangtu Chongjian* [Reconstructing Rural China], in *Fei Xiaotong Wenji*, Vol. 4: 300–440. Beijing: Qunyan Press].

关口祐子等:《日本家族史》,千叶•松户:梓出版社，1989年[Sekiguchi, Y. et al. 1989. *History of Japanese Clans*. Chiba•Matsudo: Azusa Shuppansha].

大鎌邦雄编:《日本与亚洲的农业村落-组织与职能》,大阪: 清文堂, 2009年 [Okama, K. Ed. 2009. *Japanese and Asian Agricultural Villages. Organizations and Functions*, Osaka: Seibundo].

中根千枝:《社会人类学-对亚洲诸社会的考察》,东京:东京大学出版社, 1987年[Nakane, C. 1987. *Social Anthropology – Investigation on Asian Societies*. Tokyo: Tokyo University Press].

和田传:《门和仓》全4卷, 东京:家之光出版社, 1972–74年 [Wada, D. 1972–74. *Mon and Kura, Vol. 1–4*. Tokyo: Ie-No-Hikari Press].

高永平:"传统财产继承背后的文化逻辑-家系主义":《社会学研究》,2006年第3期, 167-187 页 [Gao, Yongping. 2006. Zhongguo chuantong caichan jicheng beihou de wenhua luoji. Jiaxizhuyi', *Shehuixue Yanjiu* No. 3 (2006): 167–187].

滋贺秀三:《中国家族法论》,东京:弘文堂, 1950年 [Shiga, S.1950. *Theories of Chinese Clan Laws*. Tokyo: Kobun Do].

长谷部弘: 《近世日本的<家>的继承与相续》,见国方敬二等编著《家的存续战略与婚姻-日本, 亚洲, 欧洲》, 52–70页,东京: 刀水书房, 2009a [Hasebe, H. 2009a. 'Devolution and inheritance of family in modern Japan' In K. Kunigata et al. eds. *Survival Strategies of Family and Marriage. Japan, Asia, Europe*. pp. 52–70. Tokyo: Tosui Shobo].

—《家业、家产、家名的继承与相续》, 见长谷部弘等编著《近世日本的地域社会与共同性-近世上田领上盐尻村的综合研究之1》, 255–269页.东京: 刀水书房, 2009b [Hasebe, H. 2009b. 'The Devolution and inheritance of family business, family property and family name'. In Hasebe, H. et al. eds. *Regional Society and Commonality in Modern Japan. No. 1 of Comprehensive Study of Ueda Clan in Kamishiojiri Village*. pp. 255–269. Tokyo: Tosui Shobo].

坂下明彦, 朴红和市来正光:"中国苏南地区农业生产体制的变化和土地问题-江村追踪调查(1)":《农经论丛》2006年第62集: 15–24页[Sakashita, A., Park, H. and Ichiki, T. 2006. 'Change of agricultural production system and land problems in the Sunan area of China. a follow-up research of Kaixiangong Village (1)'. *Review of Agricultural Economics*. No. 62: 15–24].

朴红,市来正光和坂下明彦:"中国苏南地区农户就业结构的特点-第13组-江村追踪调查(3)":《农经论丛》2008年第63集: 71–84 [Park, H., Sakashita, A. and Ichiki, T. 2008. 'Plural activities of farm households in Sunan area of China – the monograph of the 13th farmers group: a follow-up Research of Kaixiangong Village (3)'. *Review of Agricultural Economics*. No. 63: 71–84].

Yan Yunxiang. 2003. *Private life under socialism—love, intimacy, and family change in a Chinese village*. Stanford, CT: Stanford University Press.

阎云翔:《私人生活的变革: 一个中国村庄里的爱情、家庭与亲密关系》, 中文简体版, 龚小夏译, 上海:上海书店出版社2009年.

王淮冰:《江村报告-一个了解中国农村的窗口》, 北京: 人民出版社, 2004年 [Wang, Huaibing. 2004. *Jiangcun baogao. Yi ge liaojie Zhongguo de nongcun chuangkou* [A report from Kaixiangong Village – a window from which to learn about rural China]. Beijing: People's Publishing House].

沈关宝:《一场静悄悄的革命》,昆明:云南人民出版社, 1993年 [Shen, Guanbao. 1993. *Yi chang jingqiaoqiao de geming*. Kunming: Yunnan People's Publishing House].

李培林: "巨变: 村落的终结-都市里的村庄研究":《中国社会科学》, 2002年第1期, pp. 168–179 [Li, Peilin. 2002. 'Jubian: cunluo de zhongjie. Dushi li de cunzhuang yanjiu' [Great change: the end of the village – a study of villages in the city], *Zhongguo Shehui kexue*. No. 1: 168–179].

DOI https://doi.org/10.24103/GCSS2.en.2016.7

The Road to the Cities

Interpreting Some Theoretical Perspectives on Migration and Urbanization from Fei Xiaotong and Ebenezer Howard[1]

Zhiming Wu and Ye Liu

Abstract: Migration has been consistently interpreted and analysed as part of research on urbanization. It has been argued that the flows of population on an 'irrational' scale could cause serious ecological and social problems. These phenomena are termed 'urban and rural diseases'. China is facing the serious consequences of urbanization, in particular those arising from the flows of population. Moreover, other factors such as the household registration system and the land system have intensified the consequences of urbanization. This article reviews theoretical perspectives on urbanization by Fei Xiaotong and Ebenezer Howard, and highlights the distinction between their standpoints and strategies. It concludes with some shared perspectives on urbanization taken from different contexts of China's and Britain's industrialization, respectively.

Keywords: population flow; urbanization; Fei Xiaotong; Ebenezer Howard

Introduction

It is widely acknowledged that China has undergone dramatic urban transformation since the 'Reform and Opening-up' policy in 1978. A rapid process of urbanization, resulting from intensive economic growth lasting more than two decades, has led to the largest migration of population from rural to urban areas in human history (Zhang and Song 2003: 386). Indeed, 'China is probably one of the fastest urbanizing countries in the world' (Chan and Hu 2003: 50).

China's urbanization process followed its own course until the early 1980s, owing to the government's strict regulation on intra-country migration. During the latter half of the 1950s, the government closed the labour market and placed strict controls on the movement of people from rural to urban areas. Over the following two decades, Chinese citizens were restricted when it came to choosing and

---

[1] This paper was originally published in Chinese by WU Zhiming and ZHAO Lu in 2010. It was submitted by the first author to the conference entitled 'Understanding China and Engaging with Chinese People – the 100th Anniversary of the Birth of Professor Fei Xiaotong'. It had been translated, revised and presented at the conference by Dr Ye Liu when she worked for LSE's CCPN in 2011. It had been proofread and updated references throughout by Costanza Pernigotti, CCPN Global's Assistant Editor and Translator before it was published in this issue.

changing their occupation and residence. These controls began to be lifted from the early 1980s as the people's commune system was eliminated. In the mid-1980s the labour market was reconstituted significantly, despite the continuing existence of the regulations affecting migration. The pattern of population mobility had begun to increasingly resemble that of other developing countries (Kojima 1995).

Many studies have demonstrated a range of different perspectives on China's rural–urban migration and urbanization.[2] However, since China has been regarded as particularly distinctive because of the size of its population and its continuous growth, more attention needs to be paid to the role of rural–urban migration in the process of urbanization and to the implications of this migration on broader development issues in China.

Reorientation of rural–urban migration in the analysis of urbanization

Generally speaking, urbanization is a dynamic process, which includes population mobility, social and cultural changes and economic reconstruction. More specifically, it is a transition from a rural or village-based population and lifestyle to an urbanized pattern (Gu and Wu 2010). Despite significant changes in socioeconomic and cultural sectors in a society, population has always been at the centre of urbanization studies. In fact, the core of urbanization is the flow and redistribution of population and the consequent changes in the economic, social and cultural domains.

Various studies have shown that cities in both developed and developing countries encounter two enduring problems in their transition to urbanization. First, large-scale rural–urban migration, which far exceeds the capacity of the city, imposes enormous pressures on urban management and further development. Second, the excessive outflow of the rural population, particularly the young, leads to the deterioration of rural areas, owing to a waste of land, a lack of labour and lower agricultural productivity.

As the world's most populous country, China is not immune from these problems. On the one hand, a large proportion of the rural population has migrated into urban areas to become migrant workers, resulting in a huge increase in the number of cities and super-cities (Huang 2007). This extraordinary phenomenon caused severe 'urban diseases', such as shortage of housing and utilities, traffic congestion, pollution and higher crime rates. Both immigrants and urban residents have somehow become victims of these 'urban diseases'. Rural migrants have often been offered jobs in 'dirty, tiring, harsh, heavy, dangerous' workplaces, and their working conditions have generally been worse than those of other urban workers (Li 2007). Moreover, their jobs have often been unstable (Huang 2009), which has resulted in a huge gap in socioeconomic and political status between

---

[2] These include Chang (2003), Chang and Brada (2002), Harc (1999), Knight and Song (1999), Sccborg et al. (2000), Song (2001), Song and Zhang (2002), Wu (1994), Zhao (1999) and Wu (2009, 2010).

migrant workers and urban workers. A considerable majority of the former are not entitled to claim social benefits such as children's education, medical care and pensions. Casualties occur significantly more often among migrant workers than urban workers (Cheng 2009). Such 'urban diseases' have also put tremendous pressure on local government to spend more on public facilities, social security, social maintenance and environmental protection (Xia 2007).

On the other hand, the outflow of rural population, with the concomitant decline/slow growth in rural income and a widening rural–urban gap (Yang 2009), will lead to more complicated social problems and have rather destructive effects on socioeconomic development (Huang 2009).

It can be argued, at least on a theoretical level, that migration has been persistently interpreted and analysed in researching urbanization. The scale and extent of the migration of the population have had a profound impact on economies, societies and lifestyles. The shared problems emerging from the process of urbanization in different countries can be summarized as follows. First, population migration tends to be 'one-way', which means a flow towards urban areas. This one-way flow results in over-concentration of immigrants in the urban areas. Second, the mass migration of the population out of rural areas negatively affects agricultural production.

At the contextual level, China's transition to a market economy starting in the late 1970s has been characterized by profound policy changes and reforms. The reforms ended the rigid household registration system and the land system, which allowed for greater movement of population between different geographical locations. In particular, rural residents flooded into urban areas for jobs, education and a different lifestyle.

China's experience of urbanization as an over-concentration of the agricultural population in urban areas can be identified as an 'irrational flow'.

To improve living standards among the growing population is the essential goal of urbanization. Changes in both urban and rural areas are inevitable. In other words, the process of urbanization is not intended to eradicate rural areas, but to achieve an integration between rural and urban areas (Xu 2006). Therefore, urbanization is neither an excessive concentration of population in urban areas, nor the decline of the rural population. Urbanization is, however, supposed to allow more people to improve their living standards, enjoy urban civilization and obtain equal opportunity of access to modern facilities.

Migration is certainly not foreign to China. China has the highest population to land ratio, calculated on the basis of cultivated acreage and rural population. This puts a great strain on the land and the rural people. The problem cannot be solved without either urban migration or significant development in the countryside. However, it does not appear to be desirable for the government to keep millions of surplus rural labourers in the countryside. The rural population has been facing poverty, poor infrastructure and much lower living standards. The problems associated with migration must be dealt with by policy enhancement, and it is for this reason that China has been facing a great challenge to improve its quality of urbanization in the twenty-first century. The increase in the size of the urban population will not cease. Therefore, serious questions have arisen. How do we find a proper way to control the flow of the population from rural to urban areas? How do we organize and manage the over-concentrated population in the urban areas? How do we achieve better living standards for a greater population?

Urbanization theorists: Fei Xiaotong and Ebenezer Howard

Fei Xiaotong (1910–2005) was a pioneer of research in the fields of sociology and anthropology in China. As one of the founders of Chinese sociology, he focused particularly on understanding the reality of Chinese society, especially regarding rural and social development. Fei is regarded as a prominent figure who devoted his lifetime to achieving a better society. Since the 'Reform and Opening-up' policy in 1978, the pace of urbanization in rural areas has accelerated. China has also seen continuous and rapid population growth overall, a huge and growing rural population, as well as massive mobility. Turning his mind to effective ways of transferring the surplus of rural labour, Fei proposed a 'small-city' strategy as an alternative to metropolitan cities in the process of urbanization in the particular context of China. Small towns were, he argued, a realistic way of channelling the excessive rural population and coordinating better urban and rural development.

Ebenezer Howard (1850–1928) was a British social activist and an urban sociologist. His experience in the USA in his earlier years contributed to his understanding of urbanization. His jobs as a farmer in Nebraska and as a reporter in Chicago enabled him both to experience rural life and to witness the enduring problems that emerge from the process of urbanization. When he returned to England, he published a book entitled *To-Morrow: A Peaceful Path to Real Reform* in 1898. This book envisioned a utopian city where people lived harmoniously together, while also preserving a natural environment. This book offered a vision of urban areas that were free of slums, where living standards were very high, with great social benefits, job opportunities, low rent and high wages, and where the natural environment was preserved.

While Fei Xiaotong was primarily concerned with the vast rural population, Howard tried to find solutions for the problems of urbanization. Thus, the 'urban disease' and the 'rural disease' were the main concerns for them both, and a consistent and rational arrangement of the excessive population was their answer to urbanization. For Fei, the building of small towns would reduce the gap between the urban and the rural areas and ultimately achieve the optimum level and quality of urbanization. Similarly, Howard's 'social cities', sometimes known as garden cities, would redistribute population from rural areas and larger cities.

The abandonment of Fei's and Howard's visions

Since the 1980s, Fei's idea of building small towns has been highly valued by the Chinese government. In 1998, the Central Committee of the Communist Party published a blueprint agenda, 'A Number of Important Issues in Agriculture and Rural Areas', in which the idea of 'small towns' was raised as part of the strategy of modernizing rural areas. The development of small towns became an important part of the government's overall plan to promote the implementation of institutionalized reform. This strategy of urbanization has achieved some success. At the time of writing, the small-town strategy has been in operation for over two decades, but the gap between the east and the west, and between the rural and the urban, has been ever widening, for which the classical theory on urbanization cannot provide sufficient explanation (Wang 2006). Since the beginning of the twenty-first century, the rapid development of China's big cities, especially the increase of metropolitan areas, has become a common social phenomenon. The national strategy of urbanization was thus changed in 2006. Central government proposed to develop medium-sized cities instead of small towns. The pursuit of big cities was back on the government's main agenda. For example, the development of Chongqing, as the key part of the development strategy in south-western China, proved to be a model of incorporating rural development into urban expansion.

In the UK, the 'garden city movement' achieved some degree of success. One of the first attempts to realize Howard's idea of the 'garden city' was the town of Letchworth, which was developed in 1904 and consisted of three villages. Another project was Welwyn Garden City, built in 1919. Howard's idea of the 'garden city' also influenced the New Town movement in the 1940s in the UK and worldwide after World War II (Osborn 1947; Osborn and Whittick 1977), but the construction of garden cities themselves was eventually abandoned (Mumford 1946). The rapid growth of a large urban population brought a corresponding upsurge in the construction of property in England. In order to meet the rising need for accommodation while avoiding an excessive enlargement of London, the government tried to build satellite towns around the metropolitan area. However, this goal of dispersing the population was not achieved. Instead, it acted as a magnet for more foreign immigrants, thus further expanding Greater London.

China has also followed a similar strategy in recent years. Building satellite cities that aim to attract rural labour has become popular. However, this trend has simply exacerbated the problems of over-concentration, traffic congestion, shortage of housing, low or underemployment and pollution, and, all the while, the migrant population in contemporary China continues to grow. Other barriers, such as the household registration system and the land policy, are also prominent in the process of urbanization in China. Thus, the question arises: To what extent is the idea of building small towns still suitable for China?

Understanding Fei Xiaotong and Howard

The Problem of Increasing Migration

Fei Xiaotong's theory of building small towns arose from contemplating how best to distribute the population. Fei argued that the population gap was too wide between the urban and the rural areas. The problem we are now facing is how to transfer the surplus rural labour force from rural areas to urban ones. Medium-sized cities have already experienced problems such as youth unemployment. However, small towns in China need support from a larger population and workforce to help them develop (Fei 1982). Although China's implementation of a family planning policy in the late 1970s has meant that population growth has slowed, it has not yet ceased, particularly in rural areas.

On the one hand, if the growing rural population tends to participate in agriculture-related production in rural areas, the limited land resources will come under ever greater strain. On the other hand, if people are transferred to the city without due controls, more 'urban diseases' will inevitably emerge.

Fei thought that the most serious problem arising from the process of urbanization was the irrational distribution of population. There was, however, little alternative urban provision between the rural areas and big cities such as Beijing, Shanghai, Guangzhou and the Yangzi Delta. This problem is closely linked to the Party's overall planning of economic development since the 'Reform and Opening-up' policy in 1978. The initial stage of the market reform simply targeted Shenzhen, where many factories were built by joint ventures and other foreign investors. The growth of Shenzhen provided a lot of low-skilled job opportunities, which gave a huge incentive for the rural population to move into inner-city areas. The 'gradual development' strategy proposed by the Party concentrated on investment and development in several areas on the east coast, which helps to explain how the cities have become over-populated and medium/small cities have experienced less development. Walker and Buck (2007) investigated patterns of formation of a Chinese working class, particularly in areas such as the Pearl River Delta and Yangzi Delta. They argued that the provision of urban opportunities in these areas had attracted a vast rural population and that the process of the industrialization of these cities was accompanied by a significant sacrifice on the part of millions of migrant workers living and working in harsh conditions (Walker and Buck 2007).

This phenomenon shows a striking similarity to the process of urbanization in the post-Industrial Revolution West. The 'urban diseases' were often seen as rapid industrial development in the urban areas, which led to a large number of immigrant labourers, over-concentration, environmental degradation and a shortage of housing. Howard predicted that cities would become slums if the population continued migrating on such a scale into urban areas. Moreover, rural stagnation and a recession in agricultural production would also be unavoidable. Howard (2000) was deeply concerned about the future of urbanization.

It is still arguable whether China has adopted a unique way of achieving urbanization, different from what the West has experienced.

The Road to Migration

When he was conducting his research work in some southern rural villages, Fei coined the term 'migrant workers' for those who lived in the towns or villages but worked in the cities. Fei predicted that these migrant workers were the key to realizing urbanization in China. He believed that this was a way of obtaining industrialization with Chinese characteristics, and that there were some characteristics shared with Western industrialization. Fei argued that any measure of social progress relied on the extent to which the gap between the rural and the urban could be reduced and a comprehensive living standard improved for the majority of the people (Fei 1983). Thus, Fei proposed a strategy of developing small towns as 'reservoirs' between the rural and the urban population. By providing these reservoirs, the problem of large migrant populations in the metropolitan areas could be eased, the gap between the regions could be narrowed and more cohesion between the urban and the rural could be achieved.

Fei argued that a close association could be developed between rural economy and urban industry. Rural areas offered some advantages for achieving industrialization, particularly with regard to the production of energy, storage, more convenient transport, market demand and distribution (Fei 1985). Township enterprises have become strong pillars of the revitalization of small cities and towns. The development of township enterprises and the prosperity of small towns can accommodate a large rural labour force, so that small towns absorb the workforce of the 'reservoir', thus solving the problem of excessive population efficiently and rationally. Two ways of doing this were proposed by Fei.

First, promoting the development of township enterprises in small towns would lead to increased job opportunities. After a longitudinal pilot study, millions of rural workers were actively engaged in the development of enterprises in the small towns. This successful pilot became the rationale for the change in the national strategy of socioeconomic development in the rural areas (Song 2000) that has taken place in the last 20 years (Ho 1994; Huang 1990), affecting the overall development of the national economy (Li and Wang 1993; Findlay et al. 1994).

Howard used the metaphor of a magnet and metal to illustrate the situation of over-concentrating the rural populace in the urban areas. Howard found it deeply disturbing that life in large cities had become so powerfully attractive that there seemed to be no other alternative for the rural population. Howard thus proposed the building of small towns with urban lifestyles and qualities, which would become attractive to the rural population. The unique advantage of small towns would be the combination of an urban lifestyle with a semi-rural natural environment. He declared in his book:

> The fullness of joy and wisdom has not revealed itself to man. Nor can it ever, so long as this unholy, unnatural separation of society and nature endures. Town and country must be married, and out of this joyous union will spring a new hope, a new life, a new civilization. (Howard 1902: 48)

The combination of urban and rural characteristics would benefit people from both environments.

Fei Xiaotong's strategy of developing small towns around metropolitan cities as reservoirs for the excess rural population in China was criticized on the grounds that this strategy might be a waste of 'resources' (Peng 2007). However, Fei's idea was based on the priority of maximizing the prosperity of the rural population and introducing modern and industrial technology to the less developed areas. Building 'satellite cities' around metropolitan areas enabled an effective connection between urban and rural markets. In Howard's view, garden cities should be built away from metropolitan areas. Hence, the main distinction between Fei's and Howard's ideas was the geographical location of small cities. Howard's idea was to develop a self-sustaining city rather than a reservoir of big cities or a commuter town. This is why Letchworth and Welwyn were developed away from metropolitan areas, with relatively independent facilities, services and provisions. By contrast, Fei's proposal of satellite cities or towns developed around metropolitan areas was intended not only to provide a reservoir of surplus migrant labour, but also to take advantage of services and facilities in the urban areas and connect rural and urban areas.

'Social Cities' as the Ultimate Goal of Urbanization
In Fei's opinion, with the development of the rural economy, small towns would grow at an even faster rate. Small towns could become economic and cultural centres in rural areas. In order to promote the prosperity of the rural commodity economy and to improve rural production, the development of agriculture and industry should be closely associated. These linkages are considered part of the process of a socialist modernization.

The development of rural areas could not be achieved without benefitting from resources and markets in the urban areas. However, urbanization could not exceed the capacity of cities. Fei Xiaotong also stressed the role of transportation in connecting rural and urban development. The only way to truly eliminate the gap between urban and rural areas and to achieve urbanization with Chinese characteristics was to comprehensively improve the level of urbanization both in quantity and in quality.

The social city is a notion developed from the ideas of garden cities, which benefit from both urban and rural advantages, particularly through the improvement of transport. The garden cities were all closely linked together, leading to the formation of a bigger network and community. However, Fei's ultimate goal was not simply the prosperity of small towns, nor the construction of a garden city.

Both concepts were ways of distributing people efficiently and rationally, and of providing them with advantages as well as development, thus reducing the gap between urban and rural areas. Urbanization does not simply mean making people live in urban areas. Instead, it means achieving greater prosperity for the majority of the population and letting more people enjoy city life, urban civilization and equal opportunities.

Conclusion

At present, China's urban development is often characterized in a popular saying as a 'suburban city surrounded by vast rural areas'. To promote development in both rural and urban areas, small towns around metropolitan areas should be closely linked. In this way, not only can the population be dispersed in the cities but also surplus rural labour can be transformed in an effective way. Metropolitan and large rural areas are unified, so that people can enjoy the advantages of both the urban and the rural. Urban agglomeration should focus on the development of large cities that can radiate to the suburbs and small towns, and join them together by good public transport systems. Building a 'big community' maximizes the redistribution of the excessive accumulation of the urban population in the city and transfers surplus rural labour. Only in this way can living standards be improved significantly in both urban and rural areas.

References

Chan, Kam Wing and Hu Ying. 2003. 'Urbanization in China in the 1990s: new definition, different series and revised trends'. *The China Review* 3(2) (Fall): 49–71.

陈甬军等：《中国城市化道路新论》，北京：商务印书馆，2009年版 [Chen, Yong-Jun et al. 2009. *New Theory of Urbanization in China*. Beijing: Commercial Press].

Cheng Xinzheng. 2009. 'Some Theoretical Considerations on the Current Formation and Development of Chinese Migrant Workers.' *Studies on Marxism* 7: 122-125.

费孝通：《费孝通文集》(八-十卷)，北京：群言出版社，1999年版 [Fei Xiaotong. 1999. *Fei Xiaotong Quanji* (Fei Xiaotong selected work, Vols. 8-10). Beijing: Qunyan Press].

— 《小城镇四记》，北京：新华出版社，1985年版 [1985. *Xiao chengzhen si ji* (four essays on small towns). Beijing: Xinhua Publishing House].

— 《小城镇大问题》，南京：江苏人民出版社，1984年版。[1984. *Xiao zhengcheng, da wenti* (Small towns big issues), Jiangsu: Jiangsu People's Publishing House].

— 《费孝通论小城镇》，北京：群言出版社，2000年[2000. *Fei Xiaotong lun xiao chengzhen* (Fei Xiaotong on small towns). Beijing: Qunyan Press].

— 《我看到的中国农村工业化和城市化道路》《浙江社会科学》，1998年第4期:4-7页 [1998. 'China's rural industrialization and urbanization.' *Zhejiang Social Sciences* (4): 4–7].

Findlay, C., Watson, A. and Xiaoying Wu, H. 1994. *Rural Enterprises in China*. London: Macmillan Press.

Gu Chaolin and Wu Fulong. 2010. 'Urbanization in China: Processes and Policies.' *The China Review* 10 (1): 1–10.

Ho, S. 1994. *Rural China in Transition*. Oxford: Oxford University Press.

Howard, Ebenezer. 1902. *Garden Cities of Tomorrow*. London: S. Sonnenschein & Co., Ltd.

埃比尼泽·霍华德：《明日的田园城市》，金经元译，北京:商务印书馆，2000年版 [2000. *Garden City of Tomorrow*. Translated by Jin Jingyuan. Beijing: Commercial Press].

金经元：《再谈霍华德明日的田园城市》《国外城市规划》，1996年第4期。

Huang, Philip. 1990. *The Peasant Family and Rural Development in the Yangzi Delta, 1350-1988*. Stanford, CT: Stanford University Press.

Huang Rongqing. 2007. 'An Outlook for the Development of China's Central and Regional Cities Based on Population Trends.' *Chinese Journal of Population Science* (6): 25–32.

Huang Qian. 2009. 'Urban Migrant Workers' Job Stability and its Impact on Salary.' *Population Research* 33 (3): 53–63.

Jin Jingyuan. 1996. 'Talk about Howard's Garden City Tomorrow.' *Urban Planning Overseas* (6):31–36.

Kojima, R. 1995. 'Urbanization in China.' *The Developing Economies* 33 (2): 121–154.

Li Peilin and Li Wei. 2007. 'Economic Status and Social Attitudes of Migrant Workers in China.' *China & World Economy* 15 (4): 1–16.

Li Peilin and Wang Chunguang. 1993. *The Growth Point of a New Social Structure*. Jinan: Shandong's People's Press.

Mumford, Lewis. 1946. *Urban Culture*. [Translated by Song Junling, 2009). Beijing: China Building Industry Press. 刘易斯·芒福德：《城市文化》，宋俊岭等译，北京：中国建筑工业出版社，2009年版]。

Osborn, F. J. and A. Whittick. 1977. *New Towns: Their Origins, Achievements and Progress*. London: Leonard Hill.

Osborn, F. 1947. *New Towns after the War*. London: J. M. Dent and Sons Ltd.

Peng Yusheng. 'What Has Spilled over From Chinese Cities into Rural Industry?' *Modern China* 33 (3): 287–319.

Song, Linfei. 2000. 'Fei Xiaotong's Small-Tow Research Methodology and Theories.' *Journal of Nanjing University Philosophy, Humanities and Social Sciences* (5): 11–18.

Walker, R. A. and Buck, D. 2007. 'The Chinese Road: cities in the transition to capitalism'. *New Left Review* 46 (July/August): 39–66.

王星：《经典小城镇理论的现实困境—重读费孝通〈小城镇四记〉》《社会科学评论》，2006年第2期：18-24页 [Wang Xing. 2006. 'The Reality of the Classical Theory of the Plight of Small Towns – Rereading Fei Xiaotong, "Four Small Towns in Mind".' *Review of Social Sciences* (2): 18–24].

Xia Yongxiang. 2007. 'Urban System and Regional Economic Space Structure.' *Jianghai Academic Journal* (2): 36-40.

许经勇：《我国城市化的目标：城乡一体化》《马克思主义与现实》，2006年第6期[Xu Jingyong. 2006. 'The Goal of Urbanization: urban–rural integration.' *Marxism and Reality* (6): 120–123].

Zhang, Kevin Honglin and Song Shunfeng. 2003. 'Rural–Urban Migration and Urbanization in China: evidence from time-series and cross-section analyses.' *China Economic Review* 14: 386–400.

DOI https://doi.org/10.24103/GCSS2.en.2016.8

A Chinese Episode in the Globalization of Sociology[1]

Martin Albrow

Abstract: The author's experience in building contacts with social scientists in China in the 1980s assisted in the editorial policy of the new journal of the International Sociological Association, *International Sociology*, establishing collaboration with the new journal *Shehuixue Yanjiu*, both founded in 1986. That policy fed into the theme of the 1990 World Congress in Madrid, 'Sociology for One World: Unity and Diversity'. Chinese papers contributed to a developing debate about the globalization of sociology, its sinification and the universalistic credentials of sociology. This episode illustrates the ongoing reflexivity of sociology when in encounters between cultures it seeks to overcome conceptual differences by attending to common features of the human condition and challenges that confront all humankind.

Keywords: Fei Xiaotong, International Sociological Association, Chinese Sociological Association, *International Sociology*, *Shehuixue Yanjiu*, universalism, internationalization, modernization, indigenization, sinification, sinicization, globalization, reflexivity

A volume celebrating Fei Xiaotong's immense achievements not only gives greater prominence to his understanding of China, but also sits within the framework of a global sociology that is bound to lead towards an understanding of a wider and, one hopes, a better world. It has indeed already done so. Writing a short book introducing sociology to a general public, I cited Fei as the sociologist whose work has produced the greatest effect on the greatest number of people anywhere (Albrow 1999: 64).

My reasoning was based on the cumulative influence that his research had exercised over the years on the introduction of the responsibility system in Chinese agriculture. He was a creative co-author at the outset of the long story of the massive release of personal and collective energies that continues to be told in China today, and which is now spreading its influence worldwide. 'For China today, for the world tomorrow': that has to be the direction of those energies in

---

[1] This paper is written specially for this issue with a theme of globalization of Chinese social sciences, based on the conference entitled 'Understanding China and engaging with Chinese people – Commemorating the 100th Anniversary of Professor Fei Xiaotong's Birth' in 2010.

the social sciences too. The brief memoir that follows will relate an early episode in such a story as it happened in sociology, from the standpoint of a participant.

As a graduate student at the London School of Economics working on Max Weber, I was familiar with his seminal study of the religion of China (Weber 1951). But my first acquaintance with contemporary Chinese scholarship and with Fei's work was inspired in 1960 by that fine anthropologist, Maurice Freedman. Because, as a rather green student in his graduate seminar, I rashly admitted a schoolboy enthusiasm for Arthur Waley's translations of Chinese poetry, he asked me to prepare a paper on Chinese social institutions. He thus led me into the mysteries (for a Westerner) of *li* via his student Sybille van der Sprenkel's thesis on Chinese law.

It was a big ask of someone whose first degree was in Western history, and an entry in my diary for 20 January 1960 reads, 'Desperation over this paper on China – contemplate giving up – why must every little setback appear a cosmic issue?' But a day later Maurice changed it all. The diary continues, 'Paper delivered – generous praise, excessive pleasure.' His kind treatment of the resulting paper was an important ingredient in my later confident belief that sociology could build a firm bridge across the West/East cultural divides – and, yes, the youthful diary writer was right, bridging those divides will determine the human future and, in that anthropocentric sense, is 'cosmic'.[2]

A fuller test of that confidence came in the 1980s after I was asked to become the founding editor of a new journal for the International Sociological Association (ISA), *International Sociology*. This was part of a renewed drive by the ISA to strengthen bridges between the 'three worlds', capitalist, socialist and developing. It reflected, and took advantage of, the lowering of international barriers at that time to the free exchange of information and ideas. Liberalization of communist regimes was being promoted in the Soviet Union by President Mikhail Gorbachev through *perestroika*.

In China, reform was being led by senior leader Deng Xiaoping, Chairman and General Secretary Hu Yaobang and Premier Zhao Ziyang through the responsibility system in agriculture. This was the geopolitical and cultural climate in which the Executive Committee of the ISA, first under its president, Fernando Cardoso, subsequently President of Brazil, and then under his successor, Margaret Archer of the University of Warwick, determined to realize sociology's potential as a universalizing agency for creating one world.

The journal aimed, in Cardoso's words, 'to offer the reader a more global and comprehensive view of contemporary sociology' but to do that 'by showing pluralistic paths of concern in sociology rooted in different historical and cultural traditions' (Cardoso, 1986: 1–2). It was therefore my privilege as its editor to

---

[2] An extended autobiographical account of the atmosphere of the LSE at that time and the stages of a journey through global sociology back to it again in the Global Governance Centre can be found in Mathieu Deflem's volume *Sociologists in a Global Age* (Albrow 2007).

follow the discipline wherever in the world it led. One direction was China, partly because of the happy accident that I was already working in partnership with a significant player in China's drive to modernize, the State Family Planning Commission.

In 1979, the Chinese Government and the United Nations Fund for Population Activities had signed a Memorandum of Understanding, which led to in-country assistance for family planning programmes and cooperation with multilateral agencies, including the International Planned Parenthood Federation, and with training centres overseas (Government of China 1987). Within that framework, the Population Centre of University College Cardiff provided courses for mid-career officials in the population programmes of developing countries and the State Family Planning Commission of China was one of the agencies that each year sent us two or three of their staff for a Diploma or Master's Degree in Population Policies. Such was the strategic significance of their work for the direction of China's population policies that we were honoured by the visit to Cardiff of the minister in charge of the Commission, Wang Wei, in February 1987.[3]

In November 1987, my wife, Sue Owen, who lectured at the Centre on the economics of ageing, and I, as Director of the Centre, accompanied by our former student, friend and translator, Li Yong, had the privilege of being conducted on visits to offices and sites of the Commission's work in Beijing, Nanjing and Hangzhou and neighbouring villages. We lectured in Nanjing College for Family Planning Administrators on 'The Education of Population Programme Professionals: the Cardiff Philosophy' (Albrow) and on 'Fertility Decline and Female Labour Force participation in the West' (Owen). In Hangzhou University we gave a joint lecture on 'The Old and the Young: the Contemporary Western Crisis'.[4]

At the same time, my visit to China provided a wonderful opportunity to renew an invitation to Chinese sociologists to join in the ISA's efforts to internationalize the discipline. I was deputed by Margaret Archer to represent the Association on my visit and met with Ding Weizhi, Deputy Secretary of the Chinese Academy of Social Sciences, and Professor Lu Xueyi, Deputy Director of the Academy's Institute of Sociology, to discuss Chinese membership of the Association.

There was a history to these talks. The ISA had for some time been seeking to bring the Chinese Sociological Research Society, of which Professor Fei Xiaotong was president, into full membership, and therefore to represent sociology for the

---

[3] In the newspaper *Western Mail* (26 February 1987), Charles Hymas, under the headline 'Experts of birth control on visit', wrote 'A Chinese leader with the toughest family planning job in the world got the chance of some on-the-spot population analysis on a visit to South Wales yesterday'. Wang Wei was pictured viewing computer population projections and the story told how 16 officials from the State Family Planning Commission had studied at the Cardiff Population Centre over the previous five years.

[4] An unpublished account of the tour was circulated as 'Report of an Observational Tour of the Family Planning Programme of the People's Republic of China' by Martin Albrow and Susan Owen, 25 November 1987.

People's Republic of China. A formal invitation was sent in August 1985 and repeated in February 1986 and Fei came to the World Congress in Delhi that year and discussed the matter with the ISA's president, Fernando Cardoso. The talks came to nothing because of the sensitive issue of concurrent membership of the Chinese Sociological Association of Taiwan. That was still the situation in November 1987 and, in explaining it, Professor Margaret Archer, the new President of the ISA, wished me well in my discussions with the Chinese sociologists, writing, 'If you could somehow find your way through this wood you will have accomplished a major geopolitical miracle in sociological terms'.[5]

It was clear to me that such a miracle was beyond my powers, but equally my experience of working relations with Chinese officials in the population field showed there was always the possibility of finding areas of cooperation across political boundaries if we sought to find areas of common interest and values.

Sociology had been suspended in 1952, politically prohibited in 1959 and re-established in China in 1979 when Deng declared that 'we neglected the study of political science, law, sociology and international politics, and it is now essential for us to catch up' (Dai 1993a: 92).

The Chinese Sociological Research Association was founded in 1979 and there was a growing enthusiasm for the subject in official circles and rapid expansion in its provision in the 1980s. The State Education Commission commissioned a report in 1986 on the future demand for sociologists from the Departments of Sociology of Nankai University and of the Shanghai College of Liberal Arts. It was published in the new journal *Shehuixue Yanjiu* (*Sociological Studies*) in July 1987, concluding that 798 postgraduates and 1,423 first-degree holders were urgently needed across government, the Party, in journalism and publishing, in large enterprises and in education (Investigation Group of Nankai University 1989). The climate was therefore favourable to an approach in 1987 that invited collaborative work rather than the formal institutional agreements that the ISA had previously been seeking

The fortunate basis for that collaboration was the new journal I edited and, with the enthusiastic support of Lu Xueyi, who visited us in Cardiff with his colleague Dai Kejing, we were able to establish a productive publication arrangement, which included Dai becoming an Associate Editor for *International Sociology.* She and I, with the generous agreement of its editor, Wang Yuming, worked together to publish five papers in English from *Shehuixue Yanjiu* in 1989 and 1990, including the report on the demand for sociology graduates.

Shehuixue Yanjiu started publication in January 1986, appeared every two months and usually included about 20 articles in each issue, so choosing just five to appear in *International Sociology* was an invidious task. What we tried to do was to find a balance between papers reporting research on Chinese society,

---

[5] Private communication from Margaret Archer, 13 October 1987.

such as market towns (Ye Kelin et al. 1989) and social security (Chen Liangjin 1990), and ones that reflected on China's place in the contemporary world, social modernization (Li Lulu 1989) and the dual structure of Chinese society (Pan Jianxiong 1990).

A further three papers by Dai (1991) on rural women, Li Lulu, Yang Xiao and Wang Fengyu (1991) on stratification, and Lu Jianjua (1991) on workers' expectations of management appeared in the last issue of *International Sociology* that I edited. These gave me particular pleasure because the latter two papers had been selected by a Chinese jury for the ISA's Competition for Young Sociologists and Lu's was one of the five eventual winners from the worldwide field of 335 entries (Bertaux 1990).

Under Dai's careful editorial scrutiny, the journal was able over the years to publish a series of academic papers from Chinese sociologists working in China. I stress 'Chinese working in China' because the philosophy underlying the journal was that there should be no political, cultural or linguistic barriers to publication. This may well appear to be the policy for so many Western so-called 'international' academic journals, but in practice those barriers exist, especially the linguistic one that requires authors to write in perfect English.

Our policy was that no paper would be rejected on language grounds, which meant that we had to assess papers in the language of their origin first.[6] Dai's bilingualism was invaluable for the journal, as it was when she translated Fei's LSE doctorate into Chinese in 1986, a volume which had previously been regarded as 'criminal evidence' of 'a widespread pernicious influence' in the Cultural Revolution when he was detained in the 'cowshed' or sent for 'retraining' in the 'cadre school' (Dai 1993b).

But bridging the language barrier was only one aspect of the way we conceived of the sociological mission at the time. A culminating moment came in 1990 with the World Congress of Sociology in Bielefeld, advertised with the theme 'Sociology for One World: Unity and Diversity'. Archer (1991) used that title for her presidential address, in which she argued for the universality of human reason, rejecting both a false unitary perspective on the world, whether as modernization or postmodernism, and also a relativism which postulated unbridgeable gulfs between cultures. Sociology, she argued, showed how global mechanisms combined with regional circumstances to create a diversity of novel configurations. Globalization was then not the effect of a new world on the old but part of the interaction of new and old to create a different world.

'Sociology for One World' had been the title of an editorial article (Albrow 1987) I wrote earlier for the second volume of *International Sociology*, in which I argued that the drive for indigenous sociologies was not a retreat from the programme of a universal science. I also touched on the practical consequences

---

[6] A fuller account of that policy appears in Albrow (1991).

of such a vision for selecting papers for the journal. One of the more contentious conclusions I drew was that intellectual excellence alone was not the sole criterion for publication. Stated so baldly, this caused considerable debate. My position was, and remains, that the universalizing mission of sociology requires knowledge to be grown from multiple viewpoints. 'The corpus of sociological knowledge is enriched by contributions from representatives of groups with distinctive social experience' (ibid.: 7).

Let me illustrate the implications of this policy in practical terms, with a necessarily invented example. Let us suppose there are 20 papers, all rated good, competing for space in one issue of a journal that can publish only ten. The 'best' 15 papers are by Western men and women on features of industrialized societies: there are three by women on women's issues in the West and two by non-Westerners, one by a man, one by a woman, in each case on issues from their own cultures. What do I choose for publication? On the basis of my principle of representing diversity, I choose six of the 15, two of the three on women's issues, and both the non-Western papers. Nine of the best papers will have to go elsewhere. Now, of course, you can query the premise of this example as follows: Why would the best papers all be by Westerners? To which my reply is that this simply represents subterranean, often subliminal processes, judgments made on language, networks, reputations and orthodox paradigms of research, which time and again will bias the judgment of what is 'best' and will lead to the exclusion of whole areas that sociology needs to take into account.

Diversity as a policy promotes the intellectual comprehensiveness and innovative excellence of the discipline as a whole, as opposed to what happens when we work as if seeking the winners of a competition between individuals. Of course when, as happened with Lu Jianjua (1991), a non-Westerner wins a competition dominated by Westerners, there is double reason for rejoicing. Even there, however, note well that we published papers explicitly to represent the younger generation of sociologists. There were older people who did not make the age limit of under 35, and were correspondingly excluded, who otherwise would have appeared in print. No apologies!

I won't carry this abstract argument further into ever deeper territory in this short memoir. Suffice it to say that it can be pursued up to, and including, ultimate assumptions about how knowledge is gained, what it is for and, indeed, what it is. And the course of that argument would take us into and beyond ideological issues about competition and collective wisdom. For these reasons, debates about editorial decisions on the content of a journal are never purely 'academic'.

Elsewhere, commenting on the editorial policy of *International Sociology*, I expressed this view provocatively and concretely: 'There is, therefore, something which the young female Indian sociologist working in her own city can give to sociology which is beyond the capacity of the senior male American sociologist working in the same place' (Albrow 1991: 111).

And further, for an illustration of the consequences of that policy for Chinese sociology we can refer to the statistics of papers received and accepted by the journal in its first four years, as reported in volume 39 of *Current Sociology* (ibid.: 116–118). From the United States, 55 papers were received and 18 accepted, from the USSR six and one respectively, and from China six received, six accepted.

Enough said. I want rather to dwell on the relatively limited topic (though still enormous in its own right) of the contribution that the Chinese collaboration made to the globalization of sociology at that time and how we can construe it now. It was only then that the discipline was beginning to reflect on the consequences of globalization for itself. The term 'globalization' was already being domesticated in the language of sociology in papers from 1985 onwards by Roland Robertson (1992). He was emphasizing consciousness of the globe as an element in the creation of global society, a product of his own dual interest in the sociology of religion and in international relations.

In the pages of *International Sociology*, Piotr Sztompka (1988) was another pointing to the globalization of society as involving the internationalization of sociology and a revision of older ideas of comparative method. Zsuzsa Hegedus (1989) pointed to the new planetary orientation of 1980s movements, 'conflictualizing' global issues and effectively 'globalizing' individuals, something she referred to as empowerment and globalization.

It was papers such as these that prompted me to recommend to the ISA that the volume to be presented to the delegates at the Madrid World Congress should be drawn from papers published in the journal and bear the title *Globalization, Knowledge and Society* (Albrow and King 1990). I believe this was the first time that 'globalization' figured in an English book title.

The volume could not have been compiled without the work of Elizabeth King, who had given editorial support from the early planning of the journal and continued through to her tragically early death (Albrow 1998). In a way, her own biography, spanning Germany, Switzerland, the UK and Greece, epitomized the way I conceptualized the globalization of sociology in the Introduction to the volume: 'It results from the freedom individual sociologists have to work with other individuals anywhere on the globe and to appreciate the worldwide processes within which and on which they work' (Albrow and King 1990: 7).

That rather general-sounding formulation actually was intended to represent a concrete stage beyond two others in the development of sociology, which, in succession, were the 'internationalism' and 'indigenization' of the discipline. The former was a post-World War II phenomenon associated with modernization in both American and socialist thought, and the latter primarily an assertion of autonomy and the values of traditional culture in Third World societies. The volume reflected both of those orientations but pointed also to an emergent one of a globalized sociology, where there is a diversity of sociological dialects and special visions within a worldwide shared discourse.

While not explicit at that point, my reflections drew on understandings that fitted with and were enhanced by what I was learning about Chinese sociology.

Li Lulu (1989) emphasized that the combination of a huge population, an ancient culture and socialism meant China was bound to develop a distinctive kind of modernization, but he and colleagues in a later paper (Li et al. 1991) argued that the old hierarchical culture still inhibited the creativity required for a successful non-Western modernization. In Pan Jianxiong's (1990) account of the dual structure of ancient Chinese culture, its combination of autocracy and a secular humanism meant that a conformity in ethics and mutual goodwill provided stability but also a barrier to Western modernization. These accounts captured cultural specifics but did not yet address the way they could frame the development of sociology.

A later round-table discussion led by Dai (1993a) directly addressed the conceptual problems of a Chinese sociology under globalized conditions. Dai wrote of a 'bumper harvest' for sociology in the previous decade, recording 15 universities where there was a department of sociology and 31 specialized research institutes. That compares with the Nankai report of 1987, which detailed only five university departments and three research institutes. She reported on the third meeting of the Board of Directors of the Chinese Sociological Association in August 1990, which emphasized the need to integrate theory and practice with the goal of creating a Chinese sociology, and Fei stressed an overwhelming need for further development.

In the other papers of that symposium we find a discussion of the sinification and globalization of sociology that could almost be taken as a textbook case of the issues involved in indigenization. Bettina Gransow (1993) surveyed the different tendencies in intensive debates among Chinese sociologists in Taiwan, Hong Kong, the United States and the People's Republic. She concluded that 'the endeavour towards the sinicization of sociology led to a learning process about sociology's cultural and civilizational ties, a learning process which sharpened the senses for the relative limits set within the context cultural semantic patterns, even if a universal approach was taken' (ibid.: 110).

For Chan Hoiman (1993), commenting on Gransow, this debate about globalization and sinification reflected a wider anxiety about the universalistic credentials of sociology, ones that we saw that Archer (1991) was concerned to reassert, and which for Chan would be advanced through a reflexive sociology, one that continually reflected on its foundations under the pressure of indigenizing and globalizing forces. Such a sociology, as advocated by Alvin Gouldner and Pierre Bourdieu, would be one of perpetual self-rejuvenation.

And that is an appropriate point to end this short account of an episode in the globalization of sociology, because the reflexivity of a discipline is fundamental to the advance of knowledge and it continues apace. However, the case of this particular encounter between China and a globalizing sociology reveals something about both sociology and reflexivity.

There is a big difference between the reflexivity that arises out of self-examination and the reflectiveness induced through partnership in conversation where each party reflects and reflects on the other. What I think we managed by introducing Chinese sociology into *International Sociology* was to bring the in-culture self-examination into an arena of multiple exchanges. It highlights cultural differences while simultaneously enhancing mutual understanding.

What does this say about universality, the quality regarded as fundamental to true knowledge? Within sociology we may employ mathematical and statistical methods that are acknowledged to have universal validity, but we fail to find the invariant relations that characterize the natural sciences. A goal of shared understandings between all human beings is not achieved by means of a science akin to that of the natural world but only through multiple encounters that are bound always to cross cultural and linguistic barriers.

The shared understandings we arrive at often arise from the recognition of a particular patterning of underlying elements that one culture selects out as strategic, the separate components of which, however, can be identified in any culture. When we recognize such a pattern in another culture, because those individual components are familiar to us in our own, we also see its potential for us in our own culture and often seek to replicate it. We discover possibilities for ourselves through understanding others. The history of East–West relations is therefore one of experimenting with each other's ways of life.

It is in this light that I see in sociology the distinction in early German theory between *Gemeinschaft* and *Gesellschaft*, which has generated a wealth of finer distinctions in English, while the original opposition remains embedded in German thought and experience and has no exact equivalent in English: this is why we retain the German terms in English-language publications. It represents a configuration of thought and feeling that may be identifiable in English-speaking cultures but never precisely replicable, and for those who speak both languages it is obvious there can be no exact equivalent.

We can expect many more such examples the more the discipline recognizes indigenous roots to social thought. Recently, Chang Xiangqun's (2010) account of the prevalence and durability of *Li shang wanglai* in a Chinese village has provided a fine example of identifying the irreducible distinctiveness of culturally transmitted patterns of social relations. And yet we can still see that this is one possible pattern of social relations, culturally defined in China, but not without approximations elsewhere.

The understanding we achieve of *Li shang wanglai* and its place in Chinese society through Chang's work illuminates cognate patterns, resemblances and differences, in other cultures. This is what is conveyed through her development of it as an analytical concept in conjunction with ideas of reciprocity and networks. In comparative work, it therefore operates for us in Weberian terms as an ideal type. Underlying this intelligibility are generic ideas of individual people, acting in social relations with one another. These are translatable into any language, belonging to a universal sociological thesaurus that conveys an unconfined diversity in the concrete manifestations of those relations in social life.

The most elementary features of the human condition are recognizable across cultures, are pre-linguistic and are shared with other species – birth, bonding, nurture, reproduction, health, death among others – and these enable us to cross cultures in our understanding. We replicate the universal features of our species as much, or even more, as we meet foreigners than we do in engaging with our own countrymen, when we are confined by the oddities of our own culture. Chinese and Westerners are of one humankind and we can rejoice in finding difference and similarity in the other.

But there is another moment in the globalization of sociology, and indeed of globalization in general, namely, that whatever differences there are between our cultures, there are supervening issues that affect the human future on this earth. Both climate change and nuclear security are challenges that require cooperation across all boundaries.

Whatever the unity sociology has found *in and through* diversity, it now has to find unity *beyond* diversity in facing the global challenges. This is what animated my concern 'to respect all peoples as potential sources of wisdom for our own time. Already the Global Age is the first period in human history when both sexes and all peoples have gone a considerable way towards asserting their equal right to make their contribution to the common stock of human knowledge' (Albrow 1996: 6).

In the 1980s the problem of how we understand each other was uppermost in our drive to globalize sociology. Since then, the need to cooperate to solve global challenges has become a more urgent priority. We cannot dwell forever on the problems of understanding one another before we work together in a common cause. In that sense, achieving an understanding adequate for the challenges facing humankind collectively is a proper ambition for sociology in our times. That has to be the main thrust of a globalized sociology today, and I am as confident of Chinese sociologists as of any national body of sociologists that they will be major contributors to that joint endeavour.

References

Albrow, Martin. 1987. 'Sociology for one world.' *International Sociology* 2: 1–12 (马丁·阿尔布劳: 适合世界的社会学. 《国际社会学》, 1987(2):1-12).

— 1991. 'Internationalism as a publication project: experience in editing an international sociological journal.' *Current Sociology* 39: 101–118 (一个出版项目的国际化主义: 编辑一本国际化社会学杂志的经验, 《当代社会》, 1991(39):101-108).

— 1996. *The Global Age: State and Society beyond Modernity.* Cambridge: Polity (also in Chinese). [《全球化时代: 现代化之外的国家与社会》, 剑桥: 政体出版社 (有中文版)].

— 1998. Obituary: 'Elizabeth King, 1949–1998.' *International Sociology* 13: 517–518. [讣告: 伊莉莎白·金,1949-1998. 《国际社会学》, 1998(13): 517-518].

— 1999. *Sociology: The Basics*. London: Routledge. (《社会学基础》,伦敦:劳特利奇出版社, 1999年).

—2007. 'Unfinished work: the career of a European sociologist', in Mathieu Deflem. ed. *Sociologists in a Global Age: Biographical Perspectives*. Aldershot: Ashgate: 15–28 (also in Chinese) ['未 完成的工作: 一个欧洲社会学家的生涯', 马蒂厄·德福勒姆编: 《一个全球化时代的社会学 家: 政治学家为何? 》,奥尔德肖特: 阿什盖特出版公司, 2007年, 15-28 (有中文版)].

Albrow, Martin and Elizabeth King. Eds. 1990. *Globalization, Knowledge and Society*. London: Sage. [与玛格丽特·阿彻合编, 《全球化、知识与社会》, 伦敦: 塞奇出版社, 1990年 版].

Archer, Margaret. 1991. Presidential Address: 'Sociology for one world: unity and diversity.' *International Sociology* 6: 131–147. [会长演讲, "适合世界的社会学: 统一性与多样性", 《国际社会学》, 1991(6):131-147].

Bertaux, Daniel. 1990. 'Designing the worldwide competition'. *International Sociology* 5: 373–378. [丹尼尔·波塔克斯. 设计世界竞争. 《国际社会学》, 1990(5):373-378].

Cardoso, Fernando. 1986. 'Foreword'. *International Sociology* 1: 1–2. [费尔南多·卡多佐. 序言, 《国际社会学》, 1986(1):1-2].

Chan, Hoiman. 1993. 'Some metasociological notes on the sinicisation of sociology.' *International Sociology* 8: 113–119. [陈好满, 一些关于社会学中国化的社会学元分析, 《国际社会 学》, 1993(8):113-119].

Chang, Xiangqun. 2010. *Guanxi or Li shang wanglai: Reciprocity, Social Support Networks, and Social Creativity in a Chinese Village*. Taipei: Airiti Press (also in Chinese).

常向群. 2010. 《关系抑或礼尚往来:一个中国乡村的互惠原则,社会支持网络和社会创造力》 , 台北: 华艺图书公司.

Chen, Liangjin. 1990. 'Social developmental mechanisms and social security functions.' *International Sociology* 5: 89–100. (First published in *Shehuixue Yanjiu (Sociological Studies)* 1987. 2(1): 85–91.) [陈良金. 社会发展关系网络与社会安全功能. 国际社会学, 1990(5):89- 100. (首版发表于《社会学研究》1987年第12卷第1期, 第85至91页)].

Dai, Kejing. 1991. 'The life experience and status of Chinese rural women from observation of three age groups'. *International Sociology* 6: 5–24. [戴可景, 通过观察三种年龄群体来看中国乡 村妇女的生活经验和地位, 《国际社会学》, 1991(6):5-24].

— 1993a. 'The vicissitudes of sociology in China'. *International Sociology* 8: 92–100. [中国社会 学的变迁. 国际社会学. 1993a(8):92-100].

— 1993b. Portrait: 'Fei Xiaotong 1910–'. *International Sociology* 8: 239–246. [肖像: 费孝通 1910. 《国际社会学》, 1993b(8):239-246].

Government of China. 1987. Leaflet 'Family Planning Program in China 1987'. Beijing: State Family Planning Commission. [中国政府. 1987年中国计划生育传单. 北京:国家计划生育委员 会, 1987].

Gransow, Bettina. 1993. 'Chinese sociology: sinicisation and globalisation.' *International Sociology* 8: 101–112. [柯兰君. 中国社会学:中国化与全球化. 《国际社会学》, 1993(8):101-112].

Hegedus, Zsusza. 1989. 'Social movements and social change in self-creative society: new civil initiatives in the international arena.' *International Sociology* 4: 19–36. [茨苏扎·海吉达 斯. 自我创造型社会的社会运动和社会变迁:国际化舞台的新的公民倡议. 《国际社会 学》,1989(4):19-36].

Investigation Group of Nankai University. 1989. 'Report on nationwide demand for sociology graduates during the period of the Seventh Five-Year Plan.' *International Sociology* 4: 393–418. (First published in *Shehuixue Yanjiu (Sociological Studies)* 1987. 2(4): 21–35.) [南开大学调查 组. 七五计划时期社会学毕业生国家需求的报告. 国际社会学, 1989(4):21-35. (首版发表于 《社会学研究》, 1987年第2卷第4期, 第21至35页)]。

Li, Lulu. 1989. 'Theoretical theses on "social modernization".' *International Sociology* 4: 365–377. (First published in *Shehuixue Yanjiu (Sociological Studies)* 1987. 2(3): 105–112.) [李路路. 社 会现代化的理论导向. 国际社会学, 1989(4):365-377. (首版发表于《社会学研究》, 1987 年第2卷第3期, 第105至112页)]。

Li, Lulu, Yang Xiao and Fengyu Wang. 1991. 'The structure of social stratification and the modern-isation process in contemporary China.' *International Sociology* 6: 25–36. [李路路，杨晓，王奋宇. 当代中国的社会分层结构和现代化进程.《国际社会学》. 1991(6):25-36].

Lu, Jianhua. 1991. 'Chinese workers' high expectations of enterprise managers'. *International Sociology* 5: 37–49. [陆建华. 中国工人对企业管理这的高期望.《国际社会学》,1991(5):37-49].

Pan, Jianxiong. 1990. 'The dual structure of Chinese culture and its influence on modern Chinese society.' *International Sociology* 5: 75–88. (First published in *Shehuixue Yanjiu* (*Sociological Studies*) 1987. 3(1): 88–96.) [潘建雄. 中国文化的二元结构及其对现代中国社会的影响. 国际社会学，1990(5):75-88. (首版发表于《社会学研究》1987年第3卷第1期，第88至96页)]。

Robertson, Roland. 1992. *Globalization: Social Theory and Global Culture*. London: Sage. [罗兰·罗伯特森. 全球化:社会理论与全球文化. 伦敦:塞奇出版社, 1992].

Sztompka, Piotr. 1988. 'Conceptual frameworks in comparative inquiry: divergent or convergent? *International Sociology* 3: 207–218. [皮奥特尔奥·什托姆普卡. 比较调查中的概念框架:幅合的还是发散的?.《国际社会学》, 1988(3):207-218].

Weber, Max. 1951 [1920] *The Religion of China*. Trans. and ed. H. H. Gerth. Glencoe, IL: Free Press. [马克思·韦伯著. 格特编译. 中国的宗教. 伊尔·格伦科：自由出版社]。

Ye, Kelin, Nongjian Zou and Nanke Ye. 1989. 'The establishment of market town sociology with Chinese characteristics.' *International Sociology* 4: 379–392. (First published in *Shehuixue Yanjiu* (*Sociological Studies*) 1987. 2(2): 36–43.) [叶克林, 邹农建, 叶南科. 中国特色的集市社会学的建立. 国际社会学. 1989(4):379-392. (首版发表于《社会学研究》1987年第2卷第2期，第36至43页)]。

DOI https://doi.org/10.24103/GCSS2.en.2016.9

Post-Nationalist Anthropology?
Anthropologies Today in their Nationalist Traditions, Cosmopolitan Ethos and Collaborative Possibilities[1]

George E. Marcus

Abstract: This article analyzes the situation of still nationally based institutions for anthropological teaching and research, and both assesses and imagines a different vision for anthropologies that are truly post-nationalist, cosmopolitan and collaborative in the production of research projects, both in the training of students and in later endeavours of comparative ethnography. The situation of China especially is assessed as a participant in post-nationalist anthropology.

Keywords: ethnography, post-national, cosmopolitan, collaboration, modernity, comparative method.

On this, the 100th anniversary of the birth of Professor Fei Xiaotong, I would like to give special greetings to and express my happiness at meeting again those friends that I made during an earlier visit to China in 2006, when I learned about anthropology programmes in Guangzhou, Shanghai, Kunming and Beijing. I returned from that visit excited by the variety of anthropology practised in China and its possibilities. I have come to this conference after a long journey of short duration through the northwest of China, where, again, I met a remarkable group of anthropologists and their students researching the rich variety of ethnic groups in those regions. I thank them for their warm friendship and exceptional hospitality. I am indebted to Professor Gao Bingzhong especially for making it possible for me to gain a vision of anthropology in China, perhaps partial and incomplete, but clearly vibrant, full of ideas and worthy of a prominent presence among world anthropologies, which is my topic of discussion today.

World anthropology does not exist as an organized project, but under this term anthropologists in many countries are reflecting increasingly upon the practice and contributions of their discipline, possibly under different conditions from

---

[1] This article is based on the author's lecture at the event 'to commemorate the centenary of Professor Fei Xiaotong Lectures - World Anthropologies and China Anthropology' on the June 20, 2010, at Peking University. It was organized by the Department of Sociology and Institute of Sociology and Anthropology, Peking University, and co-organized by the Department of Anthropology, Sun Yat-sen University, School of Ethnology and Sociology, Central University for Nationalities, School of Nationalities, Yunnan University, and Department of Sociology, Shanghai University. It has been revised by the author before it is published.

those of its historical emergence within nation-states. This kind of anthropology of anthropology is interesting and encouraging, but I do not think that any sort of grand vision of world anthropology is useful or practical at this point, given the rapid and unpredictable changes in information technologies and conditions of making knowledge that we are all experiencing today. However, it is worth thinking more incrementally, constructively and granularly about ways that anthropologists can define projects of collaboration within their existing shared cultures of professional research and teaching practices across entrenched national and transnational histories that have overdetermined patterns of relationship. There is considerable persistence in these patterns, both in their basic outline and in current attempts to transform them. I am particularly interested in the question of the training of graduate students and the subsequent shaping of research careers as a context in which considerable but still modest changes can be made in the way anthropology in its many national varieties can be practised as a world discipline.

What I have to offer, then, is a modest proposal, rather than a vision for world anthropology as an organized project. It depends on collaborations of various kinds among anthropologists within broader and more ambitious projects of global scope and import. Anthropology will certainly maintain its foundations in area studies, but its definition of its research problems cannot help but become more transnational and more globally connected in scale. The practical problem for the enterprise of anthropology anywhere is to participate in, if not create, research opportunities at this level of global implication while sustaining its traditions of area studies within national traditions.[2] World anthropology only has contemporary meaning in these small efforts and experiments within its professional cultures to create collaborations on different terms from those that prevailed in earlier, colonial, Cold War and development era contexts. I will have more to say about this at the end of my lecture, but first I want to review briefly early and recent efforts by anthropologists to reflect on and critique the global structure of their discipline.

There was a pioneering collection of articles from 1982 in the journal *Ethnos*, edited by Tomas Gerholm and Ulf Hannerz, which stands out as a first effort to discuss national anthropologies, and it seems to have set the terms for later collections after the year 2000 to both critique and advocate (or hope for) a project of world anthropology, such as those of Arturo Escobar and Gustavo Ribeiro (2006), and more recently of Aleksandar Boskovic (2008) (see also Fardon 1990 for the implication of a project of world anthropology in the examination of

---

[2] The most feasible possibility for a practiced world anthropology lies in how graduate students might be trained transnationally and how networked, modest collaborative projects are organized and managed within the academic departments and institutions of anthropology cross-nationally. At its inception, such a programme is by its nature experimental and somewhat contrary, but it tends towards the orthodox wherever anthropology is established.

traditions of ethnographic writing). The structure within world anthropology that has been both described and contested over the years posits centre or metropolitan and peripheral anthropologies, the former originating in the United States, the UK and France, and the latter consisting of the many other countries in which anthropology has been established over the past century. Also, all anthropologies, including the metropolitan ones, that have the most apparent influence over the others grew up within projects of nationalism and have been shaped by their politics.

Relationships within the world of anthropology to a degree reflect the geopolitics of the wider world. Metropolitan anthropologies are or have been those of past or present great powers. Yet their influence is worked out through smaller-scale connections, and occasionally these smaller-scale links may also happen to come about in ways that do not so immediately reflect macro-political realities.

Writings on world anthropologies have dealt most often with anthropology as it developed in India, Brazil, Japan, Latin America, particular countries of Africa, Russia/the Soviet Union and many countries of northern and southern Europe. I should note that in these discussions the rich and interesting history of anthropology in China, especially recently, has been noticeably absent. I cannot review the debates here, but just want to indicate that the effort in these studies has been directed towards opposing or correcting the view that anthropology everywhere is mainly a story of the domination of the three metropolitan anthropologies over the rest.

To a degree in the past, and considerably in the present, the power that American, British and French anthropology has had over other anthropologies is undeniable. At present it is probably American anthropology that dominates. However, US academia has long been unusually open to foreigners. It is through such immigration to American universities that some external intellectual influences are absorbed. For example, the prominence of postcolonial studies in US anthropology and related fields has depended on the recruitment of a number of the leading scholars from nations where colonialism has left its strongest legacies.

Yet there are indications of the continuing strength of national frameworks, even in an era of self-aware globalization. It is important for anthropologies to speak to several publics but it is in their national contexts where such publics seem most open to and engaged with its findings and provocations. Anthropology implicitly deals with humanity, but the media for such a cosmopolitan public commentary are still under development.

Wherever anthropology has been established, then, it has served as a screen or projection, from a marginalized cosmopolitan perspective, of the national histories and dramas in which it has grown up. This is no less true of the anthropologies of the so-called 'centre', those of the US, the UK and France, than of the anthropologies of the so-called peripheries. One of the advantages of understanding the histories of the anthropologies of the latter is that it enables one to realize more consciously how much the anthropologies of the former have also been entwined in their own national dramas.

Understanding the institutional evolution of anthropology in various states and nationalisms is an indispensable contribution in an already globalized world of instant, fluid communication. But I have found fascinating a 'reading between the lines' for the personal stories and more intimate histories of anthropology in each of those that I have visited. For example, in places like Russia and Argentina, the history of anthropology has been tied to both complicity in and struggle with authoritarian, mercurial and sometimes brutally censoring political regimes. These histories may no longer be mentioned but they are not forgotten in the professional relations that define the contours of what anthropology can say and do. In Kenya, the opportunities that anthropology provided for enquiry were entwined first with colonial rule and then with nation-building under the ideology of development. Brazilian anthropology expresses an independence and self-confidence rarely in evidence elsewhere.

I have often wondered what kind of person would pursue a career in anthropology, a self-consciously marginal discipline in academic institutions, though with huge ambitions of purpose, not well or immediately understood by the public, as opposed to, say, following a career in law, medicine or economics. What are the demographics of anthropology in each country? In the US, for example, it is increasingly pursued by women and students who are bi- or multi-cultural and -lingual. The biographies of leading anthropologists in these places must be as interesting as are the stories of the institutionalization of anthropology themselves.

Drawing on the anthropologies with which I have become familiar, I have three dimensions in mind that seem especially to have defined the character and possibility of anthropology in diverse national settings:

1. The character of the practice of fieldwork as the research modality that seems to distinctively define the ethos and identity of modern social/cultural anthropology in all the places where it has been established. Elsewhere (except for, say, Japan and Brazil), it seems, resources have rarely been available for prolonged periods of fieldwork that became definitive of anthropologies of the centre. How fieldwork has taken shape in these anthropologies in itself would be an excellent index of their special epistemological dimensions, how they defined their subjects, how they understand objectivity, how subtly they define the political and ethical commitments, typical of anthropology generally.

2. The extent to which these anthropologies have pursued and fulfilled the comparative goals that have been historically at the heart of

anthropology, or the extent to which comparison has been at the service of, and a supplement to, the nation-defining project – that is, the extent to which comparisons are produced on a universalizing canvas, or are at the service of more narrowly conceived nationalist projects of sorting out diversity within a particular historic project of nation-building.

3. The extent to which these anthropologies view themselves as having been involved in a project of modernity as well as nationalism. Do they remain across the boundary from the modern in their distinction as experts of the traditional, or even still the primitive? Or are they free to enter the historic preserves of the modern and the contemporary, allowing them to pursue their curiosities wherever they take them – even if this means moving beyond the confines of the 'other' as different according to ethos, culture or level of development (civilization)? Does anthropology have uses in these various places beyond peculiar forms of diversity management or explaining the margins relative to their own centres and mainstreams of contemporary life? What are the limits and potentialities of ordinary subjects as knowledge producers in a way that parallels the anthropologist's project? In modernity, explaining the sources and forms of heterogeneity becomes more important than accounting for difference and the cultural logics that explain it systematically. The study of the heterogeneous involving fieldwork is just as intimate and closely observed as that classically required for the study of difference, as alterity involves a different sort of engagement with subjects that presumes the critique of the systems and states that attempt to impose rational orders and categories of difference.

These are questions that could be asked fruitfully of all anthropologies, those of the so-called centres and those of the so-called peripheries. And to ask them deeply and in detail might help to soften or blur the distinctions between centre and peripheries. I think that today, for example, US anthropology should be put alongside other anthropologies in posing these questions. I would not suggest doing so if I did not think that there have been certain changes in anthropologies of the centre (in the US anyhow), occurring mostly since the 1982 *Ethnos* collection of Gerholm and Hannerz, that have made them and the anthropologies of the periphery if not more equal, then more alike in ways that matter to the practices of each.

Although it is homologously peripheral in its own context of hierarchies of disciplines and university institutionalizations of expertise, the enormous wealth invested in anthropology in the US as well as the numbers practising it make all the difference in shaping its relations with anthropologies of the periphery. Prestige, status and influence move along with the sheer weight of numbers in justifying the center–periphery distinction characterizing the way in which US anthropology exists in relation to other anthropologies. However, especially since the 1980s, social/cultural anthropology in the US has become disorganized (or rather more diffusely reorganized) as a result of critiques such as the so-called Writing Culture moment and the trends that followed them (see, for example, Clifford and Marcus 1986). Not only was US anthropology at its centre cut from its historical moorings in traditional research agendas (e.g. who in the US studies kinship or mythology now? – topics once at the centre of the discipline), but its best work since has been produced in transcultural and thoroughly interdisciplinary movements and research programmes (represented in the US university by such conglomerates as media studies, ethnic studies, cultural studies, science studies, postcolonial studies, women's studies, etc.)

I believe that this development has both nominally and substantively brought the agendas of US anthropology closer to those of the other anthropologies. No longer, for example, do US anthropologists arrive in place X to do their kinship studies while local anthropologists are concerned with issues of poverty. There is now likely to be a much greater affinity of concern and interest in a globalizing and relativizing world between anthropologists of the center and anthropologists of the peripheries even though that distinction is still held in place by the prestige of the relative wealth and status enjoyed by the former. But in a world of fluid information and access, it is less theory, concepts, and models of 'how to do it' that the center has to offer than differently inflected curiosities shared with anthropologies elsewhere. This different nature of relation and affinity cutting through and across the center–periphery distinction – the operating cosmopolitan ethos of anthropology practiced everywhere today – is worthy of more attention in continuing efforts to define or understand the possibility of world anthropology as a collective project or projects rather than a set of conditions set for anthropology by the historical conditions of its formation in various places. These certainly cannot be ignored, but they also are inadequate for conceiving the projects of research and careers that are defining younger generations of scholars and teachers everywhere.

So, in effect, the center will not hold, to evoke the poet Yeats, a condition that creates opportunities, especially in graduate training, for collaborations in designing and supervising transnational and multi-sited projects of research, such as, for example, those in which I have been personally involved with Professor Gao and his students. These projects are themselves studios of cross-cultural encounter and translation as well as pragmatic experiments in the making of world anthropologies at their most granular and grass-roots level of formation. In these projects of entry-level pedagogy neither Chinese nor US anthropology has the existing paradigms or authoritative models for producing new research in arenas such as global health, mega-cites, trade, climate change, and security. They are to be found in this most modest, but strategic level of professional activity.

So building collaboratively conceived and supervised apprentice projects of ethnographic research by which anthropologists have long entered their discipline within the agendas of larger global projects offers inevitable and feasible common grounds for communication among national anthropologies on different terms than those conceived through the longstanding center–periphery framework.

Such projects at the beginning of careers, transregional and global in scope, might create independent capacities for national anthropologies beyond the shadows of the center–periphery framework. There would of course be the difficulties of cross-cultural communication in these collaborations, but, rather than traditionally viewing these as problems of translation, we might view them more productively as processes of creolization, wherein working trading languages are devised for achieving collaborative ends. Post-nationalist world anthropology would depend on such a process, not so different from how research in the natural sciences has long proceeded across national and cultural boundaries (see Galison 1997; Fischer 2009).[3]

A nation as vast and diverse as China will always need an inward-looking social–cultural anthropology. But this need not be – in fact, logically *cannot* be – in disharmony with the edges and parts of the discipline that develop their apprenticeship projects of fieldwork in the emerging modalities of transnational, multi-sited research. There is not one local, nationally framed problem today that is not at the same time post-national. It is the job of anthropological research, always fine-grained and relating to the situated conditions of ordinary, everyday life, to move in both trajectories and to understand the careers of investigation that it spawns in this way.

World anthropology at its most pragmatic and accessible is embedded in such contemporary initiatives of collaborative, creolized training that continue to operate at a situated scale of enquiry, cultivated by and emblematic of our discipline.

References

---

[3] From my own recent experience, I have in mind participation in a three-year, French-funded collaborative ethnography inside the World Trade Organization in Geneva, consisting of a team of ten anthropologists from different countries and across generations (see Deeb and Marcus 2011). And, relevant to my current connection to China, there is my fascination with Professor Gao's interest in having his locally and internationally trained students conduct their dissertation research outside China, often on global issues. For example, I am currently supervising a dissertation project on the politics and social effects of environmental policy in the Brazilian Amazon region by a brilliant student who previously researched the effects of desertification in Mongolia for his MA at Peking University. The fact that students move internationally in their training or initial research is not what is particularly new (though it may be more so in the training of Chinese anthropologists), but the networked connections and collaborative frameworks in terms of which such projects are conceived and designed among cooperating faculty across traditions of national anthropologies, with centre–periphery associations, might be.

Boskovic, Aleksandar. Ed. 2008. *Other People's Anthropologies: Ethnographic Practice on the Margins*. New York, NY: Berghahn Books.

Clifford, James and George E. Marcus. Eds. 1986. *Writing Culture: The Politics and Poetics of Ethnography*. Berkeley, CA: University of California Press.

Deeb, Hadi Nicholas and George E. Marcus. 2011. 'In the Green Room: an experiment in ethnographic method at the WTO.' *Political and Legal Anthropology Review*. 34(1): 51–76.

Fardon, Richard. Ed. 1990. *Localizing Strategies*. Washington, DC: Smithsonian Institution Press.

Fischer, Michael M. J. 2009. *Anthropological Futures*. Durham, NC: Duke University Press.

Galison, Peter. 1997. *Image and Logic: A Material Culture of Microphysics*. Chicago, IL: University of Chicago Press.

Hannerz, Ulf and T. Gerholm. Eds. 1982. *The Shaping of National Anthropologies*. Special issue of *Ethnos* 47:1–2.

Ribeiro, Gustavo Lins and Arturo Escobar. Eds. 2006. *World Anthropologies: Disciplinary Transformations in Systems of Power*. Oxford: Berg.

DOI https://doi.org/10.24103/GCSS2.en.2016.10.1

Appendix A
Chinese for Social Sciences

Hannization *vs* Sanskritization
汉化与梵化

宋连谊 (Lianyi Song) 编[1]

中国和印度都有广阔的国土和悠久的历史，可是这两个国家的社会结构却相当不同。那么造成这两个大国内部的统一和融合的主要原因是什么呢？我认为"汉文"和"梵文"在文化传播中起了重要作用。这两种语言在古代都得到了很大的发展，而且承载和传播这两种语言和文化的人都是两个国家上层社会中的那些受过很好教育的人。但是，经过了很长的历史发展以后，这两种文化的基本观念已经逐步进入了社会的普通民众当中。汉文承载的特殊文化，可以在政治思想的伦理当中体现出来，而梵文揭示出社会制度中的哲学与宗教思想。汉文和梵文都对社会秩序和共同价值的创立做出了重要贡献。

汉文化的代表是中原的政权，"汉化"，也就是汉文化向四周的传播，在一定程度上是由皇朝政治体制的行政权力来推动的。接受了汉文化并进入到这个政治体制的人们，就成为了中国社会的组成部分。"梵化"体现的是基于印度价值的一种社会秩序，特别体现在印度的种姓制度上。不论是种姓制度内部或外部的人群，只要接近和发展出与这个秩序相似特征的人群就会逐渐成为印度社会的成员。在这个过程中，人们不能以某个个体加入印度社会，而必须以一个群体的方式成为印度社会的组成部分，成为印度人。于是，"汉化"和"梵化"就分别在中国和印度产生了与世界上其他国家都不同的社会，由于以不同的方式不断吸收新的成员，这两个社会没有像目前的民族——国家那样的明确的边界，他们的边界都是模糊的。

---

[1] 这篇中级读物的节选、改编和改写，是作者基于本刊发表的中根千枝(Chie Nakane)的原作：《中国和印度:从人类学的视角来看文化的边陲》，[第1卷第3期,刘念译(大量参考了马戎的译本，以同名发表于2007年2月期《北京大学学报》)。全球中国比较研究会助理编辑和翻译、英国埃塞克斯大学社会学系博士候选人曾育勤女士(Yu-chin Tseng),根据作者的英文原稿对全文作了详细的修改和润校]。

标签：社科汉语　　　级别：中级　　　字数：582

词汇

广阔	guǎngkuò	broad
悠久	yōujiǔ	long
结构	jiégòu	structure
相当	xiāngdāng	quite
造成	zàochéng	to cause
内部	nèibù	internal
统一	tǒngyī	unity
融合	rónghé	fusion
汉文	hànwén	Chinese language
梵文	fánwén	Sanskrit
传播	chuánbò	spread
发展	fāzhǎn	development
承载	chéngzài	to bear
上层	shàngcéng	upper strata
教育	jiàoyù	education
基本	jīběn	basic
观念	guānniàn	concept
逐步	zhúbù	gradually
民众	mínzhòng	people
特殊	tèshū	special
政治	zhèngzhì	politics
伦理	lúnlǐ	ethics
体现	tǐxiàn	reflect
揭示	jiēshì	reveal
制度	zhìdù	system
哲学	zhéxué	philosophy
宗教	zōngjiào	religion
秩序	zhìxù	order
价值	jiàzhí	value
创立	chuànglì	to found
贡献	gòngxiàn	contributions
中原	zhōngyuán	central plains
政权	zhèngquán	regime
四周	sìzhōu	surrounding
程度	chéng dù	degree; extent
皇朝	huángcháo	dynasty
行政	xíngzhèng	administrative
权力	quánlì	power
推动	tuīdòng	promote

组成	zǔchéng	composition
基于	jīyú	based on
种姓	zhǒngxìng	caste
相似	xiāngsì	similar
特征	tèzhēng	characteristics
某个	mǒu gè	(certain) one
群体	qúntǐ	groups
吸收	xīshōu	absorb
明确	míngquè	clear
模糊	móhú	fuzzy
汉化	hànhuà	The process of becoming Chinese or integrating the Chinese culture
梵化	fánhuà	The the process of lower caste seeking upward mobility by emulating the rituals and practices of the upper or dominant castes

练习1　短语学习。请把下面的短语译成英文。

国土广阔	历史悠久	社会结构	主要原因
文化传播	上层社会	历史发展	基本观念
逐步进入	普通民众	政治思想	体现出来
社会秩序	共同价值	重要贡献	一定程度
政治体制	行政权力	组成部分	不同方式

练习2　学习以下句型并造句。

1) 造成这两个大国内部的统一和融合的主要原因是……
   造成……的（主要）原因是……
   The (main) reason which (has) caused …… is ……

2) "汉文"和"梵文"在文化传播中起了重要作用。
   在……中起……作用
   to play a …… role in ……

3) 汉文承载的特殊文化可以在政治思想的伦理当中体现出来。
   在……当中体现出来
   to be reflected in ……

4) 汉文和梵文都对社会秩序和共同价值的创立做出了重要贡献。
   对……做出……贡献
   to make a …… contribution to ……

5) "汉化"在一定程度上是由皇朝政治体制的行政权力来推动的。
   由……（来）推动的
   to be promoted by/through ……

6) 接受了汉文化并进入到这个政治体制的人们，就成为了中国社会的组成部分。

成为... ... 的组成部分
to become an integral part of ... ...

详细阅读：

请参考本期中根千枝(Chie Nakane)的原作:《中国和印度:从人类学的视角来看文化的边陲》

DOI https://doi.org/10.24103/GCSS2.en.2016.10.2

Kinship, household and *gotra*: configuration of societies in China, Japan and India
家族、家户、种姓：中国、日本和印度的社会构造

宋连谊 (Lianyi Song) 编[1]

　　印度的种姓(gotra)是一个非常有特色的社会制度。在谈到这一点时，我想对中国和印度这两个国家的社会结构进行比较。关于中国的社会结构，费孝通教授曾经提出了著名的"差序格局"。在中国社会，"自我"是一个起点，社会关系像同心圆那样一波一波扩展开来，最后达到最外圈的"天下"。这些关系层具有弹性，而且在各组之间没有明确的边界。

　　当你观察印度的种姓社会时，则会显现出另一个很不同的模式。印度社会是由无数群组构成的，他们形成一个镶嵌模式。由种姓作为代表，每一个群组都是一个边界清晰的实体。群组的聚合是由各种因素促成的，如地缘联系、相同职业、在种姓等级制中相近的地位，等等。此外，印度的种姓主要还是一个职业群体，每个种姓都有一个特定的职业，这样的例子很多。为了维持日常生活与经济活动，每个种姓都需要其他种姓提供的服务，通常会需要30个以上不同种姓的配合。于是，他们和其他种姓之间保持着经济功能方面的联系，但是其中任何一层联系都不扩展到整个社会。然而，非常重要的一个特点是，不管一个人在印度社会里走到哪里，不管当地的语言和习俗如何不同，他都可以发现那里有着关于种姓体系的相同原则，也许各地会有些差异。但他们都分享着同一价值体系和行为规范的基本原则。所以他们可以辨别出其他人的身份，任何人在社会的地图中可以找到自己的位置。在这样一个体系的运作中，一个社会的整体关联性也就产生了。

　　这两个社会的图景呈现出了一个有趣的对比，尽管在两个社会组织结构的构建上存在差异，但我们在社会组织的"核心"里还是可以发现一个显著的共性，那就是"家庭"的重要地位。在这两个社会中，传统家庭结构的理想类型是相同的。在家庭的基本结构中既有家庭成员之间垂直的关系(如父子关系)，同时也有横向的平行关系(如兄弟关系)。这样一个水平和垂直交叉的结构，固定了家庭的核心，从家庭成员的亲属关系再扩展到外部的成员。在一个家庭和一个父系宗族之间，没有清晰的界限。其功能边界的产生取决于一些既定的情形，如共有的财产、成员们的个人因素。中国的父系关系的识辨根据族谱可以上溯或者下延许多代，这里我们就会想到中国的祖先崇拜。

---

[1] 这篇高级读物的节选、改编和改写，是作者基于本刊发表的中根千枝(Chie Nakane)的原作：《中国和印度:从人类学的视角来看文化的边陲》，[《中国比较研究》第1卷第3期，刘念译(大量参考了马戎的译本，以同名发表于2007年2期《北京大学学报》)。全球中国比较研究会助理编辑和翻译、英国埃塞克斯大学社会学系博士候选人曾育勤女士(Yu-chin Tseng),根据作者的英文原稿对全文作了详细的修改和润校]。

在印度，父系集团被称作"*gotra*"，他构成了一个种姓群体的组成部分，一个种姓群体由许多不同的"*gotra*"组成。他的功能就是建立起共同成员身份的认同，而不是表现与祖先之间的关系。每一个*gotra*有一个共同的神龛和名字。"*gotra*"的名字与中国的姓氏相对应，但它在日常社会生活中并不使用。不过，在印度的系统之下，妻子会被要求使用她丈夫的姓氏。

尽管我们发现在中国和印度社会中存在着不同之处，但在两个社会中对血缘(亲属)的承认，在社会组织底层发挥着重要的作用。在日本社会中则有所不同，在家庭确定内部和外部成员关系方面起关键作用的是"户"(*ié*)这个单元，而不是血缘。事实上，家庭脉络的延续是"户"的延续，在一"户"的下一代中只有一个儿子和他的妻子可以把这个"户"继承下去，其他兄弟们将分家出去，另立门户。当一个家长(父亲)没有亲生儿子来继承自己的"户"，他就选择一个男子来收养，这个男子可能来自自己的亲属中，也可能与自己没有任何亲属关系。这个收养的男子会合法地继承家长的姓氏和"户"的全部事业。同样的，尽管日本人像中国人一样有祖先崇拜的观念，但是日本人的祖先更多的是被看做是一个家户的创始人，而不一定是基于有血缘关系的人。虽然日本从中国接受了许多重要的文化成分，但是日本本土的社会架构却保持未变。

在日本社会的制度里，像"户"这样的组织在个体成员的联系中比血缘亲属关系更为重要。这一原则进一步发展成了这样的现象：个人的社会交往范围通常仅限于他现在所属的组织("户"的变种与扩展)的围墙之内。而在组织之间的那个层面上，交往网络也是存在的。例如，在一些经济界的个案中，父亲公司和儿子公司构成了一个巨大的企业集团，彼此建立起了远比经济关系更密切的忠诚关系。但是即使是在这样的例子中，人际网络的功能也被限定在机构体系的设置当中。所以，看到中国人和印度人能够拥有和运用如此丰富灵活的功能性人际关系网络，我们日本人是十分惊奇的。从日本人的眼光来看，中国和印度社会的差别和共性表现得是十分清楚的。

词语

构造	gòuzào	configuration
弹性	tánxìng	elasticity
镶嵌	xiāngqiàn	mosaic; inlay
清晰	qīngxī	clear
地缘	dìyuán	geo; local, regional
习俗	xísú	custom
规范	guīfàn	specification; pattern
运作	yùnzuò	operation
关联性	guānliánxìng	relevance, coherence
呈现	chéngxiàn	appear; show
差异	chāyì	difference
垂直	chuízhí	vertical
平行	píngxíng	parallel
交叉	jiāochā	cross

族谱	zúpǔ	genealogy
上溯	shàngsù	traced
崇拜	chóngbài	worship
神龛	shénkān	shrine
血缘	xiěyuán	kinship
脉络	màiluò	arteries and veins; context
继承	jìchéng	inherit
门户	ménhù	family; faction
收养	shōuyǎng	adopt; adoption
架构	jiàgòu	structure
差序格局		Differential pattern (cf. the ripple effect)
镶嵌模式		Mosaic pattern

费孝通(1910–2005)中国著名社会学家、人类学家、民族学家、社会活动家，中国社会学和人类学的奠基人之一

练习1　讨论题/作文题：

1) 请根据本文分别叙述一下中国、日本和印度的社会结构的特点。可以参考使用以下所给词语。

中国：
父系关系，对比，核心，共性，基本结构，既... 又...，垂直关系，横向，平行关系，交叉的结构，扩展，识辨，族谱，上溯，下延，代，祖先崇拜。

日本：
家庭内部和外部成员关系，继承，兄弟们，分家，另立门户，收养，亲属，祖先崇拜，血缘关系，本土的，社会架构，保持未变，个体成员，企业集团，人际网络，机构体系，十分惊奇，差别和共性

印度：
种姓(gotra)，特色，社会结构，观察，模式，镶嵌模式，边界清晰，实体，聚合，各种因素，地缘联系，相同职业，等级制，职业群体，特定的职业，日常生活，经济活动，配合，功能方面，扩展，整个社会，语言和习俗，相同原则，差异，价值体系，行为规范，基本原则，辨别，身份，位置，运作，呈现，对比，核心，共性，基本结构，既... 又...，垂直关系，横向，平行关系，交叉的结构，扩展，清晰的界限，功能边界，神龛

2) 你对中国、日本和印度的社会结构的了解与文章中所描述的相同吗？即：你同意作者的看法吗？如果不同意，请谈谈你的看法。

3) 本文谈论的三个亚洲国家在社会结构上的不同，请谈一下你的国家或两个不同西方国家之间在社会结构上的同异。

详细阅读：

请参考中根千枝(Chie Nakane)的原作：《中国和印度:从人类学的视角来看文化的边陲》。

DOI https://doi.org/10.24103/GCSS2.en.2016.10.3

China's family (*jia*) *vs* Japan's family (*ie*)
中国的家与日本的家

宣力 (Lik Suen) 编[1]

　　日本和中国在较早时期就已经形成了小农经济，可是，支撑小农经济的社会和经济组织并不相同：在日本，是以地缘组织为中心的村落共同体，在中国是以血缘关系结合成的同族集团。

　　日文中有"家(ie)"，中文里也有"家"(jia)。专家们一般认为，日本的家(ie)以农业生产为主要目的；中国的家(jia)以直系血缘关系的延续为主要目的。在财产继承方面，日本的家产由长子单独继承；在中国，原则上由兄弟们平均分配继承。不过，也有例外，李培林说过："历来大家族规避和抵御衰落风险的根本办法，就是不"分家"，因为"分家"就意味着产权和社会关系的重组"。

　　这篇报告的作者调查了中国江苏南部一个村子的情况，这个村子叫江村。研究的重点是房屋，由于土地少，房屋既是居住单位又是家产。通过研究这个村子29户的房屋数量和规模，作者发现，在近100年的时期内，江村房屋的变迁，也就是家产的分割是有限的。事实上，有不少多子家庭，只保留一子继承家产以外，其他的作为上门女婿，结婚离开，从而避免了分家。这种变化看起来日本的制度有些相似。

　　作者观察到，经济生活条件的逐步改善，外部环境的改进，个体家庭的经济积累的增长，导致家产的不断增加，给家产的平均分割和继承创造了条件。人们有条件分割家产，可是却没有分家。为什么会发生这种变化，真的是"为了规避和抵御衰落风险"吗？还是有别的外在原因？是一个很值得深入研究的现象。

标签：社科汉语　　级别：中级　　字数：566

词汇

形成	xíngchéng	to form; formation
地缘	dìyuán	geo-
血缘	xuèyuán	blood relation/kinship
集团	jítuán	group
村落	cūnluò	village
目的	mùdì	purpose; objective
直系	zhíxì	lineal

---

[1] 本文是作者根据发表在本刊的朴红(Hong Park)的原作：《关于农村社会的家与家产的比较研究 -- 以中日比较为中心》一文，节选、改编并改写为社科汉语的中级读物。谢谢宋连谊博士对"词汇"和"练习"部分提供的帮助。

延续	yánxù	continue; continuation
财产	cáichǎn	property
继承	jìchéng	inherit
单独	dāndú	alone
平均	píngjūn	average
分配	fēnpèi	allocation; distribution
例外	lìwài	exception
历来	lìlái	always
规避	guībì	avoid
抵御	dǐyù	resist
衰落	shuāiluò	fading; decline
风险	fēngxiǎn	risk
根本	gēnběn	fundamental
意味着	yìwèizhe	mean
重组	chóngzǔ	restructuring
调查	diàochá	Investigation
由于	yóuyú	due to; as a result of
数量	shùliàng	quantity
规模	guīmó	scale
既...又	jì... yòu	both ... and ...
变迁	biànqiān	change
分割	fēngē	segmentation
有限	yǒuxiàn	limited
避免	bìmiǎn	avoid
相似	xiāngsì	similar
观察	guānchá	observe; observation
积累	jīlěi	accumulation
导致	dǎozhì	result in; lead to
逐步	zhúbù	gradually
改善	gaishan	improve
增加	zēngjiā	increase
平均	píngjūn	average
创造	chuàngzào	create
却	què	yet; but
值得	zhídé	worth it
深入	shēnrù	thorough; in depth
现象	xiànxiàng	phenomenon

练习1 短语学习。请把下面的短语译成英文。

小农经济	同族集团	财产继承	居住单位
生活条件	不断增加	经济组织	一般认为
平均分配	通过研究	逐步改善	创造条件

并不相同	农业生产	根本办法	继承家产
外部环境	外在原因	血缘关系	主要目的
社会关系	上门女婿	个体家庭	值得研究

练习2 填空。

　　日本和中国在较＿＿＿＿时期就已经形成了小农经济，可是，支撑小农经济的社会和经济组织并不＿＿＿＿同：在日本，是以地缘组

　　织为中心的村落共同体，在中国是＿＿＿＿血缘关系结合成的同族集团。

　　专家们一般认为，日本的家(ie)以农业生产＿＿＿＿主要目的；中国的家(jia)以直系血缘关系的延续为主要目的。

　　在财产继承＿＿＿＿面，日本的家产由长子单独继承；在中国，原则＿＿＿＿由兄弟们平均分配继承。

　　这篇报告的作＿＿＿＿调查了中国江苏南部一个村子的情况，　这个村子叫江村。研究的重＿＿＿＿是房屋，由于土地少，房屋既是居住单位＿＿＿＿是家产。通过研究这个村子29户的房屋数量和规模，作者发现，在近100年的时期＿＿＿＿，江村房屋的变迁，　也就是家产的分割是有限的。事实＿＿＿＿，　有不少多子家庭，只保留一子继承家产以外，其他的作为上门女婿，结婚离开，从而避免了＿＿＿＿家。这种变化看起来日本的制度有些相似。

详细阅读：

　　请参考本期朴红原文：《关于农村社会的家与家产的比较研究 -- 以中日比较为中心》

DOI https://doi.org/10.24103/GCSS2.en.2016.10.4

Family inheritance in China and Japan
中日家庭的继承方式之异同

宋连谊 (Lianyi Song) 编[1]

将中国与日本的农村家庭与家产加以比较是很有意思义的。日本的家 (*ie*)是以农业生产为主要目的，它由家名、家产、家业和祖先祭祀等诸要素构成。日本的家产具有排他性(由长子单独继承)和永续性的特点；而中国的家(*jia*)是以直系血缘关系的延续为主要目的，作为其经济支持的家庭财产，在原则上是要在兄弟间均分继承的。当然，这种区分并非总是绝对的。

在日本和中国，较早时期就已经形成了小农经济。但是，作为支撑小农经济的社会、经济组织，在这两个国家都有不同的体现。在日本，体现为以地缘组织为中心的村落共同体，而在中国则体现为以血缘关系而结合成的同族集团。另一方面，如费孝通所指出的那样，以集镇为核心的经济网络对于中国小农经济也起到了很大的支持作用。

因此，在日本和中国，小农家庭的构成原理是不同的，并且随着家族的扩大，家产的继承方式也大不相同。本文先对中日两国间的家族、家产和继承的概念加以比较，之后通过选自两国的具体事例加以说明。

我们所选的具体事例分别是日本上盐尻村和中国江村的家与家产的继承的事例。

……

以下我们需要就这两个事例的深层含意加以表述。

首先，日本的ie是追求家业、家产、家名的永远存续的家族集团，这是日本传统家族的特点。同时，ie也是它所在的村落土地共同体的一个组成要素，如果说得形象一点，村落是一个国家，因为它具有三权，即立法，行政和司法权；而ie是这个国家里边的法人集团，每个法人都有自己的家名、家产和家业。为了家产(主要是土地)的永续，就需要家业(比如，农业)不断地再生产。家名是家产和家业的符号，作为与其他ie区别的标记。

其次，我们再看一下江村的事例。在这里，我们以第13组为事例，分析了作为居住单位的房屋的变化，并以两个典型的家族为对象分析了居住单位扩大的过程。江村地处水乡，自古以来在狭窄的土地面积上进行农业生产经营。农村居民的资产象征是房屋，随着农村工业化的发展，兼业收入的增加，3层楼房林立的村子也不罕见了。但是，解放前的江村农民大多是佃农，很少拥有自己的土地。对于他们来说，祖祖辈辈所居住的房屋就是他们的家产，这个时期的房屋具有很强的生活手段的色彩。由于经济基

---

[1] 本文是作者根据发表在本刊的朴红(Hong Park)的原作:《关于农村社会的家与家产的比较研究 -- 以中日比较为中心》一文，节选、改编并改写为社科汉语的高级读物。

础的薄弱，导致了几个家系生活在同一个屋檐下。直到20世纪70年代，由于生活条件的逐步改善和外部环境的改进，使得组内的住宅地不断从小清河岸向内陆延伸。这就为家产的分割与继承创造了条件。但是，实际上在13组的多子家庭里，包括第17户在内仅有3户分家，其他的家庭都保留一子继承家产，其他入赘他方，避免了分家。这与中国传统的多子家庭均分继承家产的观点是不符的。

那么，为什么在江村会存在这种现象呢？在这里引用李培林的一句话，应该是具有说服性的："历来大家族规避和抵御衰落风险的根本办法，就是不"分家"，因为"分家"就意味着产权和社会关系的重组"。虽然这是针对大家族的，而我们调查的13组是普通村民，但也仍然存在同一个问题。这是因为中国的家，无论大小，是以直系血缘关系的延续为主要目的，它以家庭财产作为其经济支持，当这个经济支持过于薄弱无法支撑所有家系的时候，或者如果分割之后无法支撑新的家系的时候，那么，为了使得直系血缘能够延续下去，也就是为了"规避和抵御衰落风险"，其根本办法就是不分家。在13组，村民们采用如"上门女婿"这项民间"发明"的习俗，也是村民在实践中的产物，来避免了分家。

这种"不分家"形似日本的家产继承。但是，它们有着根本性的区别。即，为了延续血缘关系的江村的"不分家"和为了延续家产永续的日本的"ie制度"存在着本质性的区别。

但是，有一点值得注意的是，由于受计划生育的影响，现今的江村家庭多是一子家庭，而且人口趋于减少，高龄化日趋严重。在这样的情况下，新婚夫妇不与任何一方的父母同住，而是单独在外独立生活。而且，出生的孩子要冠上父母双方的姓氏，以此来表示这个新的家系是同时属于两个老的家系的。另一方面，作为家产的房屋扩大了规模，为血缘关系的延续提供了(与过去相比)雄厚的经济基础，但是，原本作为被支持的血缘关系—家，却是处在一种岌岌可危的状态。对于这个问题，留作以后的课题继续研究。

注释

上盐尻村：日本长野县的一个村子。[尻 kāo]
江村：江苏省吴江县市开弦弓村，费孝通《江村经济》一书中的研究以这个村子为基地。

词汇

继承	jìchéng	inheritance
异同	yìtóng	similarities and differences
祖先	zǔxiān	ancestors
祭祀	jìsì	worship ceremony
诸	zhū	various
要素	yàosù	elements; essential factor
排他性	páitāxìng	exclusivity

永续性	yǒngxù xìng	sustainability
血缘	xiěyuán	blood kinship
均分	jūn fēn	sharing (equally)
绝对	juéduì	absolute(ly)
支撑	zhīchēng	support
地缘	dìyuán	geo; geopolitical
村落	cūnluò	villages
集镇	jízhèn	town
深层	shēncéng	deep level
含意	hányì	meaning
表述	biǎoshù	statement; expression
立法	lìfǎ	legislation
司法	sīfǎ	judicial
法人	fǎrén	legal person/representative
狭窄	xiázhǎi	narrow
兼业	jiān yè	by-business
罕见	hǎnjiàn	rare
佃农	diànnóng	tenant farmer
薄弱	bóruò	weak
屋檐	wūyán	eaves
延伸	yánshēn	extension
分割	fēngē	split, division
规避	guībì	avoid; avoidance
抵御	dǐyù	resist
衰落	shuāiluò	decline
延续	yánxù	continuation
形似	xíngsì	similar in appearance
趋于	qū yú	tends to
冠(上)	guān (shàng)	to crown (with)
雄厚	xiónghòu	strong, abundant

练习1：短语学习。请把下面的短语译成英文。

祖先祭祀	加以说明	楼房林立	外部环境
趋于减少	血缘关系	深层含意	经济基础
规避风险	日趋严重	小农经济	组成要素
大不相同	根本办法	扩大规模	具体事例
自古以来	逐步改善	上门女婿	岌岌可危

练习2： 句型学习。请试着用这些句型造句，注意口语和书面语的一些用词差别。

日本和中国在较____时期就已经形成了小农经济, 可是, 支撑小农经济的社会和经济组织并不____同: 在日本，是以地缘组

织为中心的村落共同体，在中国是____血缘关系结合成的同族集团。

专家们一般认为，日本的家(ie)以农业生产____主要目的; 中国的家(jia)以直系血缘关系的延续为主要目的。

在财产继承____面，日本的家产由长子单独继承; 在中国，原则____由兄弟们平均分配继承。

这篇报告的作____调查了中国江苏南部一个村子的情况, 这个村子叫江村。研究的重____是房屋，由于土地少，房屋既是居住单位____是家产。通过研究这个村子29户的房屋数量和规模，作者发现，在近100年的时期____，江村房屋的变迁，也就是家产的分割是有限的。事实____，有不少多子家庭，只保留一子继承家产以外，其他的作为上门女婿，结婚离开，从而避免了____家。这种变化看起来日本的制度有些相似。

练习3： 作文

试比较两个家庭的特点(如：习俗、子女教育、家务、财务收支的支配、亲属关系等)。可以是不同国家、民族或地区的家庭，也可以是你熟悉的两个家庭。

DOI https://doi.org/10.24103/GCSS2.en.2016.10.5

A Functional Approach to Social Science Translation
功能理论和社会科学文本的翻译

冯东宁 Dongning Feng

引言：社科翻译的社会作用

　　本文探讨的译稿原文是伦敦政经学院荣休教授王斯福(Stephan Feuchtwang)先生的文章——《学以致用：费孝通教授的人类学使命及埃德蒙·利奇的科研游戏》(A Practical Minded Person: Fei Xiaotong's Anthropological Calling and Edmund Leach's Game)。原文论点复杂、思想活跃、专业性强，加之个性化的笔调，给翻译带来了极大的难度。其难点主要体现在三个方面：术语概念、句法结构和内涵的表达。当这三方面在中文没有对应或约定俗成的表达法时，根据翻译目的论而构建的翻译策略和技巧的应用就显得格外重要。社科文本翻译在中国近代史的发展中起到了决定性的推动作用，其重要性是不言而喻的。而王斯福教授在本文中对文化翻译又有一番别有见地的论述，他说：

　　　　的确，想专门从事文化翻译的学者为数甚少，因此，要求他们全面掌握人类学研究的概念和系统是不现实的。希望每个人都能成为一个人类学家是荒谬的，但是任何人都有可能成为人类学家，任何语言都有可能为人类学学科所用，给我们的学科带来"震动"。因此，理想的状态是，我们应该向这种"震动"开放我们的作品……

其原文是：

It is true that few people want to be or are driven to engage in cultural translation as a profession. It is therefore wrong to expect them to have developed the concepts and generalisations which result from this activity. It is foolish to expect everyone to be an anthropologist. But it is possible for anyone to be an anthropologist and it should be possible for any language to be disturbed into anthropological usage. So we should, ideally, leave ourselves and our writings open to such disturbance.

　　这不仅说明了社科翻译的难度，同时精辟的指出了翻译不仅仅是传播知识，而且在语言的转换过程中，对研究的主体以及客体都可能带来"震动"，这种"震动"是社会发展和进步的催化剂和动力，关于这个问题我希望能有机会择文另述。

一．功能翻译理论和社科翻译

很多读者都会有这样的体会，他们发现很多社科方面的译文要么十分晦涩，要么看似简单却不知所云。一些由再通常不过的词汇组成的句子似乎很难抓住其确切的意思，这在很大程度上同翻译原则和翻译方法论的实际运用有很大的关系。一些早期的社科译者似乎着重于对原文的忠实，也就是强调译文与原文的对等。但是，他们对对等原则的理解似乎过于简单化和绝对化，缺乏对语言和语法差异的考量，同时对翻译的目的性也疏于考虑。当然，翻译的体裁论(text typology)和翻译的目的论(skopostheorie)也只是上个世纪八十年代前后才被提出来，并在翻译实践中加以应用的，所以我们不应该责怪我们翻译界的前辈。但是这些新的翻译理论的确给我们现今的翻译工作注入了新的能量，我们在这里不妨借用这两个理论来分析一下本译稿的难句翻译。

功能理论中的体裁论告诉我们社科学术体裁大体上应属于信息性体裁，而信息性体裁的翻译应该使用逻辑性强的语言，重点应该放在文章内容的传递；而译文应该表述全面的所指的概念和内容。要达到以上所说的目的，翻译的方法就应该是使用透明、简洁且明了的文体，如果有需要可以使用说明和诠释的策略。

二．词义的延伸和扩展

略通英语的学者、社科学生及双语学者不难看出原文中的难句似乎比比皆是，真有些无从下手的感觉。我们不妨先看看该文题目的翻译：

原文：A Practical Minded Person: Professor Fei's Anthropological Calling and Edmund Leach's Game

译文：学以致用：费孝通教授的人类学使命及埃德蒙·利奇的科研游戏

首先，在用词上，题目中的calling和game这两个用词的翻译颇引人注意。Calling一词的意义是"a strong urge towards a particular way of life or career; a vocation"，也就是我们中文中说的欲望或感召，但感召出现在题目中似乎有些玄奥的色彩，于是译者把它引申为使命或使命感，这用来形容费孝通教授有学者的担当及历史的责任感是非常恰当的，同时把原文的内涵表达的十分透彻。而game一词可以按字面译为"游戏"，也可按其所指的意义译为"研究"，似乎都无可非议；但是游戏一词在中文中未免过于否定，有点玩票的味道，这与原文的game的意义是有些出入的，简单译为"研究"又没有反映出原文中王斯福教授把二者研究目的作比较的中心思想。因此在"游戏"前加上"科研"，既承认了利奇的研究，又道出了他与费孝通教授治学方法和目的的不同。在此我们看到词义的延伸和适当的加词，可以将原意表达得更加清晰，这也符合功能理论的宗旨。另外题目中的 "A practically minded person" 很难说是不是"学以致用"的英译，但是回译为"学以致用"是考虑到了中文的表达习惯而且又反映了费孝通教授治学的信念。试想一下，如果把这一词译为"一个讲究实际的人"或是"一个重视实效的人"这就是对原文的忠实吗？译为"学以致用"一方面符合语篇上的对等原则，而且又达到了原文的目的。

三．社科翻译中上下文的考量

我们再来看看下一个例子：

原文：Freedman's view of the lessons which the anthropological study of China can teach will be an addition to my dialogue with Professor Fei.

译文：弗里德曼有关中国人类学研究给我们的启示的论述也是我和费教授之间要进行的学术对话。

原文中的英文词组 "teach lessons" 当然可以译为"给我们提供经验教训"，但结合上下文，翻译为"给我们启示"可能更为贴切。还有"dialogue with someone"在学术文本中也可大体上译为中文的"商榷"，但是"商榷"一词在中文中是一个负载词（loaded word），也就是说是一个富于内涵的词汇，暗含对对方的批评之意。因此使用"对话"或"学术对话"更加具有建设性和开放性。所以翻译时，应该考虑翻译的上下文以及目的性，有时一个看似简单的惯用语和套语并不能准确地表达原文的意思。

四．难句的重组

本文开始时，我们提到，功能翻译理论的文本划分和翻译原则，这里我们看一下难句的重组：

原文：From Malinowski onward, from the establishing of social anthropology as an academic profession in the 1920s, anthropologists in England have been more removed from government than is anthropology in China. But I think these differences are only relative differences, differences of priority. We share a calling to a critical, empirical discipline which is based on the study of others, respectful and curious about our differences.

译文：从马林诺夫斯基开始，从20世纪20年代社会人类学作为一门科研学科起，在英国，人类学学科与政治和政府已是相形渐远，但在中国这一学科却没有脱离政治。但我认为这些差异只是相对差异，着重点的不同。我们有着共同的使命：在对他者进行研究时，以求知和尊重他人的心态看待彼此的不同，以将人类学发展成一门具有批判精神的实验学科。

我们可以看到此处的"anthropologists in England have been more removed from government than is anthropology in China"一句拆为两句；例如："在英国，人类学学科与政治和政府已是相形渐远，但在中国这一学科却没有完全脱离政治"。这当然是为了便于理解，而又强调了两个地方的差异，这比译成一个比较句型更清晰、更符合中文的表达习惯。而最后一句的重组不但表达了原句的逻辑，亦使原文更易理解，这显然与理解翻译的目的和读者的需要分不开。我们还可以从上面的例子中的最后一句的译文中看到这一翻译策略的应用："我们有着共同的使命：在对他者进行研究时，以求知和尊重他人的心态看待彼此的不同，以将人类学发展成一门具有批判精神的实验学科"。原文的逻辑性在译文中得以还原。试想一下，如果翻译没有一个特定的目的性的话，其结果会是什么样呢？另外，此处将"curious"引申为"求知"也比译成"好奇"更能传达原文的含义，为读者所理解；"好奇"在中文中多少有些猎奇的含义，不适于应用在中文学术文体中。

我们再来看一个例子：

原文：It is a pretence of not being involved in the ideologies, governments, and common senses which make up the realities it criticises.

译文：如果批评不触及意识形态、政府及社会常识等这些现实是一种矫饰的行为……

这个例子与上面一个略有不同。为了使句子或段落明了易懂，句子段落的重组不仅是将原文的句子化解拆散，同样也可以是将原文的复杂句精简组合。上面的译文把原文中从句套从句的句子化简为一个简单明了的中文句子，同时又不损失其信息量，是翻译社科文本的有效方法。

从以上例子我们可以看到，在翻译较为复杂的社科文本时，重点应该放在对原文目的的理解，对体裁的认知上，如果有需要可以使用文内或文外的说明和诠释的策略，这样才能使译文到达其初始的目的。最后，我想借用王斯福教授的观念来结束本译评，翻译不但可以给对象学科带来"震动"，同样也可以给我们的思维方式带来"震动"，从而丰富我们的创造性思维。

参考书目

Nord, C. (1997). *Translating as a Purposeful Activity: Functionalist Approaches Explained*. Manchester: St. Jerome.

Reiss, K & Vermeer H. J. (1984) *Towards a General Theory of Translational Action*, Manchester: St. Jerome Publishing.

Vermeer, Hans J. (1996) *A Skopos Theory of Translation: Some Arguments for and against*. Heidelberg: TEXTconTEXT-Verlag.

DOI https://doi.org/10.24103/GCSS2.en.2016.10.6

Translation as a "Transcultural" Text
"跨文化"、"超文化"还是"转文化"[1]或其他?

冯东宁(Dongning Feng)

本期论文的难点是术语的翻译,在沈骑[2]的文评中对此已有说明,在此我仅从翻译的角度,继续这一讨论。文章得有一个标题,我们暂且借用文章的关键词—"Transcultural",因为翻译这一活动的确是处于一种"动态"或"过渡"文化"之中。

术语的形成和被接受有时要通过一个较长时间的磨合。比如文中提到的cross-cultural、intercultural和transcultural并非新词,但其中文的译法却仍处于一种过渡状态,一个主要原因是中文的前缀非常有限,且用法模糊;而早期的译者有时在翻译时没有使用恰当的策略给予明确的定义。

在英文中,cross-cultural和intercultural混用的情况颇多,在中文中我们也不必太过于谨小慎微,另起炉灶、重新发明轮子。在一般情况下也不会引起多大的歧义,当然在特殊情况下例外。设想如果将intercultural译为"际文化",那interracial怎么办? Intercommunal呢? Intertextual又如何翻译?

但是,我们必须承认transcultural有其特定的内涵,但有必要加以区分,而且要明确其定义。译为"超文化"或"转文化"固然是一种策略,以区分于"跨文化"。其实"跨文化"可能跟transcultural更贴近,如早期翻译时再加上原文的概念和定义,对transcultural来说,不乏是一个极佳的选择。但是位置已被cross-cultural占领,人们对其已有约定俗成的共识,想改也难。不幸的是,cross-cultural和intercultural似乎不值得占领这个位置,因为transcultural比那两个词的术语性都高,而"跨"这个字不但表达了跨越文化的状态,也包含了一个动态的内涵。

中文是表意文字,很容易望文生义。汉字用得不当,很容易令人产生误解,哪怕是在给出定义的情况下,尤其是一些与政治、社会及文化有关的词汇。所以"超文化"的译法是需要进一步商榷的,"超"字似乎离原概念甚远,有点背道而驰的感觉,而在确立这个词的定义的时候需要极大的力度来说服读者。

把transcultural译为"转文化"相对更为贴近,与其他中文概念有相同的词根trans,如转型(transformation)、转基因(transgenic)、转账(transfer)、转机等(transit)等。但是,translation(翻译)没被译成转译,transhimalaya被译为环喜马拉雅,可见,约定俗成和语境也很重要,国内已经出现媒体研究的专家在使用"转文化",作为一种约定俗成,把transcultural译为"转文化"也说得过去。

---

[1] 编者注: 本文原标题为《"跨文化"、"超文化"或其他? 》。在本文集付梓之前,征求了作者的意见,略作补充,更新为《"跨文化"、"超文化"还是"转文化"或其他? 》。

[2] 沈骑:《从跨文化、"际文化"到"转文化"研究: 兼评〈普世价值梦、民族国家梦及环球共生梦---- 中欧相逢中的跨文化生成性思考〉》,《中国比较研究》,2015年第1期。

此外，还有一个可以考虑的有效策略是创造新词 (neologism)，比如把transcultural译为"通识文化"，这是一个生造词，一方面它不具有负载(loadedness)可以塑造。另一方面，它暗含"共通认知"或"通过认识"之意，另外将trans译成"通识"亦可以说这是一个半音译半意译(phoneto-semantic translation)的词，便于记忆。当然，这只是一个设想。

社科术语译文的不确定性是难免的，这是语言在不同文化流动过程中的一个现象。作为术语的翻译的策略和概念的规范，使用术语表(Glossary)不失为一个有效的方法。例如：

跨/转文化路径 (transcultural approach)
拓扑图 (topology)
双向代理人 (double agent)
文化间代言人 (agent of in-between/*de l'entre-deux*)
多元身份 (multi-identity)
阈限灵活性 (liminal flexibility)
模糊边界效应 (fuzzy border effect)
相逢交叉场 (cross-field of encounter)
阐释型构 (interpretative configuration)
距离原理 (principle of distance)
历史性 (historicity)
镜像效应 (mirror effect)
权力游戏 (power games)
表征体系 (representation system)
主动误解 (proactive misunderstanding)
积极误解 (positive misunderstanding)
跨/转文化生成性 (transcultural generativity)

如果用中文给出以上术语的定义或说明，不但给读者提供极大的便利，而又可对术语的理解达成共识，便于学科的发展。

DOI https://doi.org/10.24103/GCSS2.en.2016.11.1

Appendix B

Globalization of Chinese Sociology and Anthropology

A Dialogue on Fei Xiaotong's Academic Contributions

Gary Hamilton and Xiangqun Chang

Editor's note: Fei Xiaotong (Fei Hsiao-Tung, 1910–2005) obtained his PhD under Malinowski's supervision at the London School of Economics (LSE) in 1938. Of the 20 volumes of his completed works (Fei 2010e), two books are well known in the West: *Peasant Life in China* (1939), and *Xiangtu zhingguo* (1947) – translated as *From the Soil: The Foundations of Chinese Society* by Gary Hamilton and Zheng Wang in 1992. As one of China's finest sociologists and anthropologists, Fei was instrumental in laying a solid foundation for the development of sociological and anthropological studies in China, and his work helped to influence China's social and economic development. Fei was awarded the Malinowski Prize of the International Applied Anthropology Association in 1980, and the Huxley Memorial Medal of the Royal Anthropological Institute in 1981.

   This is an original version of a dialogue on Professor Fei Xiaotong's academic achievements. The dialogue was arranged by Mr Wu Zitong, editor the *China Reading Weekly* (《中华读书报》), to commemorate the 100th anniversary of the birth of Fei Xiaotong in 2010. Mr Wu put a series of questions to Professor Gary Hamilton (Co-Translator of Fei Xiaotong's *From the Soil*) and Dr Xiangqun Chang (Author of *Guanxi or li shang wanglai? Social support, reciprocity and social creativity in a Chinese village* (2010), based on fieldwork in Kaixiangong Village, where Fei Xiaotong did his research for the *Peasant Life in China* (1939). Its Chinese version was originally translated by Zhang Haoyuan and Pu Yao, published in the *China Reading Weekly* (3rd and 10th November 2010). The abridged and revised version was entitled 'China and World Anthropology: A conversation on the contributions of Fei Xiaotong (1910–2005)', *Anthropology Today*, No. 6, 2011. This original dialogue covers three areas: Fei Xiaotong's academic achievements, theoretical contribution and research methods.

Keywords: *chaxugeju, tuantigeju,* pattern of pluralistic unity, cultural self-consciousness

Academic Achievements

Question 1: Professor Fei Hsiao-tung's great academic achievements in sociology and anthropology have made him rightly famous, especially his doctoral dissertation *Peasant Life in China* (1939), and his book *From the Soil* (1947). What are your thoughts about these two works?

Hamilton: I read Professor Fei's *Peasant Life in China* (1939) when I was in graduate school. I thought it was a very interesting book, but I was only at the start of my career and did not recognize Fei as a master craftsman of Chinese social science. Then in 1984–5, while I was doing a year's teaching at Tunghai University in Taiwan, I chanced on a copy of *Xiangtu Zhonggu* (*From the Soil*) in a bookstore. This encounter with Fei occurred when I was already established in my career. At the time, I was working on how to compare China with other societies without introducing a Western bias. Reading *Xiangtu Zhongguo*, I realized that Fei had not only confronted the same problem, but had gone a considerable distance towards solving it. I also saw that Fei's very complex comparisons between Chinese and Western society were stated in graceful prose, in a disarmingly straightforward way. I wondered why this book had never been translated before, and knew at the same time that it must be translated so that an English-reading public could be introduced to Fei's brilliance. I was greatly humbled to have the opportunity to translate this book.

Chang: Coincidently, it was in 1985 that I also first read Fei's *Xiangtu Zhongguo*, when I was doing a sociology master's course at the Northeastern Normal University in Changchun. It gave me a picture of Chinese society as having a vertical and a horizontal axis, the one historical, the other global. Professor Stephan Feuchtwang's paper 'Social Egoism and Individualism: Surprises and Questions that Arise from Reading Fei Xiaotong's Idea of "the Opposition between East and West"' (p??) was based on your and Wang Zheng's translation of *Xiangtu Zhongguo*. I was so pleased at the way it really brought Fei's thinking alive within the Western social scientific context. Both Stephan's previous PhD student and I had often quoted sections from the Chinese version of *Xiangtu Zhongguo*, but this hadn't shown him its true character. Your efforts to make the book available in the English-speaking world have greatly added to the worldwide understanding of Chinese society. Although it was originally published in the 1940s, some of its core ideas are as valuable now as they were then. I was writing a book about Fei, *Study of Fei Xiaotong's Theories and Restudies on Kaixiangong Village*, to commemorate the 100th anniversary of his birth.[1]

---

[1] This work has been interrupted. It will be made available in the near future.

Let's go back to Professor *Fei's Peasant Life in China*. I read the Chinese version in 1987 when it was first published, while I was teaching sociology in Beijing. At that time I wasn't very impressed by the classical ethnography. But over many years my opinion of the book's importance has often been asked by Chinese scholars and students, and finally I sought advice from Stephan. He shed a completely different light on the book's status by referring me to Maurice Freedman's Malinowski Lecture in 1962, 'A Chinese Phase in Social Anthropology' (Freedman 1963). Freedman quoted Malinowski's comment in his Preface to *Peasant Life in China* that the book 'will be counted as a landmark in the development of anthropological fieldwork and theory' (Fei 1939: xix). Freedman encouraged social anthropologists to study societies with large and complex histories of civilization lasting several thousands of years, such as China, which he believed to be the future course of anthropology. I realized that the significance of *Peasant Life in China* lay in its contribution to the development of anthropology and anthropological methodology. In 1996 I finished my fieldwork in the village where Fei Xiaotong had conducted his own. I began to follow his new writings – so-called 'self-reflections' (反省). I felt that these later papers revealed a shift in his research interests, from practical studies to theoretical reviewing and thinking. Fei himself said that the impetus behind this new interest came from rereading Malinowski's Preface. According to Fei, Malinowski had used the term 'landmark' in his preface because *Peasant Life in China* opened up 'a new field for a discipline previously confined to the study of "savages", now freed to interest itself in a wide and vast "civilised world"'. I do very much agree with this.

Hamilton: Let me echo the point you made about Professor Stephan Feuchtwang. I find that surprisingly few American- and British-trained specialists in Chinese society seem to know or cite Fei's theoretical ideas about Chinese society. So I was delighted when I read Feuchtwang's paper that you mentioned above, 'Social Egoism and Individualism: Surprises and Questions that Arise from Reading Fei Xiaotong's Idea of "the Opposition between East and West"'. It is indeed time to start a dialogue among Chinese and Western scholars that follow Fei's leadership in studying societies comparatively so that we can better understand the institutional differences that separate one society from another, as well as the commonalities that unite us.

Chang: It seems unbelievable that over recent decades hundreds of specialists all round the world have studied contemporary China and Chinese society from the viewpoint of many social scientific disciplines, but, unlike you and Stephan, it is rare for any of them to bother looking at theoretical contributions from Chinese scholars, such as Fei Xiaotong. Although such specialists produce wonderful work by social scientific standards, their ideas and methods have been in developed in the study of societies very different from Chinese society. This work is very useful, in many different ways – yet, as Chinese scholars so frequently comment, it fails to get to the root of the matter: the Chinese phrase is 'like scratching an itch from outside one's boot (*ge xue sao yang*隔靴搔痒). For me, the really important thing about *From the Soil* is that it provided a starting point for discussing indigenous Chinese theories about Chinese society. I am hoping that the many events arranged to commemorate the 100th anniversary of the birth of Professor Fei Xiaotong, both inside and outside China, and indeed our dialogue, will interest Western scholars in Chinese scholarship; 'better late than never', as the English phrase puts it.

> **Question 2: As regards ethnic issues, Fei Hsiao-tung had participated in a number of historical surveys on national identification among ethnic minorities in the early years of the People's Republic of China. After the reforms and opening up, he proposed the theory of the 'pattern of pluralistic unity'. According to this theory, consciousness of national identification is multi-layered and different layers are in parallel to each other. In his view, this characteristic of pluralistic unity works not only for China but also for other multinational societies. How do you respond to these ideas?**

Hamilton: Like other concepts that Professor Fei developed, the idea of pluralistic unity derives from his sociological understanding of Chinese society. Fei saw that differential social relationships connected Chinese people to their society in multiple ways. Some related to the closeness of family ties, some to broader lineages, yet others to regions. Fei noted in Chapter 12 of *Xiangtu Zhongguo* that all these ties represent extensions of consanguinity. He said that '[g]eographical location is actually socialized space… These are consanguineous coordinates' (*From the Soil* 1992: 121). Going beyond regionalism, we can also say, following Fei, that national identity is also a socialized space that, for Chinese, has consanguineous coordinates, and that everyone's coordinates in that space are slightly different from one another. The same concept, however, would not hold for all societies, but rather describes nationalism in Chinese societies in contrast to nationalism in many Western societies.

Chang: Yes, the rough idea of the 'pattern of pluralistic unity' (*duoyuan yiti geju* 多元一体格局) can be found in *Xiangtu Zhongguo* which was published in Chinese in the 1940s. But it was developed more fully and published to a wider audience 50 years later, when Fei Xiaotong gave a speech at the Chinese University of Hong Kong on the subject of 'The Pattern of Chinese Nationalities Pluralistic Unity'. This 'pattern of pluralistic unity' was derived from both historical documentary and empirical studies on ethnic minorities in China, made over several decades. According to Fei, China's 56 nationalities have been integrated and are interacting and coexisting within one big society. Here, '*geju*' has the same characteristics as the *geju* of *chaxugeju* and *tuantigeju*. The term '*geju*' is linked to ideas of relationships between individuals and nationalities. *Duoyuan yiti geju* (pattern of pluralistic unity) is a conceptualization derived from studies of Chinese society. By 2000 Fei had written several pieces on issues of globalization, and pointed out the need to construct a 'pattern of multi-cultural or nations' pluralistic unity within one world'. This extends the notion of 'The Pattern of Chinese Nationalities Pluralistic Unity' from Chinese society to global society. After conducting fieldwork for a project on migrants from the BRIC countries in the UK, I realized that Fei's concept of 'the pattern of pluralistic unity' is a useful addition to existing theories for studying multi-ethnic societies.

Hamilton: I guess I have a question about Fei's concept. Is the 'pattern of pluralistic unity among Chinese nationalities' Fei's dream for China's future or is it a pragmatic reality that usually works in China's present conditions?

Chang: The 'pattern of pluralistic unity among Chinese nationalities' is an outcome of Fei's studies on Chinese nationalities, and it is becoming a practical reality. But the 'pattern of pluralistic unity among nationalities in the world' is Fei's ideal or dream.

Hamilton: Following Fei's lead, I think we should make an additional point about pluralistic societies. With the exception of Japan and perhaps Korea, most Asian societies are pluralistic, so much so that the British anthropologist J. S. Furnivall coined the term 'plural society' to refer to societies containing many ethnic groups that coexist but do not combine. Furnivall developed these ideas in the 1930s when he worked as a British civil servant in South-east Asia. Furnivall's concept implicitly points to a contrast with Western societies in which diverse groups are expected to assimilate into a dominant social order. Fei's British training undoubtedly exposed him to Furnivall's writings, but as Fei began his work on ethnic minorities in Chinese society in the 1950s, he brings new insights into the study of pluralistic societies, insights from his studies of Chinese societies, some of which were made in the early 1940s when Fei was teaching and doing research in Yunnan Province.

Chang: Yes, Fei might have been influenced by Furnivall's work on 'plural society', although I haven't seen him refer to it anywhere. Interestingly, one criticism of Fei's *Peasant Life in China* (1939) from Chinese scholars is that it lacks reviews of Western literature. More than half a century later, a criticism of Yan Yunxiang's *The Flow of Gifts* (1996) by Chinese scholars is also that it lacks a review of Chinese literature. I think this shows that Chinese scholars both learn from the West and expect Western scholars to learn from them, not only materially, but also as regards ideas and ways of thinking.

Theoretical Contributions

> **Question 1: Professor Fei Hsiao-tung has made great achievements in theoretical research, and has applied these theories to the study of real society. In *From the Soil*, he described China's problems in terms of the 'Pattern of Difference Sequence' and the 'acquaintances society', ideas which attracted much scholarly attention. Can you briefly introduce the status quo of the study of Fei Hsiao-tung's thought in Western academia, and what we can learn from Fei's 'Pattern of Difference Sequence' in understanding social structures?**

Hamilton: Professor Fei's most important theoretical contribution to the sociology of Chinese society is found in *Xiangtu Zhongguo*, which I had the privilege to translate with Wang Zheng, who was then a graduate student working with me. When we finished the translation, I visited Professor Fei in Beijing. One of the things we talked about at that meeting was the English title of the book. *Xiangtu Zhongguo* does not translate well into English and gives the reader a misleading impression about the contents of the book. In our conversation, I noted Professor Fei's allusion to the fact that rural Chinese seem to spring out of the soil, and both of us suddenly, almost in the same breath, said the name of the book in English should be 'From the Soil', with a subtitle, 'The Foundations of Chinese Society'. What makes this book so important is captured in that title: out of China's rural past comes a distinctive mode of association that allows people to make sense of their place in a complex social order. This mode of association was *chaxugeju*, which I translated as 'the differential mode of association'. Fei's core insight was that this differential mode of association was quite different from the way Westerners associated with each other, a mode of association which he termed *tuantigeju*, and which I translated as the 'organizational mode of association'. These are twin concepts that should help guide our thinking about how Chinese and Western societies are very differently organized and institutionalized.

Far too few American social theorists know about Professor Fei and his work. Knowledge about Fei is primarily confined to scholars who study China. Many theorists in the United States and Europe (e.g. Kiser and Hechter 1991), like many theorists in China, continue to apply the same concepts to different societies. This undermines one of Fei's chief contributions, namely that concepts about societies should be generated from first-hand knowledge about the society in question.

Chang: I got to know of the English version of *From the Soil* from references to it in *Gifts, Favors & Banquets* by Mayfair Yang. Since I was already familiar with the book in Chinese I didn't bother to read the English version until last year, when I was writing about Fei's theoretical contributions. I immediately liked the title 'From the Soil' with its subtitle, 'The Foundations of Chinese Society'. The Introductions, Epilogue and all your notes showed how you and I had reached the same understanding of the book by different routes.

After reading all the reviews of *From the Soil* that I could find, I realized that very few Western scholars appreciated the value and effort put into the English translation. It is a shame that Fei's theories, e.g. *chaxugeju*, have had so little acknowledgment in Western academia, as you have rightly pointed out. Here I will refer to Stephan's paper again. Instead of 'the differential mode of association' and 'organizational mode of association' − your translation of the paired concepts *chaxugeju* and *tuantigeju* − Stephan interpreted these ideas as 'social egoism' to contrast with 'individualism'. This makes the comparison of relationships between Chinese and so-called Westerners easier to understand.

Hamilton: I must say that I was disappointed in the reviews of *From the Soil* as well. I remember that one reviewer criticized Fei's twin concepts as bordering on orientalism and insisted, instead, on a human rights position that all individuals are innately equal and deserving of the same individual rights. This person, who is a Chinese specialist, completely missed the point of Fei's contrast between Chinese and Western society. It is true that human rights advocacy does come out of Western traditions of political philosophy, and that *tuantigeju* is certainly a manifestation of these traditions. However, *chaxugeju* does not deny a prescriptive stance favouring human rights. It is merely a concept that describes a normative pattern of interaction.

In fact, *chaxugeju* and *tuantigeju* are not opposing concepts, are not two ends of a continuum, or polar types. They are both derived from an understanding of the social organization of two different societies. As organizational concepts, the two terms identify institutionalized patterns of interaction among members of their respective societies. In this sense, to be faithful to Fei's terminology, the translation of the terms must emphasize an institutionalized pattern of interaction in which people conceptualize themselves and which they constantly use to recreate the social order in their daily life. For this reason, Feuchtwang's translation of *chaxugeju* as 'social egoism' does not get at the interactional dimensions of Fei's concept, although it is an apt characterization from an individual's point of view in Chinese society, which Fei also uses.

Chang: Chinese is a high-context language. You translated *chaxugeju* and *tuantigeju* as 'the differential mode of association' and 'the organizational mode of association', whereas Stephan translated *chaxugeju* as 'social egoism'. It widened the meaning of the existing social scientific terms of egoism and individualism by adding Chinese characteristics. I have seen nearly ten different translations of *chaxugeju* and *tuantigeju*, and find all of them a little unsatisfactory. They are difficult terms to translate well into English, as so often happens with Chinese terms − as I know to my cost in the case of *lishang-wanglai,* my model of a Chinese style of reciprocity and networking. *Guanxi* has already become one of the foreign terms commonly used in English − bourgeois and proletariat are examples in general usage − and I am wondering whether perhaps *chaxugeju* and *tuantigeju* could be accepted into the technical vocabulary of the social sciences without the distortion of an inadequate translation.

> **Question 2: After the reform and opening up, Professor Fei put forward such theories as the variously described 'construction of small towns', 'township enterprises', 'Southern Jiangsu Mode' and 'Wenzhou Mode' as well as regional development, which made a great contribution to China's urbanization and economic development. Do you think Professor Fei's aim in his old age to 'enrich the people' is a continuation of his academic interests or rather a transformation? What is the significance of his theories for present urban and rural construction?**

Hamilton: In the same years that Professor Fei wrote *Xiangtu Zhongguo*, he also wrote *Xiangtu chongjian*, which is normally translated as 'Reconstructing Rural China'. We summarized it in the last part of *From the Soil*. Fei seemed prophetic in putting forward ideas about the rural foundations of Chinese development in the 1940s that would come true in the 1980s. That Fei could see so clearly how economic development should and could happen in China may seem amazing, but his theories are based on his clear ideas about the foundations of Chinese society.

Chang: In his paper 'Bashi Zibai' ('Self-confessions in the eighties'), Professor Fei concluded that 'aiming at enriching the people' had been his lifelong pursuit, not widely recognized until much later. It is based on his understanding of Chinese society and rooted in his early work, which it continues. His numerous 'models' are outcomes of his understanding of Chinese society with all its various cultural and regional differences. These formulations categorized economic development in contemporary China, thus enabling opportunities for comparative studies between different regions within China and beyond.

Hamilton: I am not as familiar with Fei's later works as you are, and so I find it very interesting that Fei continued to develop the implications of his earlier work much later in his life. I met Fei several times in the 1980s, once even before I thought about translating *Xiangtu Zhongguo*. I was always amazed at the robustness of his thought and at the concern he showed for people's welfare. He was a remarkable scholar.

Chang: Absolutely. Scholars from the English-speaking world always saw Fei as a specifically practically minded person. But this is a misunderstanding that comes from not having read his more theoretical writing, of which *From the Soil* is a fine example. He wrote prolifically in the last 15 years of his life, concerning himself mostly with theory. I hope he can finally be judged by scholars who have read all his later work as well as the earlier work already known in the West – but I can't imagine how these books could be translated as nicely as you and Wang Zheng have translated *Xiangtu Zhongguo*.

Question 3: In Professor Fei's later years, he paid more attention to globalization. He thought that only by establishing 'cultural self-consciousness' could the non-Western world face the challenge of globalization and form a pattern of pluralistic unity among world cultures. 'Every form of beauty has its uniqueness. It is precious to be open to appreciation of other forms of beauty. If beauty represents itself with diversity and integrity, the world will be blessed with harmony and unity'—at his 80th birthday party he succinctly expressed his viewpoint of 'living in harmony but valuing differences' and pointed out the way to achieve this goal. There are various ways of coping with globalization for non-Western civilizations, such as the anti-Western Centralism by post-colonialists and the warm embrace of Western civilization by supporters of Total Westernization. But what are the unique characteristics of Professor Fei's theories? What meaning do they have for us as regards the age of globalization?

Hamilton: I think I should not answer this question, as I am not well versed in what Fei said later in life.

Chang: I have touched on this question previously. I think Fei treated the world as one global society. His idea of constructing the 'pattern of multi-cultural or nations' pluralistic unity within one world' can be seen as part of his strategy of global governance. Fei always believed that social scientific contributions from Chinese society should be studies of Chinese people making and maintaining relationships in order to live in a peaceful environment or 'harmonious society'. He made this point in his talk at LSE in 1947, on a three-month visit to the UK. He also made the point that it had been a lack of resources in ancient China that had held it back from developing natural science. In Fei's last two papers he repeatedly stressed that the order of Chinese civilization is based on *li*-centred Confucian culture. Here the meaning of *li* is very broad, covering ceremony, gift, ritual, courtesy, propriety, rite, manners, proprieties, etc. Fei believed this philosophy of individual self-discipline promoted good social order. Coincidently, these two papers on civilization and *li* were published in 2004, when I obtained my PhD. It seemed to me that, although following different paths, we had arrived at a similar understanding of Chinese society as a civilization with *li*-centred cultural characteristics. In my own work I had explained these characteristics simply in term of *lishang-wanglai* (see Chang 2009, 2010).

Fei Xiaotong's ideas are shared with Professor Tu Weiming, Harvard-Yenching Professor of Chinese History and Philosophy and of Confucian Studies. In his lecture at the 16th Congress of the International Union of Anthropological and Ethnological Sciences last year, Tu pointed out that globalization is an extremely complex process. The enlightenment of neo-Confucianism in the East Asian communities shows that it can be helpful for reaching mutual understanding and tolerance between Eastern and Western cultures. Dialogue between different kinds of civilization should be developed as 'civilized dialogue'.

Hamilton: I am looking forward to reading your book, *Guanxi or Li shang wanglai?*, which I recently received. Even in advance of reading the book, I am fascinated by your efforts to extend Fei's theories in new directions. I am not surprised that Fei stressed the need for an analysis of societies at a civilizational level. I feel much the same way. In my recent writing, I am also trying to extend Fei's ideas to a civilizational level. More specifically, I am trying to pull together the sociological ideas of Fei with those of Max Weber, the great German sociologist who died in 1920. Although Fei does not mention Weber, his ideas are certainly compatible with Weber's notion that the 'principles of domination' best characterize a civilizational level of analysis. In my own work (Hamilton 2010), I suggest that institutions of domination in the West have a 'jurisdictional quality', meaning that legitimate authority in the West can be exercised only within prescribed organizational boundaries. This is *tuantigeju*. In China, however, I suggest that the institutions work according to the logic of relationships, which at the most basic level are controlled through what Confucius called *li*, which I define as a studied obedience to roles, to one's own roles as well as the observation of other's obedience to their roles. This is *chaxugeju*. Each principle of domination generates sets of distinctive institutions.

Chang: Thanks. Your own paper sounds very interesting; I will certainly read it. I don't know whether you are aware that Stephan has been making 'civilization' and notions linked to it a major topic for general anthropology. He and Professor Mike Rowlands of University College London gave a series of lectures on the subject in the Central University for Nationalities in 2007. These lectures were organized by Professor Mingming Wang, Peking University, and the lecture notes were published in the *Chinese Review of Anthropology*, edited by Mingming. Stephan also gave a lecture on 'The concept of civilization and civilization of China' at Fudan University last year (2009). In it he reviewed anthropological studies on civilization by Marcel Mauss and Marshall Sahlins, but didn't include Fei Xaiotong's work on the subject. I will introduce it in a section of my book on Fei's theoretical studies.

Research Methods

> **Question 1: Let us return to the comments made by Professor Fei's supervisor, the famous anthropologist Malinowski, in his preface to *Peasant Life in China*: 'I venture to foretell that [this book] will become a landmark in the development of anthropological field-work and theory.' In this book, Professor Fei turned the object of study from exotic research to local study and from primitive culture to economic life. How can we understand Professor Fei's research method and creative paradigm, which is so different from traditional studies?**

Hamilton: Professor Fei's *Peasant Life in China* was based on close, detailed fieldwork. This method was pioneered, in England, by Malinowski and others for anthropologists, and in the United States by Robert Park and others of the 'Chicago School of Sociology'. As a student, Fei studied with both scholars. He studied with Malinowski while working on his PhD degree at the London School of Economics (LSE), and he studied with Robert Park in 1934, when he was a student at Yanjing University. Recently retired from the University of Chicago, Park taught for a year in China. Both Malinowski and Park advocated fieldwork and close observation to understand the social world from the participants' points of view. Moreover, Park advised his students to study their own local society. Fei mastered this style of research and taught it to his students. It is from this style of research that all of Fei's chief contributions come.

Chang: According to philosophers and political economists, from the European Enlightenment onwards, human society has been seen as divided into three broad stages: savage, barbarian, and civilized. Early anthropologists based their research pathway on the twentieth-century version of this tripartite division, into primitive societies, ancient civilizations, and modern civilization (Stocking 1982, 1987). Fei's anthropological study of China in the autumn of 1935 started with the relatively primitive Yao Society. At that time, he was a postgraduate in sociology at *Tsinghua* University and carried out fieldwork with his new wife, Wang Tonghui. He got accidentally caught in one of the traps set by local hunters for animals, and his wife lost her life falling from a cliff on her way to seek help. This accident interrupted and certainly changed Fei's academic path. The next spring he went to Kaixiangong, where his sister Fei Dasheng had established a silk-manufacturing factory. Recuperating from this terrible event both physically and emotionally, he conducted a detailed field study of this Han village and received his PhD at the LSE with the thesis based on it, finalized as *Peasant Life in China* in 1939. In his own words, *Peasant Life in China* was an 'unintentional positive outcome' (*wu xin cha liu liu cheng yin*).

Hamilton: The tragic circumstances of Fei's early life made a deep impression on me. Out of tragedy came a new inspiration for life. Speaking of this 'unintentional positive outcome', I have always wondered how Fei was able to write his dissertation, *Peasant Life in China*, so quickly after arriving at the London School of Economics (LSE) and so well. He was only at LSE a very short time, and yet he accomplished so much.

Chang: Fei did fieldwork in Kaixiangong Village for two months, and then he spent a few weeks writing up his fieldwork notes on the ship to the UK. He completed his PhD at LSE in nearly two years under Malinowski and Firth's supervision. It saved a great deal of Fei's time to do literature reviews in English. There are four books on Chinese society written by Chinese scholars who studied in the UK and the USA, and I am sure you have read them: *Peasant Life in China* (1939), by Fei Hsiao-Tung; *A Chinese Village* (1945), by Martin C. Yang; *The Golden Wing* (1948), by Yao-hua Lin; and *Under the Ancestors' Shadow* (1948), by Francis L.K. Hsu. Sir Edmund Leach reviewed them in his *Social Anthropology* (1982). Methodologically, he was critical of scholars who know their native culture very well and may take advantage of it in their work; and of the attempt to generalize to the whole of China, and to a long Chinese history, based simply on one local study. Leach commented that Fei's work was the most successful not only because it was the earliest, but also because he was alert to quite subtle differences between the place where he grew up and the place where he conducted fieldwork, even though they were located in the same region.

The pros and cons of studying one's own native society have been of concern to Chinese scholars for decades. Outsiders studying China bring an extra dimension to their work, which comes from translating back to the languages and thought patterns of their own culture, usually Western. I raised the question of what intrinsic advantages there are in studying one's own society – which of course might be Chinese people studying China, or Europeans in Europe – when I was a discussant at Stephan's lecture on civilization at Fudan University. It remains a question.

> **Question 2: There are two research methods in sociology. One is content analysis, the other is field study. Professor Fei keenly advocated use of the latter. From his point of view, there are countless new problems and phenomena without ready approaches and solutions. Only by getting rid of prejudices, carrying out in-depth observation and understanding other ethnic cultures and civilizations could we go beyond stereotypes. There is no complicated jargon in his work, which tries 'to tell people the truth with understandable words and expressions'. What does this mean for sociology and anthropology in modern society? What methods do scholars adopt nowadays?**

Hamilton: A teacher of mine once said that one can divide social scientists into 'lumpers' and 'splitters'. On the one hand, lumpers put everything together and try to make one big pile. Most social scientists today are lumpers. They adopt a generalizing approach, which is based on formulating hypotheses and rigorously testing them using quantitative methods. They attempt to find what is generally true for the largest number of people, the big pile. On the other hand, splitters divide what they are examining, putting it into as many different piles as there are differences and as the analysis requires. Splitters look for differences between people, trying to find what is unique about this group or that group of people, and by systematically noting differences splitters develop comparisons based on contrasts. Splitters are much more unusual in social science because, in order to split human groups into different piles, you have to know a lot about different social groups and you have to get close enough to those groups to know what is distinctive about one group and what is not. In other words, you have to do fieldwork. Professor Fei was foremost a splitter. He looked closely at all groups that came into his vision, saw their differences, sought to explain those differences, and encouraged people to recognize each group's distinctiveness and to live in harmony.

Chang: 'Lumpers' and 'splitters' is a nice way of describing it. It is interesting to think of Professor Fei as a 'splitter'. It makes sense when we look at his concepts of 'the differential mode of association' for Chinese relationships, and the 'organizational mode of association' for Western relationships. His promulgation of the 'Southern Jiangsu model' for collective oriented economy, beside the 'Wenzhou model' for private oriented economy, shows a similar instinct to see theories and phenomena in localized terms. Methodologically, they can also been viewed as conceptualization or synthesis.

My training in the West under Stephan's supervision taught me that sociological research methods include quantitative and qualitative field research, secondary analysis of quantitative data, and qualitative or quantitative content analysis of media and other cultural products. For social scientific research one can gain data through indirect references or direct fieldwork or survey. There are different processes for dealing with data or materials: qualitative or quantitative, synthesis or analysis, conceptualization or scientific paradigm. Professor Fei's work looks like anthropological work based mainly on fieldwork or field visits and documentary studies, but the outcomes do not seem grounded in the rigorous process of data analysis characteristic of Western social scientific methodology. Fei's style of policy-oriented study with Chinese characteristics worked in China, though sometimes only for a short period. Perhaps this is why the huge numbers of policies in China are much more than laws and regulations, and are frequently changed. Such phenomena raise the question of whether they are due to social scientific methods in China being behind those in the Western countries, or rather to social scientific methods having been developed in studies made in Western societies and not acclimatized (*shui tu bu fu*) in a society like China.

Hamilton: It is true that Fei was not a methodologically rigorous sociologist by today's standards. However, we should not judge Fei's early work by today's standards. In the 1940s, survey research was just in its infancy, and quantitative techniques were quite primitive. Fei's fieldwork method was, for his time, an advanced empirical way to do research. If Fei had employed the quantitative techniques used today, I believe we would not be writing about him today. He would have slipped from our memory. Instead, we applaud his insights and his deep understanding of Chinese society. This understanding evades quantitative proofs. This reminds of a phrase I once read in Georg Simmel's work: 'To grasp the logical sense of things, more than logical sense is required.' That is what Fei had, a sympathetic understanding of those he studied that went beyond logical proofs.

Chang: I agree. I thought you might be interested in the following. Peking University held its 'Fei Xiaotong Memorial Lecture' in June. Professor George Marcus, UC Irvine, and Professor Judith B. Farquhar, Chicago University, both gave lectures: 'World Anthropologies Today: In Their Nationalist Traditions, Cosmopolitan Ethos, and Collaborative Possibilities' (will be published in next issue) and 'Localized Anthropology: China and Europe' respectively. This was followed by a one-day workshop which discussed issues such as how Chinese anthropologists participate in shaping world anthropology. It was coordinated by Professor Gao Bingzhong, who did post-doctoral research under Fei Xaiotong's supervision. Last year he chaired a panel 'Rewritten Culture in Chinese' at the 16th World Congress of the *International Union of Anthropological and Ethnological sciences in* Kunming. According to Gao, there were more than ten Chinese anthropologists conducting or having conducted fieldwork in countries outside China. Five of them had already published books on their fieldwork in Chinese: one on Thailand, one on Malaysia, one on the USA, and two books on India.

I remember how one of reviewers of *From the Soil* said that it seemed a waste of time and energy to put such effort into translating work Fei wrote in the 1940s, when there are so many better books by Chinese scholars of the present time waiting to be introduced to the world. I agree, but they are individual pieces, including the five books I mentioned just now. They are certainly helpful for offering different aperçus on Chinese society, but Fei Xiaotong's completed work is unique in providing an understanding of contemporary Chinese society as a whole.

> **Question 3: Professor Fei said that his lifelong motivation was to probe into Chinese society and cure social pains with reliable data from his own observation and scientific study, which gives his research great practical significance. How should we understand his exploration and analysis from the perspective of social science? What is the difference between Fei's perspective and that of other scholars?**

Hamilton: When he was a student, Fei wanted to be a social doctor, a doctor to help cure the ills of society. His faith in the usefulness of social science to help solve social problems did not diminish as he grew older. The project that he undertook in those fateful years after World War II, when he wrote *Xiangtu Zhongguo* and *Xiangtu chongjian*, showed his true character as a social doctor. He wanted all social remedies to be based on accurate social knowledge of the problem to be solved. Too often, reformers want to plan out a new world and put those plans into action with no knowledge of the society in which the plans are to be implemented. This is utopian thinking, and Professor Fei was no utopian. He was a pragmatist; he wanted programmes of action that would work in the contexts of people's lives, and to identify the right programmes for those people, you need in-depth knowledge about their society. Fei's sociological approach taught him always to be a reformer, never a revolutionary.

Chang: Perhaps this is why Fei Xiaotong was awarded the Malinowski Prize of the International Applied Anthropology Association. The conversation between Fei Xiaotong and Professor Burton Pasternak (*Pasternak* 1988) reinforced the general impression that these are the characteristics of Fei's research. In 1996 Stephan gave a talk at the ceremony for Fei Xiaotong's 60-year academic career in which he called attention to the difference between Fei's and Leach's approach to anthropology: he called his talk 'A practically minded person: Prof. Fei's anthropological calling and Edmund Leach's game' (will be published in next issue). This popular idea of Fei's work is of course based on the earlier and middle parts of his career. He wrote a great deal between his 80th birthday and his death at the age of 95. In my opinion, in his early career Fei Xiaotong, the 'social doctor', used Western medicines to cure social pains in China, and in his later life he tried to cure social pains in Western societies with Chinese medicines. Overall, Fei can be viewed as a combined Chinese and Western 'social doctor' who carried out missions to understand and help people everywhere and improve their living standards and surroundings.

Hamilton: What a nice way to end our dialogue! Yes, I agree. Early in his career, Fei may have used a social science inspired by Western academics to cure Chinese ills, but the more he worked in China, the more he saw the power of Chinese society to cure its own troubles and by extension to cure troubles elsewhere. We should remember Fei as a great humanitarian, as well as a great sociologist/anthropologist.

References[2]

常向群：《关系抑或礼尚往来？江村互惠、社会支持网和社会创造的研究》，毛明华译，辽宁人民出版社2009年12月出版。

Chang, Xiangqun. 2010. *Guanxi or li shang wanglai? Social support, reciprocity and social creativity in a Chinese village*. Taipei: Airiti Press Inc.

Fei, Hsiao-Tung. 1939. *Peasant Life in China: A Field Study of Country Life in a Yangze Valley*. London & Henley: Routledge & Kegan Paul.

费孝通：《乡土中国》，北京：三联书店，1948年版 [Xiangtu Zhongguo (From the soil), Beijing: SDX Joint Publishing Company. 1948].

—《乡土重建》，上海：上海观察社，1948年版 [Xiangtu Zhongguo (Reconstructing Rural China) Shanghai: Shanghai Guancha Publisher. 1948].

— 1989.《中国民族多元一体格局》，北京：中央民族大学出版社 [Zhonghua minzu duoyuan yiti geju (The pattern of Chinese nationalities'pluralistic unity). Beijing: Central University for Nationalities Publishing House].

— 1992. *From the Soil: The Foundations of Chinese Society* (trans.) G. Hamilton & Z. Wang. Berkeley: University of California Press.

— 1993.《八十自语》，见《逝者如斯》，苏州：苏州大学出版社 [Bashi ziyu (Soliloquy on the occasion of an 80th birthday), in *Shizhe ru si* (Essay collection). Suzhou: Suzhou University Publishing House].

— 2005.《"美美与共"和人类文明》，《群言》，第1期17-20页；第2期13-16页 ['Meimei yu gong' he renlei wenming (Common beauty and human civilization). *Quanyan* 1:17–20; 2:13–16].

— 2010a.《为和平生活做准备》，《费孝通全集》，第12卷，呼和浩特：内蒙古人民出版社，第59~66页 [Wei heping shenghuo zuo zhunbei (Preparing for a peaceful life): 59–66, in Fei Xiaotong: Quanji (Fei Xiaotong: Complete Works), vol. 12. Hohhot: Neimenggu People's Publishing House].

—2010b.《我从事社会学的经历》，《费孝通全集》，第12卷，呼和浩特：内蒙古人民出版社，第494-498页 [Wo congshi shehuixue de jingli (My experiences in a sociological career), in Fei Xiaotong: Quanji (Fei Xiaotong: Complete works), vol. 12: 494–498. Hohhot: Neimenggu People's Publishing House].

— 2010c.《关于建立长江三角洲经济开发区的初步设想》，《费孝通全集》，第13卷，呼和浩特：内蒙古人民出版社，第312-313页[Guanyu jianli changjiang sanjiaozhou jingji kaifaqu de chubu shexiang (Some tentative ideas on the establishment of the Yangtze River Delta Economic Zone), in Fei Xiaotong: Quanji (Fei Xiaotong: Complete works), vol. 13: 312–313. Hohhot: Neimenggu People's Publishing House].

—2010d.《经历·见解·反思 — 费孝通教授答客问》，《费孝通全集》，第12卷，呼和浩特：内蒙古人民出版社，第386-453页[Jingli ·Jianjie · Fansi (Experiences, opinions and reflections: A completed Chinese translation of a six-hour conversation with Burton Pasternak), vol. 12: 386–452. Hohhot: Neimenggu People's Publishing House].

— 2010e.《费孝通全集》，20卷，呼和浩特：内蒙古人民出版社 [Fei Xiaotong: Quanji (Fei Xiaotong: Complete works). 20 volumes. Hohhot: Neimenggu People's Publishing House.]

费孝通，王同惠：《花篮瑶社会组织》，上海：商务印书馆，1935年版 [Fei, X. and T. Wang 1936. Hualan yao shehui zuzhi (Hualan Yao social organization). Shanghai: Shangwu Yin Shu Guan].

王斯福：《社会自我主义与个体主义：一位西方的汉学人类学家阅读费孝通"中西对立"观念的惊讶与问题》，龚浩群、杨青青译，赵旭东校，《开放时代》，2009年第三期。

---

[2] The reason for including some references that we didn't use in this version, but did in the revised version (*Anthropology Today*, 2011. No. 6) is that the style of JCCP allows the Chinese references to be published bilingually.

Feuchtwang, Stephan. 2009. Social egoism and individualism: Surprises and questions that arise from reading Fei Xiaotong's idea of 'the opposition between East and West', 见马戎等编《费孝通与中国社会学和人类学》，第18-32页，北京：社科文献出版社[(The above article was published without translation in a Chinese book). pp18–32, in Ma, R. et al. (eds), *Fei Xiaotong and Sociology and Anthropology in China*. Beijing: Beijing Social Science Academic Press].

Freedman, M. 1963. A Chinese phase in social anthropology. *British Journal of Sociology* 14(1): 1–19.

Hall, E.T. 1976. *Beyond Culture*. New York: Doubleday.

Hamilton, G. 2010. World images, authority, and institutions: A comparison of China and the West. *European Journal of Social Theory* 13(1): 31–48.

韩格理、常向群：《从<江村经济>到<乡土中国>：纪念费孝通先生诞辰一百周年 (上)》，《中华读书报》，2010年11月3日 [Hamilton, G. and Chang, Xiangqun. 2010. Cong Jiangcun Jingji dao Xiangtu Zhongguo (From *Peasant Life in China* to *From the Soil*), translation by Chang, X et al, *China Reading Weekly*, No. 294: 3 November].

— 《美美与共，天下大同：纪念费孝通先生诞辰一百周年(下)》，《中华读书报》，2010年11月17日 [Hamilton, G. and Chang, Xiangqun. 2010. Meimei yu gong tianxia datong (Common beauty and unity of the world), translation by Chang, X et al China Reading Weekly, No. 295:17 November].

Kiser, E. & M. Hechter 1991. The role of general theory in comparative-historical sociology. *American Journal of Sociology* 97(1): 1–30.

Leach, E. 1982. *Social Anthropology*. Oxford: Oxford University Press.

Malinowski, B. 1939. Preface. In Fei, X. *Peasant Life in China: A Field Study of Country Life in a Yangze Valley*. London & Henley: Routledge & Kegan Paul.

Burton Pasternak. 1988. 'A Conversation with Fei Xiaotong', *CurrentAnthropology* 29: 637–662.

Simmel, G. 1950. *The Sociology of Georg Simmel*. Glencoe, Illinois: The Free Press: 354.

Weber, M. 1978. *Economy and Society*. Berkeley: University of California Press.

DOI https://doi.org/10.24103/GCSS2.en.2016.11.2

Comments on a dialogue about Fei Xiaotong's academic contributions

Bettina Gransow

Author's note: The dialogue on Fei Xiaotong's academic contributions between Gary Hamilton and Xiangqun Chang published in this issue, reminds me of my own experiences with some Chinese students on similar topics. I spent three years (2009–11) as a Visiting Professor at the School of Sociology and Anthropology at Sun Yat-sen University, China. I taught courses such as NGOs, Development and Anthropology, Social Scientific China Research, and so on, and engaged in discussions with students. In this comment I will address four points.

Peasant Life in China and the relationship between researchers and researchees

In your dialogue you are quoting Malinowski's preface to Fei's *Peasant Life in China*:

> I venture to foretell that *Peasant Life in China* by Dr. Hsiao-Tung Fei will be counted as a landmark in the development of anthropological fieldwork and theory. ... The book is not written by an outsider looking out for exotic impressions in a strange land; it contains observations carried on by a citizen upon his own people. It is the result of work done by a native among natives.... The book, moreover ...does not remain satisfied with the mere reconstruction of the static past. It grapples fully and deliberately with that most elusive and difficult phase of modern life: the transformation of traditional culture under Western impact (Malinowski 1939: xix).

I recently discussed this quotation with students majoring in anthropology at Sun Yat-sen University in Guangzhou. The context was Fei Xiaotong's contribution to applied anthropology and development anthropology in China and particularly the relationship between the researcher and the 'researchees' in Malinowski's writings and Fei's *Peasant Life in China* (1939). We started our discussion with a statement by Pan Tianshu, who stresses the role of Fei Xiaotong and his critical remarks regarding his teacher Malinowski (see below) as crucial for establishing a development anthropology 'with Chinese characteristics' (Pan 2009: 228).

I completely agree with you that this quotation from Malinowski can be seen as a starting point for describing Fei's later interest 'in a wide and vast civilized world', as you put it. Although Fei Xiaotong had by no means originally embarked on his study for such ambitious reasons, in the further course of his research activity – to the extent allowed by political conditions in China – he sought ways to provide a substantive basis for Malinowski's expectations (and – as I will discuss later – also for the expectations of another teacher, namely Wu Wenzao).

Fei's study represented an advance not only by virtue of examining a rural village (as part of a national context) as opposed to tribal societies, but also because it incorporated precisely that proximity between researcher and 'researchee' that Malinowski himself had never been able to generate in his own field research. Given his cultural distance from the 'natives' that formed his object of study, the method of participatory observation that he developed ran up against an insurmountable barrier. Fei's advantage initially consisted of collecting facts in and about a society from which he came, whose local dialect he knew, and to which he had a positive connection via his sister and her active reform project. The social or intellectual distances that still existed were nothing in comparison to Malinowski's research situation, which was limited by general colonial conditions – regardless of whether Malinowski himself identified with the aims of the British colonial system (Hsu 1980) or had a compromised relationship with it based on his self-image as an intermediary (Kohl 1987: 57).

According to Fei, Malinowski envied his research conditions, which seemed so much more satisfactory in respect of both the access to information and the personal situation (Fei 1981: 9). These different research conditions were what made Malinowski describe Fei's study as a milestone or landmark – i.e. a demarcation along a linear progression – in the history of social anthropology. But there was another difference, one which Malinowski himself did not or perhaps could not reflect upon, namely personal motivation. In contrast to other sociological studies and especially to Malinowski's work, Fei reports that he was interested not so much in the condition or the history of people, but rather in the people themselves and thus in the consequences of those very studies (Fei 1981: 9ff.). Fei locates the source of Malinowski's frustration not in the possibility of the latter experiencing an ethnocentric sense of superiority but rather in the fact that his studies lack any significance for the 'objects' of his study. After all, what became of the Trobriand Islanders? Malinowski's interest, Fei noted, was not in the living individuals but rather in their history and their relationships. What remained was 'the mere shadow of these people dancing under my tutor's pen nib' (Fei 1981: 9ff.).

The crucial difference that Fei himself saw between his own research and previous social anthropological studies did not lie in the more favourable conditions brought by social scientists who know the local dialect, come from the same area, and in the best case enjoy good personal relationships with the community being studied, but rather, and especially, in a new quality to the relationship between researchers and 'researchees', in shared motivations and aims to improve the living conditions of the (local) population. In David Arkush's interpretation Fei viewed social research as a means of controlling and guiding processes of social transformation induced from outside, in contrast to Malinowski's 'romantic escapism', which tended to emphasize maintenance as opposed to change of native culture (cf. Arkush 1981: 55ff.). A sense of responsibility is an integral part of Fei's research. Here is where Fei sees the actual and liberating turn (not landmark) that his 'Jiangcun' study represented in the history of social anthropology. Therefore, Fei construes 'applied anthropology... as a science that concerns itself with the transformation of human society via knowledge of the social studies' (Fei 1981: 3). Emphasizing Malinowski's part in creating this type of applied anthropology only barely disguises the break that Fei made from his teacher's understanding of science.

Pragmatic approach or theoretical programme?

A concern for the living conditions of the researchees should nevertheless not be confused with a pragmatic approach. Identifying with an academic community study approach, Fei distanced himself from the various reform projects going on during the 1930s. Examples are Yan Yangchu's educational reform project in Dingxian with Li Jinghan's social surveys as a mainly quantitative approach, or the philosophical reform project undertaken by Liang Shuming in Zouping, Shandong Province, where Fei, I think, turned down an offer to participate. This becomes clearer when looking at the role of Fei's teacher, Wu Wenzao.

Wu Wenzao (1901–1985), the éminence grise of Chinese community research who himself belonged to the first generation of Chinese sociologists, devoted sustained efforts in the 1930s to establishing a systematic link between sociology and anthropology. He was interested in combining field research à la Malinowski with the Chicago School's approaches to community studies, emphasizing especially Radcliffe-Brown's idea of comparative sociology (cf. Kuper 2003: 363). Given the extreme spectrum of social and cultural relations in China, he thought that comparative sociology should focus on juxtaposing different Chinese communities, starting with those in the coastal regions, which at that point were under direct Western influence, and extending to those in relatively untouched areas in the interior of the country (Sun 1940: 259).

For reasons less political than methodological, Wu Wenzao and the faculty of the social anthropology wing[1] of the sociology department at Yanjing University dissociated themselves explicitly from the social survey approach. Although they, too, recognized the fundamental need for social reforms in Chinese society, they sharply criticized the quantitive surveys for what they viewed as unscientific methodology. Neither did they support the dovetailing of science and social work, of university and administration. Wu Wenzao became dean of the sociology department at Yanjing University in the mid-1930s, replacing Xu Shilian, who

---

[1] It was particularly because of Wu Wenzao's programme of linking sociology and anthropology that I spoke of a social anthropology wing of the sociology department at Yanjing University (see Chiang Yung-chen's criticism of my 'renaming his "sociology wing"' (Chiang 2001: 46, fn.1; Gransow 1992).

had given the department a social-work orientation. In the second half of the 1930s, Wu initiated a sea change in sociological research in China. Influenced by social anthropology in Great Britain and the United States, he criticized the lack of scientific autonomy in social survey methodology up to that point and stressed the advantages of social–anthropological community studies. Wu Wenzao supported a systematic linking of sociology and anthropology in China and saw the introduction of functionalistic community studies as the appropriate path towards a sinicization of sociology. He worked towards a comparative methodology[2] to relate the different developmental stages within Chinese society to one another. Wu argued that sinicization was possible for sociology only after independent scientific competence had been developed, which could be identified through a scientifically founded hypothesis and verified by field research. Many of his students achieved international acclaim, among them Lin Yuehua (*The Golden Wing,* 1944), Yang Qingkun (C.K. Yang) (*A Chinese Village in Early Communist Transition,* 1959), and Xu Langguang (Francis L.K. Hsu) (*Under the Ancestor's Shadow,* 1948).

   The foundation for this type of comparative sociology was to be provided by ethnographic studies of tribal societies in border or colonial areas, studies by agrarian sociologists of village communities in the interior or of emigrant communities, and studies by urban sociologists of municipal communities on the east coast of China (Wu Wenzao 1982: 48). As Wu Wenzao described it, comparative sociology thus comprises agrarian sociology and urban sociology, social anthropology and cultural anthropology, and ethnology or folklore studies. The cornerstones of its conceptual matrix (*gainian geju*) are the notions of community, culture, system, and function (Wu Wenzao 1944: 1ff.). This type of programme extended far beyond the capabilities of individual scientists, and Wu spent a lot of energy establishing a broader basis for implementing his ideas, by such means as acquiring funding sources and channelling targeted support to his students. The fact that this approach succeeded only up to a point was due initially to the chaotic nature of the war period and subsequently to political restrictions. Wu Wenzao's research programme also helps us to a certain degree to understand better Fei Xiaotong's later research on small towns and the links between *Peasant Life in China* and his later research.

---

[2] Wu's methodology followed Radcliffe-Brown (1937).

Small-town research

In *Peasant Life in China*, Fei describes the village of Kaixiangong (Jiangsu Province), the name of which he changed to 'River Village' (Jiangcun), as a harmoniously functioning cultural unit into which conflicts were introduced from outside. Fei understood social change here as the destruction of social harmony leading to confusion in social roles. For him, culture was not an expression of national essence, as it was for e.g. Sun Benwen, but rather – entirely in accord with the social–anthropological school – functionally conditioned, i.e. he started with the assumption that specific cultural forms would disappear as they lost their functions. In order for culture to fulfil its function of adaptation, reforms must be based on a functional analysis of existing institutions or customs.

Following up on his earlier research, Fei later refined his theory of rural industrialization as a modernization strategy suitable for China and added a concept of rural urbanization. The small-town studies by Fei Xiaotong are outstanding among the empirical projects of the initial phase of reviving Chinese sociology after the opening up of the country at the beginning of the 1980s (Fei 1984; Fei Hsiao-Tung et al. 1986). Based on a functionalistic analysis of local economic traditions, paths of modernization were sought in which (spontaneous) micro developments and (regulated) macro developments were adapted to each other. At the same time it represented an implicit attempt to extract elements for a theory of adapted modernization from an empirical analysis of the revival of traditional economic activities. The project was also a starting point for a number of studies on rural industry, conducted in cooperation with the World Bank.

Xiangtu Zhongguo and *chaxugeju*

This lecture series is a brilliant piece of thick description of the rural Chinese society at the time and an extraordinary example of comparing Chinese and Western cultures. I came across *Xiangtu Zhongguo* in the mid-1980s and gave a reading class on the text at FU Berlin. I was also fascinated by the text and during a research stay in Hong Kong at the beginning of the 1990s I learned that this booklet was a kind of broadly shared secret knowledge of the Chinese-language social science community in the Greater China region. So I very much welcomed the English translation by Gary Hamilton and Wang Zheng, because it introduced the text to the international social science community and because it made it much easier for me to discuss the 'Fei Xiaotong complex' in class. I also liked the translation of the title as 'From the soil', because the translation as 'Earthbound China' was always leading to confusion with Fei Hsiao-Tung and Chang Chih-I's *Earthbound China: A Study of Rural Economy in Yunnan* (London, 1945).

On translating and introducing *chaxugeju* in class I normally use Fei's metaphor of the stone thrown into the water with rings spreading around it for the Chinese egocentric network pattern and the straw bundle for the Western mode of individual association in organizations. Although I find Fei's lecture series very appealing, from today's perspective this kind of comparison of cultures appears to essentialist cultures as static and to highlight the dualism between tradition/China and modernity/West. Today it has become necessary to frame the entanglement of cultures in a dynamic pattern from a global perspective that takes into account the fact that more and more people are living out of context (as Clifford Geertz once put it). Maybe this is something that comes close to Fei's idea of the 'pattern of pluralist unity' that you are identifying in *Xiangtu Zhongguo*.

References

Arkush, David. 1981. *Fei Hsiao-tung and Sociology in Revolutionary China*. Cambridge: Harvard University Press.

Chiang Yung-chen. 2001. *Social Engineering and the Social Sciences in China 1919–1949*. Cambridge: Cambridge University Press.

Fei Hsiao-tung. *Peasant Life in China. A Field Study of Country Life in the Yangtze Valley*. New York: E. P. Dutton & Company.

费孝通:《乡土中国》, 北京: 三联书店1985年版 [Fei Xiaotong. 1985. Xiangtu Zhongguo (*Rural China*), Beijing: Sanlian Shudian].

— 《小城镇, 大问题: 江苏省小城镇研究论文选》, 南京: 江苏人民出版社1984年版 [Fei Xiaotong. 1984. *Xiao chengzhen, da wenti. Jiangsu sheng xiao chengzhen yanjiu lunwen xuan* (Small Towns, Big Problems. Collection of articles containing research on small towns in Jiangsu province). Nanjing: Jiangsu People's Press].

Fei Xiaotong. 1992. *From the Soil: The Foundations of Chinese Society*. A translation of Fei Xiaotong's *Xiangtu Zhongguo* with an introduction and an epilogue by Gary Hamilton and Wang Zheng. Berkeley: University of California Press.

Fei Hsiao-Tung and Chang Chih-I. 1945. *Earthbound China: A Study of Rural Economy in Yunnan*. London: Routledge & Kegan Paul.

Fei Hsiao Tung. 1981. *Toward a People's Anthropology*. Beijing: New World Press.

Fei Hsiao Tung et al. 1986. *Small Towns in China—Functions, Problems & Prospects*. Beijing: New World Press.

Gransow, Bettina. 1983. *Soziale Klassen und Schichten in der Volksrepublik China* (Social Classes and Strata in the PR China). Theoretische Transformationskonzepte und reale Entwicklungsformen von 1949 – 1979 unter besonderer Beruecksichtigung der staedtischen Arbeiterklasse, Muenchen : Minerva Publikation Saur.

— 1992. *Geschichte der chinesischen Soziologie*. Frankfurt / New York: Campus.

Hsu, Francis L.K. 1980. 'Malinowskiana. A Reply to Dr. E.R. Leach', in *Royal Anthropological Institute News*, Vol. 38.

Kohl, Karl-Heinz. 1987. *Abwehr und Verlangen. Zur Geschichte der Ethnologie*. Frankfurt/Main: Qumran.

Kuper, Adam. 2003. 'Anthropology', in Theodore M. Porter and Dorothy Ross. eds. *The Cambridge History of Science*. Vol. 7. The Modern Social Sciences, Cambridge: Cambridge University Press: 354–378.

Malinowski. 1939. 'Preface', Fei Hsiao-tung. *Peasant Life in China. A Field Study of Country Life in the Yangtze Valley*. New York: E.P. Dutton & Company.

潘天舒:《发展人类学概论》, 上海: 华东科技大学出版社, 2009年版 [Pan, Tianshu. 2009. Fazhan Renleixue Gailun (Development Anthropology Outline), Shanghai: East China Technical University Press].

Radcliffe-Brown, Alfred. 1937. Proposals for a Sociological Survey of Village Life in China. *Shehui yanjiu* (*Social Research*) Vol.1, 2: 4f., 9 (Guangzhou).

孙以芳：《中国社会学的发展》，北京：燕京大学社会学论文，1940年 [Sun, Yifang. 1940. Zhongguo shehuixue de fazhan (The Development of Chinese Sociology). Thesis, Beijing: Yanjing University].

吴文藻：《社会学丛刊总序》，见马凌诺斯基《文化论》，1944年，重庆 [Wu, Wenzao. 1944. Shehuixue congkan zongxu (Introduction to a Sociology book series), in Malinuosiji (Malinowski). Wenhua Lun (*Theory of Culture*). Chongqing].

— 《吴文藻自传》，《晋阳学刊》，1982年第 6期：44–52页 [Wu Wenzao. 1982. Wu Wenzao Zizhuan (Autobiography of Wu Wenzao), *Jinyang Journal* (*Taiyuan*) No. 6: 44–52].

DOI https://doi.org/10.24103/GCSS2.en.2016.12

Appendix C

Important Conferences Held 2015–2016 to Commemorate the 80th Anniversary of Fei Xiaotong's Fieldwork in Dayao Mountain and Kaixiangong Village

18-19 October 2015, Chinese Social Science Forum: International Conference on Theoretical and Methodologic Innovation and Development of Ethnology and Anthropology to commemorate Mr. Fei Xiaotong's 80th Anniversary of Fieldwork in Dayao Mountain, Beijing, organized by the Academy of Social Sciences, CASS Institute of Ethnology and Anthropology, and International Cooperation Bureau.

8-10 July 2016, The Second Symposium of Fei Xiaotong's Academic Thinking to commemorate Mr. Fei Xiaotong's 80th Anniversary of Fieldwork in Kaixiangong Village, and book series lunch of *Studies of Fei Xiaotong Thought*, Shanghai. It was organised by the Chinese Sociological Association, the CASS Institute of Sociology, Shanghai University, China Democratic League Shanghai Municipal Committee, the Research Center for Fei Xiaotong Academic Thought, Shanghai University, Society, etc.

22-23 October 2016, Village Fieldwork and Chinalization of Social Sciences to commemorate Professor Fei Xiaotong's 80th Anniversary of Fieldwork in Kaixiangong Village, organised by the Sociology Department of Peking University, School of Social and Behaviour Science of Nanjing University, Propaganda Department of CCP Wujiang City, etc.

DOI https://doi.org/10.24103/GCSS2.en.2016.13

Appendix D

Speech at the Symposium of Philosophy and Social Sciences (17th May 2016)

Xi Jinping[1]

Xi Jinping, General Secretary of the CPC Central Committee, President of the PRC, Chairman of the PRC Central Military Commission, chaired the symposium on philosophy and Social Sciences, and delivered an important speech on May 17 in Beijing.

Today we are holding a symposium on philosophy and social sciences. Most of the attendees are Chinese experts and scholars in the philosophy and social sciences. Some of them are prestigious senior experts and academics with remarkable achievements to their name, others are promising young talents, and they include consultants or leading experts in Marxist studies and construction projects, representatives of Chinese high-level think tanks, PhDs, university graduates and undergraduates and the heads of relevant departments. First and foremost, please accept my warm greetings to all those who are engaged in philosophy and social sciences in China.

Since the 18th National Congress of the CPC, in order to strengthen and improve the work of propaganda and thoughts, as well as culture and theoretical research, the Central Committee has held a series of conferences such as the National Conference of Propaganda and Thought Work, the Forum on Literature and Arts, the Symposium on News and Public Opinion and the Cybersecurity and Informatization Work Conference: I have delivered speeches on all of these occasions. The purpose of these meetings and conferences is to listen to opinions from all quarters, to analyse the situation collaboratively, to communicate ideas, to gather common consensus and to plan for the future.

Philosophy and social sciences are important tools by which to know and reform the world. They are important forces in advancing historical development and social progress. The level of development of the philosophy and social

---

[1] Translated by Anna Zhenping Yu (余珍萍), translator of CCPN Global

sciences reflects a nation's capacity for thought, its spiritual character and the quality of its civilization and mirrors its comprehensive power and international competitiveness. The development of a country depends on that of both natural sciences and philosophy and social sciences. A country cannot take the lead in the world without advanced natural sciences; nor can it take the lead in the world without flourishing philosophy and social sciences. We must uphold and develop socialism with Chinese characteristics, continuously exploring in both practice and theory, and guiding the practice with developing theory. Philosophy and social sciences play an important and irreplaceable role in this process, and so do researchers working in these fields.

The speakers have just made wonderful presentations, which were insightful, heartfelt and very inspiring. Now I will present my views on some issues, which I wish to communicate and discuss with all of you.

First Issue: Great importance should be attached to philosophy and social sciences in adhering to and developing socialism with Chinese characteristics

Engels said, 'A nation cannot go without theoretical thinking if it wants to be at the peak of science.' The Chinese Communist Party has always valued philosophy and social sciences. At the time of the revolutionary war, Mao Zedong said, 'We must use social sciences to understand society, transform society and carry out social revolution.' Mao Zedong was a great philosopher, thinker and social scientist. His famous philosophical writings, including *On Contradiction* and *On Practice*, still have instructive significance. Many of his well-known investigations and studies made a penetrating analysis of Chinese society and are regarded as classic works of social sciences. During the new era of economic reforms and opening up, Deng Xiaoping pointed out, 'Science certainly includes social sciences,' and, 'Research into politics, the law, sociology and world politics has been neglected in the past. Now is the time to make up for this lost learning.' Jiang Zemin indicated, 'During the process of understanding and reforming the world, philosophy and social sciences and natural sciences are equally important. It is also important to foster high standards for both philosophical social scientists and natural scientists. It is equally important to enhance the whole nation's disposition for both philosophy and social sciences and natural sciences. Both philosophical social scientists and natural scientists should be appointed to appropriate positions in order to give full scope to their professional knowledge.' Hu Jintao said, 'In response to intense and wide-ranging international competition between national powers and in order to continuously strengthen China's economic power, we must also enhance Chinese cultural creativity and national cohesive force, and increase the influence of Chinese civilization. There is an urgent need to develop academic discipline systems and academic thoughts with Chinese characteristics in philosophy and social sciences.' Since the 18th National Congress of the CPC, the Central

Committee has continued to issue policies and take measures aimed at greatly enhancing the development of philosophy and social sciences.

Modern Chinese philosophy and social sciences should be observed from a broader perspective, in the context of the history of the world and of Chinese development. No great leap in human society or important development in human civilization would have taken place without advances in knowledge and pioneering thoughts in philosophy and social sciences. From the perspective of Western history, the ideas of Socrates, Plato, Aristotle and Cicero came into being in ancient Greece and ancient Rome. During the Renaissance, there were Dante, Boccaccio, da Vinci, Raphael, Copernicus, Bruno, Galileo, Shakespeare, Sir Thomas More, Campanella and other famous cultural scholars and thinkers, many of whom were giants in literature and the arts. Their works were deeply infused with their thoughts about social construction. Around the time of the Industrial Revolution in England, the French Revolution and the American War of Independence, a lot of capitalist thinkers whose ideas and views reflected the new capitalists' political demands came into prominence, such as Hobbes, Locke, Voltaire, Montesquieu, Rousseau, Diderot, Helvetius, Paine, Jefferson, Hamilton and others. The creation of Marxism was a great event in the history of human thought. Marxism critically absorbed the philosophical thoughts of Kant, Hegel and Feuerbach, the utopian socialism of Saint-Simon, Fourier and Owen, the classical school of political economy founded by Adam Smith, David Ricardo and so on. Without the development of European philosophy and social sciences in the 18th and 19th centuries, there would have been no possibility for the emergence and development of Marxism. In the 20th century, social conflicts intensified. In order to soften social contradictions and repair the disadvantages within the system, various schools of thought brought forth new ideas, including Keynesianism, neoliberalism, neoconservatism, democratic socialism, pragmatism, existentialism, structuralism and postmodernism, which were both products of the development of the Western societies and deeply influenced them.

Chinese civilization has a very long history, with several periods rich in academic thought, such as the academic thoughts of pre-Qin thinkers, the classical study of Confucianism in the two Han dynasties, Xuanxue philosophy or the metaphysics of the Wei and Jin dynasties, Buddhism in the Sui and Tang dynasties, the integration of Confucianism, Buddhism and Taoism, and neo-Confucianism in the Song and Ming dynasties. During this long history, different schools of thought appeared, such as the Confucian, Buddhist and Taoist doctrines, Mozi and the teachings of Mohism, the Logicians of the Warring States period, the Legalists, the theory of yin and yang, the academic group reflecting agricultural production and the ideas of farmers of the Warring States period, the pre-Qin synthesis integrating all the different schools of thought and the philosophy of war, and more besides. There were thinkers who left an extensive cultural heritage, such as Laozi, Confucius, Zhuang Zi, Mencius, Xun Zi Han Fei, Dong Zhongshu,

Wang Chong, He Yan, Wang Bi, Han Yu, Zhou Dunyi, Cheng Hao, Cheng Yi, Zhu Xi, Lu Jiuyuan, Wang Shouren, Li Zhi, Huang Zongxi, Gu Yanwu, Wang Fuzhi, Kang Youwei, Liang Qichao, Sun Zhongshan and Lu Xun. Those great ancient Chinese writings included rich ideas on the philosophy and social sciences, as well as the wisdom of state governance, which provided important foundations for ancient people to understand and transform the world. They also contributed greatly to Chinese civilization and to human civilization in general.

After the Opium Wars, foreign powers invaded China, forcing it to open itself to the world. China gradually became a semi-feudal and semi-colonial country, and Western thought, culture, science and technology swept in. From then on, China and the Chinese nation underwent a painful period of history, in which traditional Chinese culture and thought underwent drastic changes. In order to seek ways of survival and avoid destruction, people such as Lin Zexu, Wei Yuan and Yan Fu turned to the West, going from 'learning from the technologies in the West in order to resist the invasion of Western powers' to the idea of 'Chinese essence and Western utility', which entailed keeping Chinese traditional thought, culture and systems as the foundation while simultaneously introducing and applying advanced Western science and technology. There was a 'Chinese Westernization Movement' at the end of Qing Dynasty and the 'New Culture Movement'. Western philosophy and social sciences were translated and introduced into China. Quite a few scholars began to study China's social problems with a modern social scientific approach. Different disciplines in social sciences were gradually developed.

As the cannon blasts marked the start of the October Revolution, Marxism and Leninism were introduced into China. Chen Duxiu, Li Dazhao and others actively disseminated Marxism and advocated using Marxism in reforming Chinese society. Many advanced scholars applied Marxism in their research on the philosophy and social sciences. In the long period of practice and exploration that followed, a series of famous scholars emerged, such as Guo Moruo, Li Da, Ai Siqi, Jian Bozan, Fan Wenlun, Lu Zhenyu, Ma Yinchu, Fei Xiaotong and Qian Zhongshu, all of whom made pioneering efforts in the development of China's modern philosophy and social sciences. These sciences were based on Marxism from the time when it was introduced into China and gradually developed under its guidance.

At present, China's academic discipline system in philosophy and social sciences is becoming more sound and better organized. Research teams are expanding and research standards and creative ability are increasing steadily. Many achievements have been made in Marxist theoretical research and construction. Vast numbers of people engaged in the philosophy and social sciences have emancipated their minds and are seeking to draw out the truth from the facts so as to advance with the times. They adhere to Marxism as their guide and uphold the policy of serving the people and socialism. In line with the policy of 'letting a hundred flowers bloom and a hundred schools of thought contend', they make rigorous studies and try to address the important theoretical and practical issues the CPC faces in the development of our country. They have achieved a great amount and made huge contributions to upholding and developing socialism with Chinese characteristics.

Under these new circumstances, the status of China's philosophy and social sciences seems more important, and their mission weightier and more arduous. The choice of social ideological concepts and values tends to be more dynamic and exciting. The mainstream and non-mainstream co-exist, and the social trends of thought are more diverse and complex. There is an urgent need to give philosophy and social sciences full play in consolidating the leading position of Marxism in the ideological field, fostering and practising socialist core values, solidifying the common ideological foundation to encourage the Party and people all over the country to unite and work vigorously together. In the new era, China's economic development has become a new normality and the international developmental environment has undergone rapid changes. Therefore, philosophy and social sciences should play their full role in implementing new developmental ideas, in speeding up the transformation of economic developmental methods, in heightening developmental quality and performance, in better guaranteeing and improving the living standards of the people and in promoting social justice and fairness. Faced with the new situation in which Chinese reforms have entered a period of overcoming major difficulties and a deep-water zone, with various contradictions and problems appearing at a deep level and different kinds of risks and challenges increasing, philosophy and social sciences are expected to operate more effectively and fully in enhancing the standard of reform and policy-making and modernizing the state's system and capacity of governance. Under the new global circumstances, in which all kinds of ideological and cultural ideas communicate, converge and clash, philosophy and social sciences should urgently seek to exert their influence in quickening the building of socialist cultural power, increasing its cultural soft power and enhancing its discursive power globally. In the new situation in which the CPC is strictly and comprehensively managing discipline within the Party as it faces risks and challenges, philosophy and social sciences should waste no time in developing their role in increasing the Party's leading and governing standards, strengthening the Party's capacity to resist corruption and risks and prevent upheavals, and assuring the Party's position as the core leadership in the cause of socialism with Chinese characteristics. All in all, to uphold and develop socialism with Chinese characteristics, to plan the 'Five Constructions of economy, politics, culture, society and ecology' as a whole, to enhance harmoniously the 'Four Comprehensives of a moderately prosperous society, deepening reform, the rule of law and governing the Party' in order to realize the 'Two Centenary (foundation of the Party and the PRC, 1921–2021, 1949–2049, respectively) Goals' and attain the Chinese Dream of great rejuvenation of the Chinese nation – in all of these, philosophy and social sciences can play a leading role.

      In facing these new demands, there are still issues needing to be addressed urgently in the field of philosophy and social sciences. For example, the developmental strategy of philosophy and social sciences is not clear. The overall level of development in the scheme of academic disciplines, a canon of academic historical and practical knowledge and a framework for traditional discourse remains low. . The capacity for academic creativity is not strong. Systems of training, fostering and teaching in philosophy and social sciences are incomplete and imperfect. Academic evaluation is not scientific. The management and operational mechanisms are not perfect. The overall quality of scholars needs improving. There are significant problems in academic atmosphere and discipline. Generally speaking, the quantity is sufficient but the quality is insufficient in China's philosophy and social sciences. We have experts but we lack great masters in the field. The role of philosophy and social sciences is underplayed. To reverse this status, the large numbers of those engaged in the philosophy and social sciences should redouble their efforts in order to make significant progress in addressing the prominent issues affecting the development of these sciences in China.

      History demonstrates that an era of great social transformations is one of great development for philosophy and social sciences. Contemporary China is experiencing unprecedented profound and widespread social changes and carrying out the most enormous and extraordinary exercise in practice and creativity in human history. This unprecedented great practice provides a strong impetus and vast scope for theoretical creativity and academic prosperity. Our era needs theory, and theories are bound to come into existence in this era. Our era needs thoughts, and thoughts are bound to come into existence in this era. We should live up to the expectations of the times. From ancient times, Chinese intellectuals have maintained this ambition and tradition – 'Be determined to establish a whole set of ethical values accepted universally, to secure life and a future for the people and to pursue the rare, lost knowledge of past scholars, to establish peace for all future generations.' All philosophical social scientists who have lofty aspirations and ambitions should lead the trend of the times, thoroughly comprehend ancient and present changes and also be the heralds of new ideas. They should actively comment and present their arguments, expressing their views and submitting advice for the Party and the people to undertake the glorious mission that history bestows upon them.

Second Issue: Upholding the leading position of Marxism in the field of China's philosophy and social sciences

To adhere to Marxism as a guide is the fundamental feature that distinguishes contemporary China's philosophy and social sciences from others, and we must have a clear-cut stance on this.

Although Marx was born over a century and half ago, history and reality prove that his theory is a scientific one and shows great vitality even today. Marxism exposes the general laws of nature, human society and the development of human thinking and provides the correct direction for the development and progress of human society. Marxism insists on the liberation of the people and on defending people's interests. It regards gaining freedom for the people to achieve overall development and emancipating the whole of mankind as its responsibility. It reveals the beautiful longing of humanity for an ideal society. It discovers the essence of things, their inherent ties and developmental laws. It is a 'great epistemological tool'. It is a powerful thinking weapon for people to observe and analyse the world. It has the distinctive feature of practice and aims at not only scientifically 'explaining the world' but also at positively 'changing the world'. Never in the ideological history of humanity has such a theory as Marxism evolved which has had such a vast and extensive impact on the progress of human civilization.

The introduction of Marxism into China was a trigger for both drastic changes in Chinese civilization and the gradual process of the sinicization of Marxism. At different historical stages of revolution, construction and reformation, the CPC adhered to the policy of combining Marxist fundamental principles with Chinese practice. The CPC applied a Marxist stance, views and epistemology to study and address important theoretical and practical issues and enhance the sinicization of Marxism. As a result, Mao Zedong's Thoughts, Deng Xiaoping's Theory, the 'Three Representatives', the 'Scientific Outlook on Development' and other theories came into existence. The Party and the Chinese people attained the great successes of the New Democratic Revolution, the Socialist Revolution and construction, reforms and opening up. In China's philosophy and social sciences, the application of Marxism as a guide is a prescription and a necessity in modern Chinese history. Without Marxism as our guide, philosophy and social sciences will lose their 'soul' and their way and will not play their role. As the saying goes, 'If one wants to learn Daoism, one should not learn and think about other things. Otherwise one's mind is filled with miscellaneous ideas, and one becomes confused. The more confused one is, the more upset one becomes. Then one becomes hopeless. So it is better to focus on one doctrine.'

Although the sinicization of Marxism scored great successes, the task remains incomplete. One of the most overwhelming tasks in China's philosophy and social sciences is to continuously enhance the sinicization, modernization and popularization of Marxism, thereby developing Marxism in the 21st century and Marxism in contemporary China.

The great majority of comrades are sober-minded and steadfast in upholding Marxism as our guide. But there are a few who do not have a thorough and complete comprehension of Marxism. The lack skill in the application of the Marxist stance, viewpoints and methods; the lack high-level achievements; they do not yet have all the skills for establishing a scheme of academic disciplines, a canon of academic historical and practical knowledge and a framework for traditional discourse, using Marxism as their guide. Some vague and even erroneous understandings still exist. Marxism is regarded as out of date and not pursued in China; Marxism is thought to be mere ideological preaching and non-systematic, deficient in academic and scientific theoretical rigour. In practice, in some fields, Marxism is marginalized, generalized and over-simplified. Marxism is outside the discourse of mainstream disciplines, 'missing' from teaching materials and 'losing its voice' in the forums. This situation demands our close attention.

Marxism still exerts an important influence on the Western world. At the beginning of this century, Marx was esteemed in the West as the 'first thinker in a thousand years'. The American scholar Robert Heilbroner expressed in his book *Marxism, For or Against* that advice and consultation should be sought from Marx in order to explore the developmental prospects of human society, whose laws Marx expounded. The practice also proves that, no matter how many rapid changes there are with the times and no matter how much progress the science has made, Marxism continues to show its great scientific force in ideology and occupies the commanding heights of truth and morality. Deng Xiaoping pointed out, 'I firmly believe that more and more people will favour Marxism because Marxism is a science.'

China's vast number of philosophical social scientists should consciously uphold Marxism as their guide, apply the socialist theoretical system with Chinese characteristics throughout their research and teaching and transform it into a sober theoretical consciousness, firm political beliefs and a scientific way of thinking.

In upholding Marxism as our guide, first we must make sure that we truly understand and firmly believe in it. The development status of philosophy and social sciences is closely related to our world outlook and the research epistemology. We can better observe and explain those phenomena of the natural world, human society and human thinking, exposing the laws in them, when we have the correct outlook on the world and epistemology. Marxist principles on the materialism of the world, human society and the essence of epistemology and their respective developmental laws provide the fundamental outlook on the world and epistemology in the study and mastery of every field and every discipline in philosophy and social sciences. Only through a thorough understanding of Marxism can we gain new ideas in revealing the Party's governing law, socialist construction law and human societal development law, distinguishing all kinds of idealism and withstanding the fallacies of all kinds of nihilism.

The classical Marxist writers had broad visions and profound erudition. Marxist theoretical and knowledge systems are broad, extensive and profound, covering numerous fields in nature, human society, human thinking, as well as all aspects of history, economics, politics, culture, society, ecology, science and technology, military affairs and the building of the Party etc. It is impossible to grasp its true essence and gain a thorough understanding without the greatest effort and hard work. As the famous Chinese sayings go, 'Thinking is the root and foundation in learning,' and, 'One does not know the truth if one does not think profoundly. One can easily lose what is learnt without deep thought.' I have read some books on Marxism by those who have studied it in the West. Their conclusions are not necessarily correct, but their study and textual criticism of Marxist texts are careful and solid. By contrast, some Chinese researchers' work is insufficiently thorough. Engels once said, 'The development of materialist views just on a simple historical case is a piece of scientific work that requires many years' intensive and dispassionate study. Obviously empty talk is of no use at all. We can only fulfil this task by critically reviewing and fully understanding a large amount of historical information.' In the study and research of Marxism, we cannot adopt this attitude of stopping after making minimal effort and gaining just a little knowledge, or going into the matter superficially like a dragonfly skimming over the water. There are a few people who have read little of Marxist classical writing and have a half-baked knowledge of it but who have created a hullabaloo of their views. This is an irresponsible attitude, which goes against the scientific spirit.

In order to uphold Marxism as our guide, the core fundamental issue is whom the philosophy and social sciences serve; this is a matter of principle. It must be made clear for whom philosophical social scientists write books and expound ideas in China, whether this serves a minority of the people or the great majority. There are no pure philosophy and social sciences that exist for their own sake. All the greatest achievements in philosophy and social sciences have resulted from responding to and addressing the critical issues that humans and societies were faced with. What the researchers study and advocate bears the marks of the society in which they are living. The CPC serves the people's heart and soul. The people are the masters of China. The starting point and finishing point of all the work for the Party and the State is to attain, maintain and develop the greatest number of the people's fundamental interests. If China's philosophy and social sciences strive to achieve, their research orientation should be centrally towards the people. Detached from the people, the philosophy and social sciences will no longer carry attraction, appeal, influence and vitality. Philosophical social scientists should stick to the stance that the people are the creators of history. So they should engage in research for the people, respecting the fact that the people hold the principal status. They should focus on practice and creation by the people.

They should consciously and closely link their personal academic pursuits with the development of the country and the nation and exert themselves to attain as much as possible, such that their achievements can withstand the tests of practice, the people and history.

To uphold Marxism as our guide, we should follow the Chinese saying that, 'The value of knowledge lies in its application.' Marxism has the theoretical feature of advancing with the times. Under new circumstances, the great imperative is to adhere to Marxist fundamental principles and the Marxist stance, views and methods, which are the quintessence and living soul of Marxism. Marxism is an open theoretical system that unceasingly develops with time, practice and science. It has not exhausted the truth. Instead, it opens up the route to the truth. Engels had already said, 'The whole Marxist outlook of the world is not a doctrine. It is about methods. What it provides is not ready-made doctrines. It is the starting point for further study and the method for its study.' To integrate the upholding of Marxism with its development, to make new theoretical creations in the light of new practice, is the very reason why it keeps its vitality forever.

We must not adopt dogmatism or mere pragmatism with respect to the theory of Marxism. If we do not take the historical conditions or real situation into consideration and if we rigidly adhere to certain inferences and concrete action programmes proposed by those classical Marxist writers according to certain historical conditions and specific situations, we will not make smooth progress, or we may make mistakes because of the divorce of thought from reality. It is not a Marxist attitude if we only follow the quotations by classical Marxist writers and dare not say something that they have not discussed. On the other hand, it is not a Marxist attitude either if we refer to lots of quotations according to our needs, giving the excuse that everything was said by Marx and Engels, and rigidly 'tailor' lively practice development and creativity.

Problem orientation is a salient feature of Marxism. Problems are the starting point and motivation for innovation. We should listen to the voices of the times and respond to their call to earnestly study and address important and urgent issues. Only in this way can we grasp the historical arteries and veins, discover development law and push forward theoretical innovation. Marxism as our guide should be applied to the study of the important theoretical and practical issues relating to the development of our country that face our ruling Party, to correct thinking and to effective ways of solving problems. Matters that have to be dealt with should be looked from the perspectives of co-relation and development. Strategic and systematic ways of thinking should be strengthened. The essence and the phenomena, essential or main aspects and minor or nonessential ones should be distinguished. Both the existing problems and their developing trends, both the partial and the overall situation should be taken into consideration. The views proposed and the conclusions drawn should be objective and accurate and should be able to withstand the test. After a comprehensive and objective analysis, the most important underlying principles and tendencies of China's social development and human social development can be exposed.

Some say that Marxist political economics and *Capital* are out of date. This is a subjective assertion. Just judging from the international financial crisis, the economic downturn in many Western countries continued afterwards, the gap between the poor and the rich widened and social contradictions deepened. This proves there still is an inherent contradiction between socialization of production and private ownership of production materials in capitalist countries, although the form of presentation and the present features look different. After the international financial crisis burst upon us, quite a few Western scholars turned to the study of and research into Marxist political economics and *Capital* to think about the disadvantages of capitalism. The French scholar Thomas Piketty has written a book entitled *Capital in the Twenty-First Century*, which has stirred up international academia and generated extensive discussions. The full and detailed data presented in the book indicate that inequality in the United States and other Western countries has reached or surpassed the highest level in history. Unrestrained capitalism will deepen and worsen wealth inequality. Piketty's analysis is mainly done from the perspective of distribution, even though it does not study the fundamental issue of ownership. But the method used and the conclusion drawn are worth thinking about.

Third issue: Speeding up the construction of philosophy and social sciences with Chinese characteristics

The features, style and manner in which philosophy and social sciences are pursued are the product of development when it reaches a certain stage, a sign of maturity, a symbol of strong capabilities and also the embodiment of confidence. China is an important player in philosophy and social sciences. Its research teams, the number of dissertations published and government investment rank high in the world. But the standard and level of academic proposition, thought, views and discourse and the academic standards do not match China's comprehensive power and international status. We should exert efforts to construct philosophy and social sciences with Chinese characteristics, following the idea of using China as a base, drawing on the experience of foreign countries, delving into history, seizing the opportunity of contemporary times, caring for mankind and looking forward to the future. Chinese characteristics, Chinese style and Chinese manners should be fully reflected throughout the scheme of academic disciplines, the realm of academic historical and practical knowledge and the system for conducting discourse.

What are the features of philosophy and social sciences with Chinese characteristics? In my opinion, there are three aspects.

First, they are a reflection of succession and national character. The current situation of philosophy and social sciences is the result of integration of the knowledge, concepts, theories and methods of ancient and modern times. We must gain a thorough understanding through comprehensive study of all of kinds of Chinese and foreign resources from ancient and modern times. We should especially take full advantage of the following three types of resources. One is Marxist resources, including Marxist fundamental principles, their consequences and the cultural status of the sinicization of Marxism, such as the CPC's theory, line, principles and policies, the socialist road, the theoretical system and institutions with Chinese characteristics, the thoughts and achievements of philosophy and social sciences in the fields of China's economy, politics, law, culture, society, ecology, foreign affairs, national defence, Party construction and so on. They are the major contents of philosophy and social sciences with Chinese characteristics. They are also the maximum increments of the development of philosophy and social sciences with Chinese characteristics. The second resource is the resource of China's excellent traditional culture, which is valuable and rare. The third is foreign resources, including the positive achievements in philosophy and social sciences attained by all countries in the world, which could benefit the philosophy and social sciences with Chinese characteristics. We should make ancient things serve present-day China and adapt foreign things to Chinese needs. We should integrate all kinds of resources and carry on enhancing knowledge innovation and theoretical creativity and the production of new methods. We should not forget our roots. We should learn from foreign countries. We should look forward to the future. We should thoroughly study the important matters vital to the nation's well-being and the people's livelihood. We should look to foreign countries and explore those key issues that are related to human prospects and destiny. We should look forward and correctly judge the tendency of developing socialism with Chinese characteristics. We should look at the past and inherit and carry forward the refined essence of the traditional culture of the Chinese nation.

Chinese culture, extending back thousands of years, is the solid base for the growth and development of philosophy and social sciences with Chinese characteristics. I have said that, standing on a vast land of 9.6 million square kilometres with 1.3 billion Chinese people, which constitutes a monumental power, and absorbing the cultural nourishment accumulated by the Chinese people, we Chinese should go our own way and have confidence in ourselves; every Chinese should have this confidence, as we act on a very broad stage, have a profound historical background and enjoy extremely strong willpower. What we should have is firm self-confidence in the socialist road, theory and system with Chinese characteristics, and ultimately in our culture. Cultural self-confidence is a fundamental, deep and everlasting force. History and reality demonstrate that a nation that has abandoned or betrayed its own history and culture will never be able to grow and develop, leaving the possibility of a historical tragedy instead.

The Chinese nation has a deep cultural tradition, with a characteristic system of thinking, which reflects the knowledge, wisdom and rational speculation accumulated by the Chinese people for thousands of years. This is China's unique advantage. The Chinese civilization carries on the state and the nation's spiritual blood, which needs to be passed on and guarded by generation after generation, and to be improved with the times as the new culture emerges and the old one is pushed out. The Chinese nation's fine traditional culture should be thoroughly explored and elaborated, so that the most fundamental Chinese cultural gene conforms to modern culture and is harmonized with modern society. The cultural spirit is transcendental in time and space, transnational, possessing an everlasting charm and at the same time contemporary value, which should be promoted and developed. The Chinese civilization should be propelled forward into creative transformation and innovative development, with its vitality activated. Let Chinese civilization, side by side with rich cultures created by the people of all countries, provide the correct spiritual guidance to mankind. Proposals, ideas and programmes that mirror the Chinese standpoint, wisdom and values around the critical issues that China and the world all face in development should be promoted. *A Bite of China* should be well-known worldwide. *Academic China, Theoretical China* and *China's Philosophy and Social Sciences* should be widely known too, as should *Developing China, Open China* and *China and its Great Contributions to Mankind*.

Putting emphasis on nationality does not mean rejecting other countries' academic research achievements. Nationality can meet the needs of development in conformity with contemporary China and the present world on the basis of making comparisons, contrasts and criticisms, and absorbing and distilling. The pride of a nation is also the pride of the world. If national issues can be addressed, world issues can be addressed more efficiently. If we have the ability to summarize Chinese practice, we will have more capacity to provide ideas and ways to solve world issues. This is the developmental law from specificity to generality.

We should base ourselves on China's reality and conduct open-door research. We should absorb and learn the theoretical views and academic achievements of mankind. But we should not regard one kind of theoretical view and academic attainment as the 'sole criterion' of value. We should not try to remould the whole world using one model. Otherwise we will slip into the quagmire of mechanicalism. Some theoretical views and academic achievements can be used to explain the developmental history of certain countries and nations, which is reasonable in certain regions and in certain historical cultures. But it would be absurd if they were applied blindly and indiscriminately to all countries and all nations, or if human life was conventionalized and judged by those. We should analyse and distinguish foreign theory, concepts, discourse and method and only apply those that are suitable, never mechanically applying those that are unsuitable. Philosophy and social sciences have a critical spirit, which is the most precious spiritual trait of Marxism.

Philosophy and social sciences as a research category are extensive. Each discipline has its own knowledge system and research methods. All the useful knowledge systems and research methods must be studied and learnt. We should not exclude anything without any analysis. Marx and Engels absorbed and learnt tremendously from their predecessors' academic attainments in the establishment of their own theoretical system. We can and must make good use of those beneficial knowledge systems, model deduction, quantitative analysis and other effective measures accumulated in modern social sciences. What must be noted is that we should never forget our ancestors nor lose scientific judgement in applying such knowledge and methods. In Marx's *Capital*, Lenin's *Imperialism* and Mao Zedong's series of rural investigative reports and other writings, large amounts of statistical data and fieldwork materials were applied. In order to address Chinese issues and put forward Chinese proposals in solving the problems of humanity, we should uphold the Chinese outlook of the world and epistemology. There is no possibility for creativity if foreign academic thoughts and methods are taken without analysis as a universal 'bible' and standard. There is also no possibility for creativity if foreign methods are applied and the same conclusions are drawn. In order to gain creative research achievements, we must proceed from China's reality and adhere to practical, historical, dialectical and developmental views to understand, test and develop the truth from practice.

Second, Chinese philosophy and social sciences should reflect the originality and the spirit of the times. Whether Chinese philosophy and social sciences have Chinese characteristics is judged essentially by their subjectivity and originality. If we follow others' every move and blindly follow suit, we can never establish philosophy and social sciences with Chinese characteristics and never solve any of China's actual problems. Mao Zedong said in 1944, 'Our attitude is to critically accept our own historical heritage and foreign thoughts. We oppose both blindly accepting all such thoughts and indiscriminately resisting such thoughts. We the Chinese people should think with our own heads and then determine what can be grown in our own land.' We should start our research from Chinese reality and propose subjective and original theoretical views. Only in this way can we construct a scheme of academic disciplines, a canon of academic historical and practical knowledge and a framework for traditional discourse, with their own features, and only then can China's philosophy and social sciences with their characteristics and strengths be developed.

A theory's vitality lies in creativity, which is the eternal theme in the development of philosophy and social sciences. Creativity is also the inevitable demand of social development, deepening practice and historical advancement. Society is always developing, and new circumstances and problems are emerging one after another all the time. Some of the problems could be dealt with and addressed by applying old and past experiences and methods, while others cannot. If we cannot study, raise and apply new thoughts, ideas and methods in time, the theory will appear pale and powerless and philosophy and social sciences will suffer from 'myasthenia gravis' (muscular weakness). Creativity in philosophy and social sciences could be large or small. Revealing one law is creativity. Bringing forward one kind of school of thought is creativity. Expounding a principle is creativity. Producing a method of solving a problem is also creativity.

The starting point of theoretical thinking determines its result, which can only originate from the problem. In a way, the process of theoretical creativity is one of discovering, screening, studying and solving problems. Marx once pointed out, 'The major problem is the question, rather than the answer,' and, 'A question is the slogan of the times and is the most practical voice for revealing its state of mind.' I have read or glanced over the following and other writings: Plato's *The Republic*, Aristotle's *Politics*, Thomas More's *Utopia*, Campanella's *The City of the Sun*, Locke's *Two Treatises of Government*, Montesquieu's *Spirit of the Law*, Rousseau's *Social Contract*, *The Federalist Papers* by Hamilton and others, Hegel's *Elements of the Philosophy of Right*, Clausewitz's *On War*, Adam Smith's *An Inquiry into the Nature and Causes of the Wealth of Nations*, Malthus's *Essay on the Principle of Population*, Keynes's *The General Theory of Employment, Interest and Money*, Joseph Schumpeter's *Theory of Economic Development*, Paul Samuelson's *Economics*, Milton Friedman's *Capitalism and Freedom*, Simon Kuznets's *Economic Growth of Nations*. I am deeply aware that all those writings are the product of their times and they are the result of thinking over and studying prominent social contradictions and problems in those times and places.

Since the reforms and opening up, we have upheld theoretical creativity and correctly answered the following and other important questions. What is socialism? How do we build socialism? What kind of party should we construct? How do we build our Party? What kind of development should we achieve? How do we achieve development? We have continuously put forward new theories according to the new practice and provided the scientific guidelines for implementing all kinds of avenues of enquiry and policies, and promoting the progress of all such work. We have proposed the following and other original and up-to-date concepts and theories: to modernize the state's governance system and governing ability; to develop a socialist market economy; to develop socialist democratic politics; to develop socialist negotiation and consultative democracy; to build a socialist legal system with a set of laws on governing with Chinese characteristics; to develop an advanced socialist culture; to foster and practise the core socialist values; to construct a harmonious socialist society; to construct an ecological civilization; to establish a brand new and open economic mechanism; to implement the view of the state's comprehensive safety; to build commonality for human destiny; to promote the construction of 'One Road and One Belt'; to uphold the 'right view of justice and interests'; to strengthen the capability of the Party in power; to adhere to the route of building a strong military force with Chinese characteristics; and to achieve the goal of building a strong military force in the new circumstances.

China's philosophy and social sciences have made great contributions to this work and constituted an unparalleled strength to underpin it.

China's contemporary great social changes and reforms are not merely a simple continuous copy of Chinese history and culture. It is not a simple and blind application of the model envisaged by classical Marxist authors. It is not another version of other states' socialist practice. It is not a re-production of foreign modernization development. There are no ready-made textbooks. China's philosophy and social sciences should concentrate on what we have been engaged with: to dig up new materials, expose new problems, propose new views, construct new theories from practice in China's reforms and development; make a systematic summary of the practical experience of China's reforms and opening up and the construction of socialist modernization; carry out further studies and research on developing the socialist market economy, democratic politics, an advanced culture, a harmonious society, ecological civilization and the construction of the Party's governing power and other fields; reinforce the study and explanation of the Central Committee's new views, thoughts and strategy in governing the state; refine new theories in scientific principles; and summarize new practice with the law. This is the main force and focus in constructing philosophy and social sciences with Chinese characteristics. It would be futile to mechanically copy or perform things such as 'marking the side of a moving boat in order to retrieve the sword in the river', 'portraying the picture of a tiger with a cat as the model', 'copying blindly, disregarding specific conditions' or 'drawing the gourd from the gourd as an example'.

Third, the philosophy and social sciences reflect systemization and specialization. Philosophy and social sciences with Chinese characteristics should cover history, economics, politics, culture, society, ecology, military affairs, construction of the Party and other fields, as well as traditional disciplines, emerging disciplines, frontier disciplines, interdisciplinary subjects and less familiar subjects. We should promote the construction and creativity of the academic disciplines, a sphere encompassing all academic historical and practical knowledge and a system of conducting discourse, striving to constitute a philosophical social scientific system in all aspects, fields and elements.

The basic academic discipline system of philosophy and social sciences has been established in China, but there are issues that need to be addressed urgently: mainly the setting up of some subjects is not closely related to social development. The academic discipline system is not complete, and the construction of emerging disciplines and interdisciplinary subjects is fairly weak. What has to be done next is to give prominence to the advantages, expand the fields, bolster weak spots and perfect the system. One ambition is to strengthen the building of Marxist subjects. A second is to speed up the improvement of those subjects that support the philosophy and social sciences, such as philosophy, history, economics, politics, the law, sociology, anthropology, journalism, demography, religion and psychology, to forge the academic discipline system with Chinese characteristics but also of universal significance. A third is to develop predominant key subjects. Fourth, we should accelerate the development of emerging disciplines and interdisciplinary subjects of important realistic significance to allow those disciplines to break through in China's philosophy and social sciences. Fifth, we must greatly value and develop the 'lost or vanishing' body of knowledge and those rare or less familiar subjects, which are of great cultural value and traditional significance. These subjects seem to be remote from reality. But we make them ready for possible use when in need by 'maintaining the army for a thousand days just for the use of an instant'. Enough attention should be paid to these subjects in relation to cultural heritage, for example studies of oracle bone inscriptions and other ancient Chinese writing, to ensure the tradition is transmitted to our successors. All in all, the basic disciplines should be solid and complete, key disciplines should be prominent, emerging and interdisciplinary subjects should develop creatively, rare or less popular disciplines should be carried on, fundamental research and application research should supplement each other, and academic research and the application of achievements should propel each other forward.

Academic discipline systems and teaching material systems are closely related. If the academic discipline system is not improved, the level of teaching materials cannot be raised. The reverse is also true: if the level of teaching materials cannot be raised, the academic discipline system has no power or potential for future progress at a later stage. According to statistics, the subjects of philosophy and social sciences are offered in almost all Chinese colleges and universities and students of arts account for a great percentage of university students. They are the reserve force for China's philosophy and social sciences. During their time in school, if they are not armed with a correct outlook on the world and epistemology and lack solid basic knowledge, it is out of the question for them to be able to shoulder greater responsibilities in the future. Higher education institutions' philosophy and social sciences function as a means of nurturing and educating students, which helps all students form a proper outlook on the world, life and values, cultivate their morality and spirituality, foster the habit of scientific thinking and promote healthy physical, spiritual and personal development. Appropriate teaching materials are needed to train talents of tremendous promise in philosophy and social sciences. With strenuous effort during the process of implementing Marxist theoretical research and construction, much has been achieved in the construction of teaching materials, although overall, this area represents a shortcoming. Close attention must be paid to the creation of teaching materials so that a comprehensive system of teaching materials in the philosophy and social sciences can be formed, which is adapted to the needs of developing socialism with Chinese characteristics, and based on international academic frontiers. In the compiling, promulgation and use of teaching materials, attention should be given to creativity in the institutional system and its mechanisms. The initiatives of scholars, schools and publishers should be encouraged to this end.

The construction of a framework for discourse should be enhanced in order to make China's philosophy and social sciences fully effective. In the interpretation of Chinese practice and construction of Chinese theory, we are best qualified to speak about it. But in fact, China's voice in the philosophy and social sciences is fairly small in the world. We are still caught in the dilemma of being voiceless, even though we are qualified to speak. Our utterances are not widely disseminated. We should be adept in refining logographic concepts, forging new concepts, categories and expressions that can be easily comprehended and accepted by the international community to facilitate research and discussions in the international academic field. This task should be performed by the construction of academic disciplines, and every discipline should have its own systematic disciplinary theory and concept. Philosophy and social sciences' institutions should be encouraged to participate and set up international academic organizations. The establishment of overseas Chinese academic research centres should be supported and encouraged. Overseas learned societies and foundations should be supported to promote Chinese studies. Exchanges between domestic and foreign think tanks should be strengthened to promote Chinese studies overseas, focusing on issues of shared interest for the international community, proposing research projects and taking the lead in them to increase China's international influence in philosophy and social sciences studies. The creation of outstanding foreign-language academic websites and journals should be advanced and high-quality research achievements should be recommended and introduced overseas. Scholars should be supported to attend international academic conferences and to publish academic articles.

It is a systematic and weighty task to construct philosophy and social sciences with Chinese characteristics. We should support top-level design and promote the advancement by co-ordinating efforts in all aspects. We should implement innovative projects in philosophy and social sciences and build effective platforms for innovation in all fields. The following and other platforms for ideological and theoretical work should function fully: Marxist theoretical research and construction projects, centres of research into a theoretical socialist system with Chinese characteristics, an academy of Marxism, and theoretical propaganda via periodicals, newspapers and networks to deepen and expand Marxist theoretical research, dissemination and education. By applying internet and big data technology, we should speed up the construction of book collections, networks, databases and other infrastructure and information, as well as documentation centres for the state's philosophy and social sciences, and formulate convenient and speedy, resource-shared information platforms for the research of philosophy and social sciences. We should innovate in the area of research funding allocation, sponsorship and management systems to make better use of the state's social sciences funding by combining financial grants with special funding, combining universal funding with competitive funding, and combining governmental funding with social donations, to increase investment in scientific research and improve our efficiency in spending funds. We should set up a scientific, authoritative, open and transparent evaluation system for attainments in philosophy and social sciences, and establish a recommendation and introduction institution for excellent academic achievements, so that outstanding research achievements are singled out for recognition and popularized.

Fourth issue: To strengthen and improve the leadership of the Party in the work of philosophy and social sciences

Philosophy and social sciences are an important cause and battleground of the Party and the people. It is essential to strengthen and improve the Party's leadership in philosophy and social sciences to make this cause promising and prosperous.

The Party committees at all levels should include the work of philosophy and social sciences in their agendas to underpin its political leadership and guide its work. Prosperous development, guidance and management should be done side by side. The reform of institutional management should be extended. The institutional and mechanism systems should be formulated to ensure the correct direction and stimulate the vitality of scientific research. Overall planning work should be done for the management of important talents, key fronts and positions, core research planning, significant research programmes, the distribution of important funding and major evaluation and awards activities. Research at both national and local levels should be taken into account. The design of scientific research should be optimized and resources should be rationally allocated. Relations between investment and benefits, quantity and quality, size and structure should be well handled to increase the developmental capacity of philosophy and social sciences. Leaders at all levels and especially those in charge should be armed with rich natural sciences knowledge and extensive social sciences knowledge in order to constantly raise the level of leadership and decision-making.

The Party committees and governments at all levels should put philosophy and social sciences at the forefront in the governance of the state. It was pointed out during the 3rd Plenary session of the 18th Central Committee of the CPC that the construction of a new think tank and the establishment of the healthy policy-making and consultation system should be boosted. It was emphasized at the 5th Plenary session of the 18th Central Committee of the CPC that innovative projects in philosophy and social sciences and the establishment of new think tanks with Chinese characteristics should be implemented. In November 2015, I presided over the meeting of the Central Leading Group for Comprehensively Deepening Reforms. The 'pilot' project of founding a national high-profile think tank was approved and the first batch of high-level think tanks has been established and is in operation. I emphasized during the meeting that a series of characteristic and innovative high-profile think tanks, which can lead development and which the state urgently needs, should be constructed, with the focus on forward-looking, targeted and specific policy research around the State's strategic needs. In recent years, there has been great enthusiasm for constructing think tanks in the field of philosophy and social sciences and much has been achieved, which is hugely beneficial for the policy making departments of the Party and the government at all levels. Meanwhile, however, some problems remain. Some think tank research focuses on quantity instead of quality; some value more the forms of dissemination than innovative content; some engage in 'only setting up a rostrum' as a formality, without performing real actions, or inviting VIPs, holding forums and other formalistic approaches. The essential point in the establishment of think tanks is to enhance research quality and innovative content. Information sharing and exchanges between the policy making departments and the think tanks should be furthered. Policy research in the departments of the Party and the governments should be closely linked with the countermeasure research of think tanks, guiding and enhancing the healthy and efficient development of think tanks.

In the constitution of philosophy and social sciences with Chinese characteristics, special attention should be paid to the personnel who are expected to persevere with continuous drive. Intellectuals congregate in the fields of philosophy and social sciences. Currently there are five main forces in China's philosophy and social sciences. We should show concern for them, foster them well and use them as the advocates for our advanced thoughts, make them pioneers in academic research, leaders of social fashion and firm supporters of Party rule. The overall developmental strategy to nurture people and talents as a priority in philosophy and social sciences should be implemented, formulating a comprehensive development system to integrate students, academia and academic disciplines. The talent project of philosophy and social sciences should be implemented with great effort to discover, foster and gather together a number of thinkers and theorists who have profound Marxist accomplishments and who are well versed in Chinese and Western learning, as well as academic leaders with solid theoretical foundations who are pioneering and innovative, senior and young key academic members who are energetic, ambitious and dynamic – all with a view to forming a cohesive echelon of a range of the best talents in philosophy and social sciences. Academic title ranks and a system for selecting personnel should be elaborated. An appropriate award system should be devised to reward prominent people and increase their sense of honour, responsibility and achievement. Propaganda or publicity, HR and educational departments and higher educational institutions, research organizations in philosophy and social sciences, Party schools and administrative institutions, research centres attached to the departments of the Party and governments and military academies should all work together. An effective system to motivate and foster talent among philosophical social scientists should be formulated to promote continuous progress.

The Party's intellectual policy should be properly implemented to show respect for work, knowledge, talent and creativity. We should completely trust our intellectuals politically, guide them in ideology, create good working conditions for them, tend to their needs in daily life, help them in practical ways and assist them in solving their problems. Leaders should regard philosophy and social sciences with a scientific attitude and respect scientists' diligence and research attainments. Leaders should recognize that the subject matter in philosophy and social sciences is not unduly profound and is within their reach and should have the ability to make comments and give opinions on it. Leaders should have more interactions with experts and scholars and make friends with them, raise topics with them and listen to their views and suggestions. They should make full use of outstanding talents and let those with both ability and integrity play a vital role in important positions.

'Let a hundred flowers bloom' and 'let a hundred schools contend' are important policies in the prosperous development of China's philosophy and social sciences. We should advocate theoretical and knowledge innovation, encourage bold exploration and launch equal, healthy, lively academic and rational discourse within an active academic atmosphere. We should uphold and develop academic democracy, respect differences, tolerate diversity and recommend mutual learning from different academic viewpoints and discussion among different schools of learning on an equal footing. We should distinguish properly between academic and political matters. We should neither regard general academic matters as political ones nor regard political matters as general academic ones. We are opposed to academic falsehoods or actions taken against academic ethics and in breach of the Constitution and the law, under the banner of academic research. We are also opposed to simplified actions that mix academic and political affairs and deal with academic issues by offering political solutions.

The style and atmosphere of learning should be rectified for the sake of the prosperous development of China's philosophy and social sciences. Nowadays, a bad atmosphere prevails in the field of philosophy and social sciences, for example, pomposity, academic misconduct and corruption. Some are eager to pursue instant success and fast profits; some produce cut-and-paste work; some manufacture shoddy and rough work; Some shut themselves behind closed doors to do things blindly irrespective of external circumstances and objective conditions; some try to avoid reality; some merely sit and pontificate; some plagiarize others' work or even misrepresent documents and fabricate data. Accordingly, some very sharp comments have been made, implying that, at certain times, many researchers put solely their 'body' into the work, whereas only a few put their 'soul' into it. We should vigorously promote a fine style of learning and combine soft restrictions and tough measures to enhance the development of a style of learning that advocates good-quality work, pursuing study strictly and precisely, laying stress on honesty and trust and being responsible. We should create a pure and healthy academic environment of mutual learning and positive progression. The vast number of philosophical social scientists should set up fine academic morale, norms and criteria and abide by them consciously , and strive for erudition, a spirit of enquiry, discretion, clear distinctions and perseverance. We should advocate for the precept that 'scholars should be responsible for expanding teaching' and integrate good behaviour and conduct with doing research. With commitment and dedication, with persistence and perseverance exemplified by 'sitting on a cold stool for 10 years to study', philosophical social scientists could avoid empty vacuity in their writings. They should be able to put up with boredom, resist temptation and defend the bottom line. They should have the ambition to acquire broad and authentic learning, keeping their social responsibilities as a priority. They should take the social effects of academic research seriously and put core socialist values into practice. They should become the seekers and disseminators of truth, kindness and beauty. They should win respect with their profound and wide-ranging learning and knowledge. They should take the lead in creating a pleasant and elevated social atmosphere with their refined personal charisma, realize their own value and attain their own achievements while promulgating virtues and expounding their views and ideas for the country and for the people.

Comrades, in the historical course of developing socialism with Chinese characteristics, there are plenty of opportunities for the great number of Chinese researchers working in philosophy and social sciences to develop their abilities to the full in this great field. I expect you to work fearlessly, in the face of all kinds of hardships, and live up to your mission, and with your efforts and with your wisdom make ever greater contributions to the realization of the 'Two Centenary Goals' and making the Chinese Dream of a great rejuvenation of the Chinese nation come true!

17-05-2016 23:24:00 Source: Xinhua
BEIJING, May 18 (Xinhua)
http://news.xinhuanet.com/politics/2016-05/18/c_1118891128.htm

DOI https://doi.org/10.24103/GCSS2.en.2016.14

List of Contributors

Martin Albrow (马丁·阿尔布劳) FAcSS, Emeritus Professor of the University of Wales and Senior Fellow of the Käte Hamburger Centre for Advanced Studies, Law and Culture, University of Bonn. He is an Honorary Vice President of the British Sociological Association and Fellow of the Academy of Social Sciences. Professor Albrow was Founding Editor of the journal of *International Sociology*. He is author of *The Global Age* (1996), *Bureaucracy* (1970) and *Max Weber's Construction of Social Theory* (1990). His most recent books are *Niklas Luhmann: A Sociological Theory of Law* (Routledge 2014), co-edited and co-translated with Elisabeth King-Utz, and *Global Age Essays on Social and Cultural Change* (Klostermann 2014).

Xiangqun Chang (常向群) is President of Global China Institute, Editor of *Journal of China in Comparative Perspective* (JCCP), and Chief Editor of Global China Press; Honorary Professor at University College London, Professorial Research Associate at SOAS, University London, UK, and holder of several professorships and senior fellowships at Peking, Renmin, Fudan and Sun Yat-sen universities in China. Her publications amount to two million words and include *Guanxi or Li shang wanglai?: Reciprocity, Social Support Networks, and Social Creativity in a Chinese Village* (2009; 2010).

Dongning Feng (冯东宁) is a Senior Lecturer in Translation Studies at SOAS, University of London. He has taught a range of subjects in China, Japan and Britain. His current research interests focus on critical discourse analysis and translation, translators' autonomy and literary and screen translation. His publications include works on aesthetics and political communication, politics of translation and translation as political discourse, Chinese cinema, Chinese cultural and literary studies, and a monograph on literature as political philosophy and communication (*Literature as Political Philosophy in Contemporary China*, 2002).

Stephan Feuchtwang (王斯福) is Emeritus Professor of the Department of Anthropology, London School of Economics and Political Science (LSE), where he established the MSc China in Comparative Perspective Programme in 2006, to date the only one of its kind in the world, and acted as founding director of the China in Comparative Perspective Network (CCPN), LSE. He was President of the British Association for Chinese Studies (BACS). In recent years his interests have covered charisma, making place, transmission of loss due to state violence, comparing civilizations, temporalities, regimes of visibility and invisibility, and urbanization. He is author of *After the Event: The Transmission of Grievous Loss in Germany, China and Taiwan* (2011), and *Popular Religion in China: The Imperial Metaphor* (2001).

Bettina Gransow (柯兰君) is Professor of Chinese Politics at the East Asian Institute and the Otto-Suhr-Institute of Political Science, Free University Berlin, Germany. She has published in German, English and Chinese since the 1980s, covering the topics such as migrants and health in China, migrant communities and social change in Chinese megacities, social assessment, risks of impoverishment; and involuntary resettlement in rural China.

Gary G. Hamilton (韩格理) is Henry M. Jackson Professor, Department of Sociology and The Jackson School of International Studies, University of Washington (Seattle), formerly Associate Director of the School. He is the author of Emergent Economies, Divergent Paths, Economic Organization and International Trade in South Korea and Taiwan (2006), Commerce and Capitalism in Chinese Societies (2006), and The Market Makers: How Retailers Are Changing the Global Economy (2011). He is also well known in China for introducing Fei Xiaotong's book From the Soil – The Foundations of Chinese Society (1994) to the English-speaking world.

Ye Liu (刘烨) is a Lecturer in International Education and Development at Bath Spa University, UK. She also taught at the University College Cork, Ireland, and was a research associate for the China in Comparative Perspective Network, London School of Economics (LSE). Her research interests primarily focused on the role of education in shaping a transitional society with regard to social inequality, life chances, social mobility and social harmony. She has conducted survey studies, extensive interviews and in-depth observations in China.

George Marcus (乔治·马尔库斯) is Chancellor's Professor and Chair of Department of Anthropology, University of California, Irvine, USA. He is Founding Editor of *Cultural Anthropology*, Editor of *The Late Editions Series of Annuals* (1993-2000). His research interests are in the fields of elites, ethnography, cultural critique and Pacific studies. His publications include *Writing Culture: The Politics and Poetics of Ethnography* (1986, co-edited with James Clifford), *Anthropology as Cultural Critique: An Experimental Movement in the Human Sciences* (1986, co-authored with Michael M. J. Fischer), *Rereading Cultural Anthropology* (1992), *Ethnography through Thick and Thin* (1998), *Critical Anthropology Now: Unexpected Contexts, Shifting Constituencies, Changing Agendas* (1998, with the contribution of Paul Rabinow), *Designs for an Anthropology of the Contemporary* (2008), and *Fieldwork Is Not What It Used to Be* (2009, co-edited with James Faubion).

Chie Nakane (中根千枝) is Professor Emeritus at the University of Tokyo, Japan, where she taught Social Anthropology, and also became Director of the Institute of Oriental Culture. She was a Visiting Professor at the University of Chicago and the School of Oriental and African Studies (University of London), as well as Professor-at-Large at Cornell University. Professor Nakane is also an honorary member of the Royal Anthropological Institute of Great Britain and Ireland. Her research is dedicated to cross-cultural comparisons of Asian societies, particularly

Japan, China and India. She is mostly known for her book *Japanese Society* (1970).

PARK Hong (Ko Paku in Japanese 朴红) is an Associate Professor of Agricultural Economy at the Graduate School of Agriculture, Hokkaido University, Japan. She is mainly interested in conducting fieldwork for long-term follow-up studies on agricultural and rural development in the East Asian area (China, Japan, South Korea and Taiwan). She has published more than 70 articles (in Japanese, Chinese, Korean and English) and six books (in Japanese), including *The Revival of Family Business and Establishment of Rural Organizations in Northeast Rural China* (1999), *Peasant Association in China* (2001), *The Export Strategy of Vegetable Processing Enterprises in China* (2006) and *Rural Cooperatives in Taiwan* (2010).

Lianyi Song (宋连谊) is Principal Teaching Fellow in Chinese at the Department of the Languages and Cultures of China and Inner Asia, School of Oriental and African Studies (SOAS), University of London. Dr Song has taught Chinese as a foreign language in the UK for over 20 years, both before and after he obtained his PhD. He is author and co-author of many books, such as *Teach Yourself Beginner's Mandarin Chinese*, *Get Talking Mandarin Chinese in Ten Days*, *Speak Mandarin Chinese with Confidence*, *Beginner's Chinese*, *Mandarin Chinese Conversation* and *Read and Write Chinese Script*.

Charles Stafford (石瑞) is Professor and former Head of the Department of Anthropology at The London School of Economics and Political Science (LSE). He focuses on the anthropology of China and Taiwan, with particular interests in child development, learning, kinship, religion and economics. He has conducted fieldwork both in Taiwan and in mainland China, and published *The Roads of Chinese Childhood: Learning and Identification in Angang* (1995), *Separation and Reunion in Modern China* (2003), *Ordinary ethics in China* (2013). Currently he is working on the book *Logic and Emotion in Chinese Economic Life*.

Lik Suen (宣力) is Principal Teaching Fellow in Chinese at the Department of the Languages and Cultures of China and Inner Asia and Deputy Director of the London Confucius Institute at SOAS, University of London. She has taught Chinese as a foreign language in Hong Kong, the USA and the UK for nearly 20 years. She is Chief Examiner in Chinese for a major examining body in the UK, editor of *Get Ahead in Chinese*, and co-author of *Chinese in Steps*.

Cary Zhiming WU (吴志明) PhD candidate in Sociology and a fellow of the UBC Institute of Asian Research, University of British Columbia, Canada. He was Research Assistant at the Department of Sociology, University of Illinois at Chicago, USA. He has studied at the Department of Sociology, Renmin University of China with a Fei Xiaotong Scholarship for Outstanding Students. He was Editor and Journalist on *China Social Science Today*, Chinese Academy of Social Sciences (BACS), China, and was a Research Assistant for the China in Comparative Perspective Network at LSE. His research interests are urban sociology and political culture. He has published many journal articles, mainly in Chinese.

Dr Xi Jinping (习近平**)**, General Secretary of the CPC Central Committee, State President, and Chairman of the Central Military Commission. He graduated from the Department of Chemical Engineering of Tsinghua University in 1979; he did his PhD (1998–2002) part time in the Department of Sociology of the School of Humanities and Social Sciences of Tsinghua University. He has served in Beijing, Hebei, Fujian, Zhejiang and Shanghai since 1979 in differents posts at different levels. From 2007 to 2012, he served as the Principal of the Party School of the CPC Central Committee. He is author of *Xi Jinping's Governace of China* (Chinese 2014, English 2015), *Zhejiang, China: A New Vision for Development* (Chinese 2007, English 2019), *Research on China's Rural Marketization Construction* (Chinese 2002), *Up and Out of Poverty* (Chinese 1992, English 2019).

DOI https://doi.org/10.24103/GCSS2.en.2016.15

About the Editors

Stephan Feuchtwang (王斯福) is Emeritus Professor of Anthropology at the London School of Economics (LSE). He established the first centre for social scientific study on China in the UK (1973) at City University London, and the MSc China in Comparative Perspective Programme (2006) at the LSE, to date the only one of its kind in the world. He was Present of the British Association of China Studies (BACS). He has been engaged in research on popular religion and politics in mainland China and Taiwan since 1966, resulting in a number of publications on charisma, place, temples and festivals, and civil society. He has recently been engaged in a comparative project exploring the theme of the recognition of catastrophic loss, including the loss of archive and recall, which in Chinese cosmology and possibly elsewhere is pre-figured in the category of ghosts. Most recently he has been pursuing a project on the comparison of civilizations and empires. He has published more than ten books and a few dozen articles, including *Popular Religion in China: The Imperial Metaphor* (1991, 2001) and *After the Event: The Transmission of Grievous Loss in Germany, China and Taiwan* (2011).

Xiangqun Chang (常向群) is Director of Global China Institute, Editor of *Journal of China in Comparative Perspective* (JCCP), and Chief Editor of Global China Press; Honorary Professor at University College London, Professorial Research Associate at SOAS, University London, UK, and holder of several professorships and senior fellowships at Peking, Renmin, Fudan and Sun Yat-sen universities in China. To date the only UK-based sociologist trained in both China and the UK, she has been working at universities on social scientific studies of China interdisciplinarily since 1991, when she came to the UK as a Visiting Fellow. In the past two-plus decades Xiangqun has conducted about two dozen research projects and published over two million Chinese characters and English words. Based on a thorough and detailed ethnography of a Chinese village with longitudinal comparisons, she developed a general analytical concept – 'recipropriety' (*lishang-wanglai* 礼尚往来) – a Chinese model of reciprocity, relatedness and social networks (see *Guanxi or Li shang wanglai? Reciprocity, Social Support Networks, & Social Creativity in a Chinese Village*, 2010). This 'recipropriety model' is being tested in many projects with both interdisciplinary and comparative approaches.

ZHOU Daming (周大鸣) is Professor of the School of Anthropology and Sociology, Chang Jiang Scholar Distinguished Professor of Ministry of Education, Director of the Ethnic Group Study Centre, Sun Yat-sen University, Deputy Director of Historical Anthropology Research Center, Ministry of Education Humanities and Social Science Key Research Base at Sun Yat-sen University, and Vice-president of the China Union of Anthropological and Ethnological Sciences (UAES), China.

He was co-editor of the US-based *Chinese Sociology Anthropology* (1981–2011). He has published nine books and a few dozen articles. His academic contributions have mainly focused on aspects of migration and urbanization, ethnic groups and regional culture, applied anthropology, and construction of anthropological discipline. He is the initiator of urban anthropology research in China and constructed the theme, method and theoretical basis for the study of urban anthropology in China. He has also used the theory of ethnic group and ethnic group relations to carry out regional cultural studies in China. In the field of applied anthropology, he has undertaken various commissioned projects of the World Bank, the Asian Development Bank, relevant ministries and commissions of the State Council, the Guangdong Provincial Government and other institutions and departments.

www.ingramcontent.com/pod-product-compliance
Lightning Source LLC
Chambersburg PA
CBHW080133270326
41926CB00021B/4468